# Smartass

# Smartass

MEMOIR
OF A
MOUTHY GIRL

Emily Sayre Smith

SHE WRITES PRESS

Published in 2025 by
She Writes Press, an imprint of The Stable Book Group

32 Court Street, Suite 2109
Brooklyn, NY 11201
https://shewritespress.com
Library of Congress Control Number: 2025909823
ISBN: 978-1-64742-982-9
eISBN: 978-1-64742-983-6

*Interior Designer: Stacey Aaronson*

Printed in the United States

Names and identifying characteristics have been changed to protect the privacy of certain individuals.

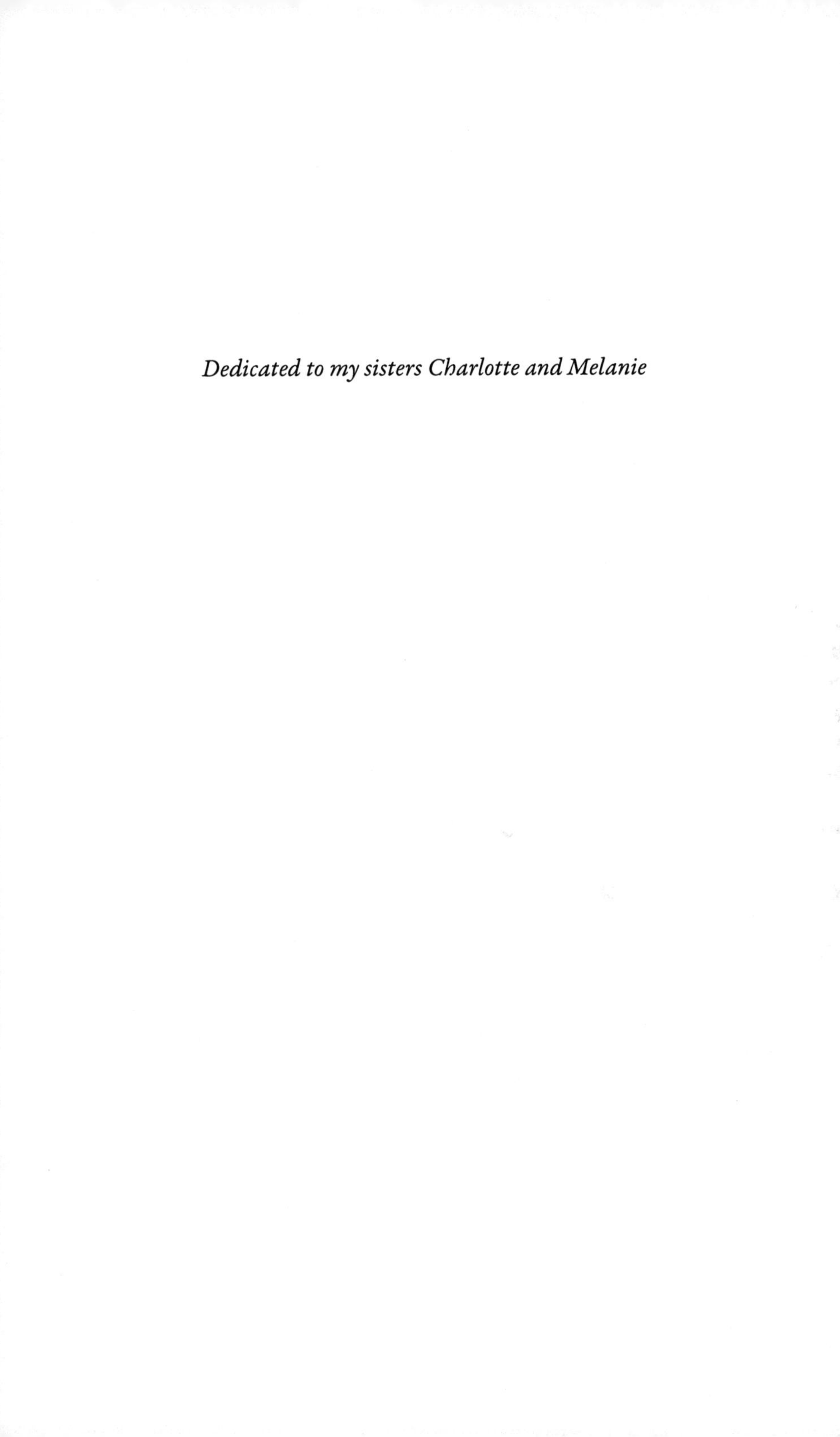

*Dedicated to my sisters Charlotte and Melanie*

# one

TEXAS IN THE 1950S IS A VERY GOOD PLACE TO BE BORN. The people are big and bold and enthusiastic. They have flags and songs and flowers. Hats and horses. Festivals and rodeos. All around, everyone seems to be very impressed with where they are and what they're doing.

I enter the state on an unremarkable spring day in April 1956. My mother, being the kind of woman she is, is telling the doctor how to go about his business while he tells her how to go about hers. "Hey, what are you doing down there, Buster?" she snaps.

"Doctor Buster, if you please," he responds.

I clock in at 10:00 a.m., weighing seven pounds two ounces. I am chubby, red, and have a full head of rather dark hair. I look more like an Eskimo than a Texan.

I have only vague memories before four years old, but I know my father is an Episcopal priest in town and my mother is beautiful and full of magic. My father wears his priest uniform at the church: embroidered capes and dresses. But he still has his shirt and trousers on underneath. I know he's special because he stands up at the altar in church on Sundays and does all sorts of chanting and magic incantations. "Let us pray" seems to be one of his favorites, and everybody does. Then he gets out the fancy silver dishes and everyone lines up for a dry, tasteless cracker and a sip of wine. For a snack, it seems rather disappointing.

I have a sister Charlotte who is two years older than me. She is fair, blond, and skinny, whereas I am dark, ruddy, and chunky. I follow her around, but I don't think she likes me. We play prince and princess a lot—me being the prince mostly. We wear outfits created from the dress-up box, hers being some sort of long gown made from our mother's old skirts and petticoats, while mine are mostly baby blankets pinned around my neck as a cape and an old hat. I am not allowed to have a sword.

Playing prince and princess involves a lot of parading around and giving homage to the princess. She makes me special sun tea in old mayonnaise jars out of leaves and twigs she finds on the ground.

This morning we are on the front porch about to set off on an epic journey to slay a dragon. In my mind the dragon lives in the backyard, and we need to go around the house to the side gate and into the yard to find him. I have stolen a broken yardstick from Mother's sewing room to use as a sword, which I wear in a belt around my waist in anticipation of the battle. Charlotte decides, in a rather unprincess-like fashion, that I am not supposed to have a sword. "You could put somebody's eye out," she chastises and tries to wrestle it away, which escalates to "I'm going to tell Mommy!" There is a struggle over my weapon—she won't let go and she's winning—so I bite her. I am four years old. I don't have many moves, and biting her hand to get her fingers off my sword seems quite logical.

There is a power struggle that underlies all our stories. She's older and smarter. I'm happy to play along (just to have her to play with)—until I'm not. I ruined her life the day my parents brought me home from the hospital. This resentment gets played out over and over again by the princess seeking revenge on the prince for her very existence.

When Charlotte goes to our mother to tell on me, a scenario

that gets repeated time and again, my first line of defense is deny, deny, deny. I stand before my mother, trying desperately to invent in my mind some story to justify my crime. The princess is wailing and crying (far beyond what the injury requires), "She bit me!" The princess snivels.

Magic Mommy is consoling the princess (which is the entire point of this melodrama) and asks the prince, "Did you bite her?"

"Noooooo," I respond, but there between her thumb and forefinger lies the irrefutable evidence of my crime. Teeth marks like some record on file at the dentist clearly detailing my upper baby teeth.

At five, things get more interesting. We move to Bay City to a basic three-bedroom, two-bath ranch-style house. I am small but strong. I have matching shorts and shirts and my red Buster Brown sandals. My hair is cut in the every-damn-kid-in-the-neighborhood bowl haircut, just under the ears with bangs.

My mother tells me she always knows where I am as there is always a soundtrack to my life. Either I am playing my little RCA record player in my bedroom, singing songs you never heard before, like "I'm As Happy as a Little Clam," or I am about to go on some adventure and sing the accompanying operatic soundtrack: "I'm the prince and I'm going on my horse to see the princess. I will save her from the monster and we will live happily ever after."

I play outside every day. Our backyard is unremarkable, with the exception of a swing set made of what seems to me to be very large piping. It's very tall, so I can swing high, which makes the pipes in the ground lift slightly when I hit the top of my swing. This has the dizzying effect of making me wonder if the whole thing is going to fly right out of the ground, but surely if this were true, they wouldn't allow kids to swing here. But I worry. Five years old seems too young to worry, but I do.

Texas summers are very hot and humid, but I don't know anything else. I am covered in a light coating of sweat, like when you get out of the tub and there is no towel. My shirt sticks to my back and my underpants are stuck to my butt. There is water everywhere. Streams to hunt crawdads. A small pond between the houses across the street. The older boys in the neighborhood have made a rope swing tied to a large overhanging branch so they can swing across the pond to the other side. I am very excited to try this, but they tell me, "There are water moccasins that will bite you if you fall in. See the ripples in the surface there? That's them. Snakes!" Although I am five, I am not prepared to die in a pond where I fall off a rope swing, then am bitten by a deadly snake.

We run in gangs determined by age. No seven-year-old is going to be caught dead with some stupid five-year-old. The admonishment from the older boys is, "You stay here. You're too small and scared to cross the highway on your bike. You're too scared to stick your hand in the creek to catch crawdads." I have actually never seen a crawdad, nor do I know what they look like, but I am told they are there, so this is five-year-old fact.

Everyone has a bike. Mine is a green Huffy with training wheels. Training wheels don't actually train you to ride a bike. They just encourage you to rock back and forth from training wheel to training wheel. My tires are solid rubber, not the inflated kind, so it's like pedaling a small tank. The best part of my bike is the playing cards and clothespins attached to the spokes so they make the sound of a deck of cards being shuffled as I ride along.

Nobody locks their door. Dogs run loose and chase cars as they drive down the road past my house, and kids run wild through the neighborhood from dawn to dusk.

# two

THESE ARE THE DAYS OF POLIO. WE HAVE JUST GOTTEN OUR vaccinations at school. The terror of swimming pools and iron lungs is waning. We have been vaccinated at the doctors against diphtheria, pertussis, and tetanus (DPT). We get whooping cough and smallpox vaccinations.

My mother has a degree in bacteriology, and she's all over the medical advances of the time. She sometimes takes us to visit families with children we don't regularly play with. (I learn later she was intentionally exposing us to mumps, measles, and chickenpox, which were considered harmless childhood illnesses and are rampant in the neighborhood kids.) Charlotte and I both come down with measles.

I have itchy red spots all over me and run a high fever. This is my first experience of illness. We are miserable and sleep a lot, but as we get better we are served chicken and rice soup in bed. We get crackers and ginger ale when we want. These are remarkable firsts in my life, but they are eventually tempered with a new, more important first: We get better and suddenly our mother is sick. Very sick. My mother has never had measles as a child, and in the process of making sure we get it, infects herself. Measles in small children is not a big deal. A rite of passage. A box to tick on the list. In adults, it can be deadly.

She is in her bedroom and we are not allowed in. Daddy is

home from work. I can see next to her bed a tall silver stand with a clear bottle and a long tube like they have in the hospital. They are afraid she could die (no one tells us this of course), but she can't go to the hospital because she is too contagious, so we are left to ride it out on our own at home.

My days are the same. I play outside. Someone makes my lunch. I have to take a nap. I don't really notice her absence or my father's stress. It's just the way it is. What is happening today. Everything is new. Nothing is "normal." What do I know? I'm five for God's sake.

My mother returns and everything is right again. My peanut butter and jelly sandwiches are made correctly and there are mommy kisses. Daddy goes back to work. No one tells us how close we came to disaster.

Shortly thereafter my mother goes blind in one eye and takes me with her for a long car ride over to the next county to see the doctor. She is wearing a patch on one eye, so I am to sit on her lap and "drive the car." Okay, no problem, I've seen this done. "I will work the pedals and you will help me steer the car," she tells me. She will steer the car, but I am to help her "see." I feel very important.

If my mother had known the impact that this illness would have on her, she wouldn't have exposed herself so cavalierly. But she didn't know. Nobody knew. For now, it's just measles and she survives the attack, but her illness plants a seed left to grow that would change her slowly, rob her of all abilities, and leave her gutted.

I start school in the fall. Not real school in my mind, as they call it "kindergarten," which sounds good but not the same as school. I have a Mickey Mouse lunchbox. Every day I have the same lunch—a peanut butter and jelly sandwich, a bag of Fritos, three Oreo cookies, and a Mickey Mouse thermos of milk.

My school is named after the patron saint of kindergarten, Miss Payton. Miss Payton is glamorous in a black and white houndstooth skirt, a wide black belt, and a crisp white shirt, her graying hair pulled starkly back in a tight bun. She wears black loafers and white socks and cuts a striking figure. Miss Payton teaches first grade. My teacher is Miss Yancy. This is my first disappointment but probably the reason I learn my letters and numbers. I am starstruck by Miss Payton, and she is my first crush.

One afternoon after recess, we are given a picture of a bird. We are instructed to get a blue crayon and color our bird blue. I dutifully comply, making a reasonable effort to stay inside the lines. Next, we are instructed to get a yellow crayon and color our bird yellow. I think this is particularly strange as my bird is already blue, but again, I go along. What? The ground shakes. The earth moves. My bird is turning *green* with every stroke. What hocus pocus is this? This is the day I decide that school might not be so bad. These people know things! There is magic to be learned here.

Like any good kindergarten of the time, we have classes in the morning: recess, band, and something to do with numbers in the afternoon. Band is my favorite. Every day we are assigned to our sections. You either get "tone blocks," a triangle, tambourine, or some other rhythm instrument you are to hit as Miss Yancy plays the piano. Miss Payton conducts.

About midyear it is determined that we will have a band recital at the high school auditorium. We are all to wear the same outfit (God, I love an "outfit"): gray pleated skirt, white blouse, navy blue blazer, blue knee socks with black shoes, and a blue beret. I am to be the conductor and have to learn an introduction in French. "*Bonjour, mes amis. Je m'appelle Emily Smith. Parlez-vous français? Oui? Non?* Then I will speak to you in English. My name is Emily Smith and I am the director of the Payton School

Rhythm Band. Our first selection tonight will be "March of the Wooden Soldiers.'"

Come the big day we are all seated on the stage, but I am up front at the microphone. I have a baton. Not the twirling kind but the orchestra conductor kind. I give my little speech in French and turn to my classmates. On the downbeat we play along with Miss Yancy on the piano to "March of the Wooden Soldiers." My mother takes pictures of everything, so for years to come this night will be memorialized. We even have a movie camera, which has to be wound, and God forbid the subject of the film lasts longer than the winding. "Do that again, honey," encourages my mother, as if my leaping from rock to rock precariously over some fatal gorge can ever be recreated.

Our parents' big night out in this small Texas town is to go to the high school auditorium and watch a bunch of kindergarteners hit tone blocks and triangles? They were just happy to be alive. Happy to have homes and children. Happy not to be buried in Normandy.

Because of my father's job we get late-night phone calls and people coming to the house at odd hours. Tonight, after being put to bed as usual, I have wandered down the hall and am lurking along the edges of the kitchen toward the den.

"I can't sleep," is my plea when they notice me leaning against the wall, looking as pathetic as I can muster. I want to be allowed to stay up with my parents. When no objection is raised, I patter into the room and deposit myself cross-legged on the rag rug of the den facing the TV. There is a knock at the back door. My mother opens the door and says, "Come in," to the as-yet-unseen visitor.

"Thank you," a man's voice says. An apparition appears in our den. He is tall, dressed head to toe in black leather, zippers all over, black boots, and carrying a white motorcycle helmet. He is offered a chair, and I stare in stunned amazement as he takes an armchair directly facing me. I am dressed in puffy turquoise two-piece pajamas, and I'm suddenly ashamed. He is what is right. He is what I want to be, but I don't have the words to say so. And I am terrified. As if with some kind of mystical understanding to calm my nerves, he unzips a pocket on his sleeve, pulls out a small carton of milk, and proceeds to down it.

My mother starts a polite conversation. "Where are you from?"

"Nottingham, England," he replies softly. "I am traveling across the United States on my motorcycle."

Just the ordinariness of the conversation soothes me. He has an English accent, which I have heard in the movies, and it's beautiful. He is an ordinary man, but nothing about him is ordinary. He is handsome and so tall his knees come up to his chest as he sits in the low chair. His sandy hair is sweaty and slightly stuck to his head from his helmet. He has removed his gloves and they rest on his knee. I begin to count the zippers on his jacket and pants and wonder what is in each one. If he can produce a carton of milk, what other magic might he produce? He is from a faraway land across the sea. The land of Arthur and princes, yet here he sits in our den exchanging pleasantries with my mother.

My father appears in his coat with the keys to the parish hall and off they go. The gentleman is only seeking shelter. Somewhere to sleep for the night. I want him to stay. Is he here to show me there is more to the world than swing sets and water moccasins? I hear the unfamiliar roar of his motorcycle as he drifts off down the road following my father to the church.

# three

IN THE LATE SUMMER OF '61 MY FATHER GOES INTO THE HOSPITAL for a "bad back." He'd fallen and hurt his back on my parents' wedding day. There was an ice storm in Houston that day, and he slipped on the ice outside the church and fell onto the curb. He'd lived in constant pain since then. A given in my life was, "Daddy can't lift that. Daddy can't sit that long. Daddy has to go lie down."

When we visit him in the hospital, my father is in a bed tied to pulleys with little black bags of sand hanging from his legs. It is explained to me that this is "traction" designed to alleviate the compression in his lower spine and relieve the pain in his back. To further complicate matters, Hurricane Carla is bearing down on the Gulf of Mexico heading straight for Galveston with Bay City just a short jaunt north. On our next visit to the hospital, we have to stand on wooden tomato boxes outside so we can see in through the taped-up windows as we are not allowed inside. My father's bed is in the hall outside his room and all we can see are his feet. The hospital is on lockdown. Everything is on lockdown. Carla is coming and we need to get home!

Hurricane Carla hits Bay City with the force of a Category 4 hurricane. The wind howls, the house shakes, it rains sideways, and the glass doors and windows bend. We are in the dark with hurricane lamps and candles. We eat peanut butter and jelly sandwiches for days.

At some point Mr. Arlet, a man from our church, comes to our house to stay the night. I assume this is because my father is in the hospital and we need a man at our house, but I wonder—*if he is at our house, who is at his house?* He and my mother practice taking the hall door from its hinges and pretending to jam it into one of the glass windows along one side of our house that might be blown in by the hurricane-force winds. I hear them whisper, "If one window gets blown in, all the other windows in the house will blow out from the force of the wind." I sit cross-legged on the floor and watch the glass doors and windows bend because this is what my mother is doing. I am very focused.

Charlotte and I play "jump the drip." This is a game where you follow a path around the house and jump over all the pots and pans strewn about the floor that are catching the water leaking from the roof and through the ceiling. There isn't much light because we have no power and the storm has all but blocked out the sun. We don't light the lamps and candles in the house until it's really dark, so I navigate the course with care, timing my jump over each pot between drips. You win if you finish the course without getting dripped on. Charlotte inspects my head.

When the eye of the hurricane passes over us, Mother knows there is a period of calm, so we race to the grocery store. We take the Old Gray Goose, an ancient oxidized gray Buick from the '30s, but she runs. We drive through flooded streets with trees down all over town. My mother gives a running commentary on her fear of "losing the breaks." "Pump the breaks," she says to no one in particular.

We go to the grocery store, and Charlotte and I are instructed to "stay in the car and pump the breaks." Charlotte explains we have to do this because the streets are flooded all the way to the car floorboards and the brakes are wet and could fail. My mother returns with fresh supplies, and we retrace our path back home.

Mr. Arlet returns to his family, assumedly to jamb doors into their windows. The eye passes, and Carla returns again.

Roofs have been blown off, tornadoes have touched down in town, and people are killed. My parents' friends in Texas City, who we call Aunt Sally and Uncle Amos, have four feet of water in their house and snakes taking refuge on top of the refrigerator, but the storm has passed, the flooding is over, the trees are cleaned up, and my daddy is home from the hospital. God's in His heaven and all's right with the world.

# four

THE SUMMER BETWEEN KINDERGARTEN AND FIRST GRADE WE move to Houston. No one tells us why. We just move. The blue Chevy station wagon is loaded up with the basics of life, and a Bekins Van Lines truck comes to collect all our furniture and boxes of dishes and books. We will spend years thereafter peeling Bekins stickers off all our furniture.

As is typical of road trips, Charlotte and I are taken from our beds by my parents, still asleep in our PJs, and carried out to the car before dawn. We are loaded in the back, the seat folded down so we can sleep on the way. We wake up on some two-lane highway passing fields of cows, horses, cotton, rice, beans, and bluebonnets. Bluebonnets are particular to Texas. My mother says people try to grow them in other states, but bluebonnets aren't happy if they're not growing in Texas, a point of great pride for Texans. The flowers are a deep blueish purple and grow in great numbers in any uncultivated field. A single bluebonnet is pretty but unremarkable, but a field of bluebonnets set against the green Texas hills and a warm spring sky will make you gasp in wonder or sigh with delight. They are my mother's favorite flower, so they are also mine.

These are the days when driving is a skill, not the mind-numbing experience of the multi-lane interstate highway. There is one lane in each direction, and if you get stuck behind a slow car or a pig truck, well, this is your lot in life. Passing is an adventure and not for the meek of heart. You drift over to the left, make sure the road ahead is clear—no hills or curves to obscure your vision—then gun it to get around the pig truck in front of you, which smells like, well, pigs!

Pig trucks are only for pigs, as no other self-respecting animal, be it sheep, cow, or horse, will set foot in a truck used to haul pigs. There is concentrated pig pee and poop soaked into the metal floors that cause a chemical reaction, creating a smell heretofore unknown to the earth. Acrid, pungent, and permanent—a smell that coats your nostrils and gets stuck in your throat. Pig truckers throw down a little dirt or straw on the truck beds to soften the stench, but it only eases their conscience. Theirs is a trail of tears as they drive along the highway. Even just passing a pig truck you know that your eyes will water and you'll involuntarily stop breathing until you can eventually break out and pass them into fresh air and freedom.

Driving is a family affair. On a trip like this my father usually drives, while colorful commentary and driving suggestions are provided by my mother. "Slow down, Parke." "Watch this guy. He doesn't seem to be paying attention." "Look at the bluebonnets!"

These are the days before seat belts, so my mother sits sideways in the front seat talking to my father. We are in the back, perched precariously on the folded-down back seat and leaning over the front seat for a better view. My father smokes, so he has the little tiny "wing" window open to pull his cigarette smoke out of the car, but then he takes a drag and blows the entire car full of smoke.

At every car or truck passing opportunity, we all participate. Drift left, check the road ahead, curve—can't see—drift back into our lane. Drift left. Seems clear. No curve, no hills, no cars, gun it! This does not always turn out as planned. Driving is an adventure, a group sport on the road, and some drivers are more competitive than others. Now and again you'll come up on some guy that doesn't like being passed. As soon as we get alongside, he guns the motor and races us down the highway. This is scandalous and we are all having fun yelling at him, my mother pointing out the flaws in his moral character, my father shaking his head in disbelief at his irresponsible behavior, my sister Charlotte and I disparaging his family and friends, using the full capacity of our knowledge and vocabulary. I think my father will pull this off—until we hit a hill. Will the guy next to us back off? Will my father have to retreat and pull back behind him, admitting defeat in our pass? We all watch and will the old Chevy down the road until it is finally safe to pull in ahead of the offending car. It is understood that we're all required to participate and successfully achieve the pass. Not one of us could have been asleep or not paying attention. Everyone has to be on board and pulling for the team. This is what it means to be a family.

We play "I Spy" and "Twenty Questions" and sing "The Eyes of Texas" and various church hymns favored by my parents. My mother peppers the time with, "Look, bluebonnets!" "Look, they're growing beans," as we drive the rural highways toward Houston.

My contribution to most car trips is vision and vomit. Mother and Daddy both wear glasses (Charlotte will by third grade), but my vision is sharp. I can read street signs at half a mile. The vomit part is less attractive and not at all useful. I get "car sick" and my mother carries medicine in the glove compartment for this, but invariably she forgets to give it to me until it's too late. I regularly decorate the side of the car with my half digested breakfast or lunch. One memorable time I chucked up plums and the whole back quarter panel was a lovely shade of purple, reminiscent of flames on a hot rod.

The new house in Houston is on Elm Street in Bellaire with

the grade school at the end of my block. We arrive well ahead of the Bekins truck, so we have to camp in the house until the furniture arrives. My mother makes frozen green peas for dinner in the coffee percolator as we have no pots or pans. Daddy grills burgers on the hibachi. We have improvised beds on the floor.

The whys and wherefores of our new life are unknown and not discussed with children. My daddy doesn't have a new church. He goes to work, but I don't know where, and it's not the same somehow. "God, God the Father" are the words we hear in church, and it's a little confusing. He's my dad, but he also stands at the altar in church with consecrated fingers so he can touch the "host" and give out communion. He baptizes babies, marries couples, and signs kids up for the big dance with confirmation. It's a gray area. He's supposed to be God's representative or messenger on Earth, but without his own church, he is suddenly just Daddy.

Life in Houston is unremarkable with the exception of it being huge. There are freeways that crisscross each other like a layer cake. Mother drives the Old Gray Goose and we cruise along them. There are more freeways than cars. Charlotte and I rumble around in the back seat. We have discovered a hole in the floorboards where you can take a Kleenex, shove it through the hole, and watch it fly out of the car, surprising and obscuring the vision of the car behind. We think this is big fun and regularly terrorize our fellow travelers on the freeway. Mother says nothing about this game, so she either doesn't notice or doesn't care.

After a month or so Daddy gets a church! It isn't "his" church, but we go every Sunday. We don't know these people, but we are the preacher's family and must dutifully attend. I like the beauty of churches—the architecture, the art, the choir, the singing, the pageantry—but I hate my clothes and this ruins the experience. I am required to wear a dress that is itchy and involves some sort of petticoat, invariably organdy or tulle, puffy, fluffy kinds of dresses designed to make you look like a ball of cotton candy.

One of the benefits of Daddy's new job is that there is a Cuban family that has been adopted by the church. They're here because of some guy called Castro, and they're part of the first great migration of Cubans fleeing to the United States. Our president, Mr. Kennedy, doesn't like Mr. Castro and sent a bunch of pigs on an invasion that doesn't work out.

Carlos and Aleda Alonso fled Cuba with the clothes on their backs. Carlos owned a garage in Cuba, and they are salt of the earth, hardworking middle class. Aleda would tell the story of officials taking her nail kit at the airport. They weren't allowed to leave with anything of value, so they showed up on our shores destitute but hopeful.

My mother speaks fluent Spanish, the result of four years of Catholic School in a high school with a very good language department and wants desperately to use it, so we go to visit the Alonsos regularly. I don't understand a word that is being said, but I understand Coca-Cola when offered. We are invited for Sunday dinner (which is lunch) and all sit down for a feast. There is a large plate of rice and beans and a plate of sliced fried bananas, which Aleda serves proudly. My mother advises Aleda that I need to have my rice with the beans on the side not on top. It's possible my mother's Spanish is insufficient to communicate this information, but it's more likely the case that this way of serving the rice and beans is so foreign to Aleda that my mother has to reach over and prepare my plate herself. I have never seen black beans before, but I know rice.

I ask please for butter and sugar. Aleda is too polite to question me and brings the requested condiments. I proceed to butter my rice, which seems to raise the level of tension at the table, but when, like a good Southern child, I put sugar on my rice, Aleda actually shrieks. I sit in humiliated silence, sugar spoon frozen in midair, not knowing what I have done wrong but sure I have caused some sort of offense. There is much excitement back and forth in Spanish, none of which I understand, but then there are smiles and laughing and much merriment. I get over my humiliation quickly. I am hungry. I am always hungry.

The experience with Carlos and Aleda brings the idea to Mother that she needs to start using her Spanish. At home she starts speaking, sometimes exclusively, to my sister and me in Spanish. At first Charlotte and I are taught simple phrases to use when we visit the Alonsos. "*Yo no comprendo*," I say proudly. Later she just speaks to us as if we understand, hoping we do. We do, over time, ferret out a few things. "*Te quiero*" means I love you. "*Vamonos*" is "let's go." Simple stuff, but when she rattles off an entire sentence in the grocery store pertaining to what kind of cereal we are buying, I've had enough. "Speak English!" I yell at the top of my lungs.

Probably the only reason I speak even passable Spanish today is not the two years I studied in high school but the Spanish my mother spoke to me as a child. When a *gringa* makes an effort to speak to you in your native tongue and not just assume that everyone speaks English, it is generally a moment of note and considered with some affection. Saying "*Que es esto*?" or "*Que esta haciendo*?" to a worker using a tool or a technique I have never seen and would like to understand often leads to a conversation—in his bad English and my bad Spanish—but we get there. He explains, I understand, we laugh together knowing we are slaughtering the languages we are attempting, but it's the effort toward each other that matters . . . the human interaction. He might be a low-level guy in the crew, but somebody bothered to note his existence and interact with him. Your mother is right. Your mother is always right about such things.

Mother is late almost everywhere we go. It invariably has to do with her hair, which she wears up in a French twist. Think Audrey Hepburn in *Breakfast at Tiffany's*. I am dressed for church in my scratchy, uncomfortable dress pacing in the hall just outside the bathroom door where she is waging war with her hair. I know the Sunday routine. We get sweet rolls for breakfast and are required to put on "church dresses" with petticoats, white socks, and either white or black patent leather shoes, depending on the season. Gloves, if you can find two that match, and a little purse to carry your quarter for the collection plate completes the outfit.

There is always tension as Mother goes to do her hair. A lot of frustrated cursing as it is brushed and twisted. Hairpins and hair spray. A lot of hair spray. It's up, it's done, but then, no, she tears it all down and starts over. Codependent doesn't properly describe my feelings as I watch her struggle. It's like watching a boxing or tennis match when she does her hair, where you involuntarily bob and weave with the players, flinch with the punches. "You can do it. Just that little bit there. Another hairpin here. Almost. Almost." Then she tears it all down and starts over. We are going to be late to church.

The women of this postwar generation have very little left but their looks. Gone is Rosie the Riveter, gone are the jobs they had during the war: transporting planes around the country, building battleships, packing munitions, winning the war, being part of something big and good and important. They have been stuffed back into stylish shirtwaist dresses, into the home with only the drudgery of housework, family, and children. My mother wanted to be an engineer like her father—to build things. Engineering wasn't considered appropriate for a girl, though, so they made her take bacteriology instead. Her first job out of college, while my father went to seminary in Berkeley, California, was testing mayonnaise for Kraft foods. Not the life she aspires to. Not the kind of job her generation of women is hoping for. Not the career they have in mind. They go insane.

The lucky ones are the nurses. Invaluable during the war, caring for the innumerable injured soldiers. They came home and went back to work in hospitals and doctors' offices, but their transition is often just as frustrating. A nurse who improvised under battlefield conditions to save limbs and lives and suffered through the trauma of the dead and dying is now working in a hospital under a fresh-out-of-school, half-her-age doctor whose word is gospel. No one asks her what she thinks. She's just supposed to stand behind the doctor looking pretty.

Because of my mother's frustration, every house we ever move to or live in is subject to her whim. "That's not a bearing wall," she says. "Emily, bring me that hammer." Walls are removed, fuse boxes rewired, backhoes rented, thermostats repaired, heating systems redesigned and reworked. It seems like my mother can do anything, and she always elicits my help. "Hold this." "Stand up here and holler if it goes on." Maybe she isn't going to be an engineer and build bridges or invent the catalytic converter, but she is going to do her damnedest to try. She is also passing her bravery on to me. She is creating a fearless child.

# five

ALMOST ALL OUR RELATIVES LIVE IN HOUSTON: MY GRANDPARENTS on my mother's side, my father's aunt and uncle, his mother, my mother's brother and his children. The two sides of our family are decidedly different. My father's people are from Galveston. Solid, blue-collar, Gulf Coast folks. My mother's people are East Coast–educated, country club Episcopalians who aspire to money and status. Her parents live in River Oaks, a fancy suburb for wealthy folks in Houston.

My father's mother, "Grandma Smith," I do not like. Grandma Smith's house is dark and smells of mildew. She is needy and cloying. She wears her hair pulled back in a tight bun, is a little chubby, pulls Kleenex of some dubious condition from her cleavage, and smells funny. I met my grandfather at some point, but the only lasting memory I have of him is seeing him sitting on the front porch of their red brick craftsman house in Houston. He was in a bathrobe, smoking and coughing, and I would later recall there was a bottle next to him. No one ever talked about it, but he was an alcoholic. He died almost immediately after we moved to Houston. Grandma Smith, now retired, is a very hard worker and supported my Grandpa and my father, putting him through college and seminary. She sold Mrs. Grass Soup out of the trunk of her car, saved all her money, bought government savings bonds, and landed in Houston. She benefitted from the war years when so many women were working.

We regularly visit my father's Uncle Frank and Aunty. Grandma Smith has lived with them since my grandfather died and she had pacemaker surgery. Uncle Frank and Aunty have a daughter, Muriel, who is spoken of in hushed tones. "She couldn't deal with life at an office job. People were all talking about her." Apparently, she had a beau at one time but they broke up, leaving Muriel forever brokenhearted. All I really know is that Muriel is odd but nice. She plays the organ when we come over—"Yellow Bird" and "Alley Cat"—and Charlotte and I dance around the living room.

Aunty is diabetic but I don't know what that means. I know it has to do with food and ice cream in particular. She isn't supposed to eat it but does regularly. She seems to live in the kitchen, and the fruits of her labors are as mysterious as the characters who live in this house. They grow their own food in the back garden—eggplant, okra. Things I have never heard of, much less eaten.

Their dining room table is huge and occupies most of the room. Glass doors separate the space from what used to be a porch but is now enclosed and serves as Uncle Frank's office. The only air conditioner in the house is a window unit on said porch, but try as it may, it cannot keep up with the Texas humidity or the human heat load.

We're all seated at the table, Charlotte and me each on two phone books, and Aunty comes through the swinging door that separates the kitchen and dining rooms with a huge caldron of something that smells divine. Gumbo. Shrimp gumbo. I love shrimp. If you live on the Texas Gulf Coast, you better love shrimp—and seafood in general because we have a lot of it.

Everyone is served from a large pot of rice, then from the divine-smelling gumbo. I am one of those unfortunate children who don't like my foods to touch, though I don't know why. Did

I come by this predilection myself, or is it the product of the '50s three piles of food mentality—meat, vegetable, starch. At my house, you are very likely to be served a hamburger patty, baked potato, and green peas. I eat each category individually. I like them all, but I am not a food mixer. I am very hungry. I am always hungry.

After all, it is one o'clock and I have spent the last hour or so dancing around the living room to Muriel's organ playing. The bowl set down in front of me is beautiful. To one side is the mysterious red concoction of shrimp, vegetables, and spices, and the other, a bed of bright white rice. Aunty knows I don't like my food to touch and serves accordingly. The horror that explodes in my mouth is topped only by the disappointing realization that I will soon starve. There are spices and peppers I have never tasted. They sear my tongue and numb my mouth and lips. Gulps of water wash away the current offense, but the infestation remains.

I have the palette of an infant. I cannot drink a chocolate soda because it burns my mouth. I cannot stand the smell of black pepper, much less have it touch my food. My father's use of pepper at the dinner table is liberal, so much so that it aerates and drifts around the room. The smell alone is sometimes enough to drive me from the table.

Charlotte has no issue and gobbles up her gumbo and rice. I am encouraged by all to "Try again, Emily. It's not that hot." I try, but not really. My mouth is still burning from the first bite. No one notices after my first mouthful that I'm not eating as they are all enjoying the delights of Aunty's gumbo.

I dig at the center of my rice for a mouthful that has not absorbed any of the gumbo's juices. I add butter in an attempt to eat something familiar. Eventually, I give up, and those beautiful shrimp swimming in a sea of fire are taken away. My only hope is the ice cream that is sure to follow.

In the fall, I start first grade at the elementary school at the end of the block. This seems more advanced than kindergarten. This is school. Real school. I am six, dressed in my little brown dress with a red rooster on the collar. Charlotte and I walk together down our street to school and then I'm abandoned in the hall to find my own way to class.

My teacher is young and pretty but does not make the same overwhelming impression as Miss Payton. No houndstooth skirt. No black loafers. We read Dick and Jane. We're introduced to Spot the Dog and learn to read in little circles at the side of the classroom.

The children in my class are strange. There is a girl who eats paste and a boy who is continually in trouble for putting paste on another girl's chair. Paste seems to be a big thing. These seem to me to be advanced ideas, things to do that I would never have thought of. I am continually hungry but I would never eat paste. I consider putting paste on my sister's chair, but the consequences are evaluated and the idea rejected. It's not like biting, where no real harm is done.

One of our extra activities in class is the bomb drill. We line up against the walls of our classroom, then squat down on our haunches with our heads on the floor against the wall. The most important instruction seems to be to cover our necks with our hands. This is all fine and good and I want to play along, but my brown dress with the red rooster on the collar is very short, and when I bend over my underpants show. I spend the entire drill trying to pull my dress down in the back, which of course means exposing my neck, which will surely result in my being killed in the nuclear holocaust.

My parents float through my life as the great mysteries, the providers, the gods of life. They are the center and safety of my world. My father, it is well-known, is beyond special. He is a priest. Not a fireman or an insurance salesman, but a priest. He doesn't wear regular clothes to work but instead a black suit with a black vest over his shirt and a stiff white collar. He works at church, for goodness' sake. My mother is stunningly beautiful and knows everything. Not just how to make food but how to fix electrical stuff and how to make clothes. Our home is nice and cozy. I don't realize that we are poor. My mother does a lot with very little.

My mother's parents' big fancy house in River Oaks has a bay window in the front and wall-to-wall carpeting. There are oil paintings of long-dead relatives, antique furniture, and a grandfather clock that strikes the hour with some sort of church-sounding holy chime. There is a front entry hall that has furniture in it and a massive gold-framed mirror that goes from the floor to almost the ceiling. There are beautiful rugs, a large white porcelain elephant by the fireplace, and vases of roses grown in the rose garden outside. There is no yard to play in, just a huge bricked patio with rose beds everywhere. They are rich. We are poor.

These grandparents are called "Granny" and "Pompy." There is no way my grandmother is going to be called "Grandma." My parents are nervous every time we go to their house. Daddy gets dressed in his best suit, Mother in her best dress, and Charlotte and I in church clothes, which itch and are uncomfortable. There is a palpable tension from my grandparents when we arrive, but Charlotte and I seem to be the peace offering that smooths the way.

I am excited to visit, as I truly love my Granny and Pompy. There will be candy orange slices from the glass jar in the kitchen, and there is a toy cabinet under the window seat in the living room. The living room is massive, with another bay window looking over the rose garden. There is no real fun to be had here, just quiet playing. We never eat a single meal at their house. Probably because it would be too messy and disturb the magnificence of their home. It is beautiful. It is sterile. It is cold. My grandmother is the magnolia in charge.

Mother and Daddy sit stiffly in the living room. Pompy is there but not. Granny directs Charlotte and me to the toy cabinet under the window seat. There is an old box camera to play with that I love. I mostly love the sound it makes as I open and close the back, turn the wheel that would advance the film, and push the button to click the shutter. I pretend to load film and take pictures, but there is nothing to take pictures of. The adults all sit rigidly upright in their chairs, my parents trying to give the illusion of our life being better than it is and Granny and Pompy judging it all.

Eventually snacks appear: tiny crackers and some cheese. Nothing that will make a mess, but also not enough. I hop up to avail myself of the food provided, but I'm met with a withering glance from Granny. These are grown-up snacks, not for children, but I persevere, gingerly taking one cracker and piece of cheese, carefully putting it all in my mouth so as not to leave any crumbs on the carpet. This is met with approval from Granny's force field. I return to the floor and my camera knowing I am not to eat any more or risk the mess that comes with children.

Charlotte knows better than to attempt an approach. She stays on the carpet playing tea party with an old china doll with a chipped nose and a tiny little china tea set. She knows how to portray perfection. She has game. Blond, thin, quiet, and careful, deliberate in her aura and demeanor. By contrast, I vibrate unexploded energy like my mother. We are both in control now but known to be dangerous if let loose.

When I was four, I stayed overnight at Granny and Pompy's house, a special treat. They had come to Bay City to visit and I drove back with them to Houston. During the visit I got angry with Granny for being chastised for running on the patio and falling in the rose garden. Being escorted to the bathroom for first aid for my skinned knee and elbow, I lost my temper that there was no sympathy for my injuries, just scolding for my behavior.

"You are not to run in the garden or in the house," was Granny's unspoken law.

"I'm gonna throw you in the alligator water," I hollered. It was my threat to gain power in this situation, but it backfired horribly as I was yanked up by my wrists and spanked there on the spot. Grannies don't spank! They fuss over you, compliment your long eyelashes, and give you delicious orange slices. My illusion vanquished on the spot. I was met with a powerful and skilled opponent who is not to be toyed with. I would not win. I would be outmaneuvered at every turn. I began to understand my mother's frustration. No one is allowed to be who they are if who they are is not exactly what Granny wants them to be.

Our visit is approaching the allotted two hours, and Granny is clearing away the snack. She gives the silent signal that she has had enough and the visit is over. Good, because I can't pretend to be having fun anymore, and there have been no orange slices. Let's get out of here and out of this dress. We are escorted to the front door, where everyone hugs and kisses. Pompy shakes my father's hand, and we walk properly to the car. Once in the car, and having driven out of sight, we all sit in silence for quite some time. It takes a while for Granny's smothering blanket of civility and etiquette to evaporate; we don't recover that day. There is a pall of disapproval that follows us and takes a good night's sleep to dissipate. It lurks; Granny's magic is strong. Her spells are powerful and meant to last. My mother is slowed and more refined; I don't run in rose gardens. But eventually it wears off. There is more than one wizard in this family.

# six

THE HANGOVER OF THE VISIT TO GRANNY AND POMPY'S HAS WORN off and I am back to myself. Back to the rambunctious child seeking adventure at every turn, and Saturday mornings are the stuff of legend. Charlotte and I wake up early as there are cartoons and independence awaits. My parents sleep in. The TV is in a little step-down room off their bedroom, with the living room on the other side. We sprawl on the couch and select our favorites from the three-channel selection. Charlotte likes *Johnny Quest*, while my favorites are *Underdog* and *Mighty Mouse*. Duh! "Here I am to save the day. That means that Mighty Mouse is on the way." I love Mighty Mouse. He's not like Mickey, who seems boring in comparison. This guy is a hero and saves people. That's for me.

At some point my parents stir and we hear their rustling, but we're glued to our television adventures until we hear a joyful roar from my mother, followed by a painful shriek. When we run into the room to see what's happened, our father looks sheepish and our mother is holding her face with both hands.

My parents' bedroom is dominated by a king-size bed. The room is small but the bed is the size of an aircraft carrier. My father's back requires a special mattress, purchased at some expense. It also has plywood placed underneath it for support. Turns out, my father was reluctant to disembark the ship this morning. My mother, in an attempt to rouse him, launched herself across the bed. He procured an elbow in defense which struck her with deadly precision on the nose. There was an audible crack, and here we are.

My parents return from the doctor later that day with stories of overcharging and a "cast" on my mother's nose. This is a plaster apparatus that spans the distance between her forehead to her upper lip, taped to her face to protect and immobilize her nose. She is supposed to wear it for two weeks, which is a ridiculous idea proposed by the doctor who obviously knows nothing about my mother. She wears it periodically when it suits her, but mostly she does not. She obviously knows more than the doctor.

Houston is a bog. A swamp. It is always raining, or the rain has just stopped, or it's about to start again. In Bay City there was water everywhere, too, but it was contained in ponds and streams. Stayed where it belonged. In Houston it hangs in the air, runs in the gutters, and squishes up out of the heavily matted Saint Augustine lawns. Add the heat, and you live in a perpetual steam bath.

Since we live in suburbia, we play in the gutters instead of the ponds and streams of Bay City. I float little paper boats down the block, build dams, and make puddles until some car comes along, drives through my puddle, and soaks me for all the effort. Ringworms are the new water moccasins. I am told they live in the gutter and that I'll surely catch them. Jimmy Joe, who lives next door, tells me this isn't true, but since he had pneumonia last year and recently cut his toes off helping his father mow the lawn, he's not considered a reliable source of information.

My parents are off to Arkansas. There is a church there for my father, so they are off to check things out, my mother being first and foremost concerned about the schools. They take an airplane with tickets provided by the church and are gone Friday night to Sunday afternoon. Charlotte and I are shuffled off to Granny and Pompy's, but being such a short visit and without my parents, the atmosphere is lighter and we have each other to play with.

Sunday night back home, Charlotte and I eat our traditional Sunday night dinner of graham crackers and peanut butter and overhear my mother's list of objections to Arkansas. "Parke, it's too rural. I like the countryside and it's beautiful—but boring. Plus, the schools seemed old, rooted in some 1930s mentality of reading, writing, and arithmetic. I just get a feeling that Arizona might be just what we need. Let's get out of Texas, out of the South, and start fresh."

"The diocese wants me in Arkansas," Daddy counters. "I think Arizona is just being offered to look like we have a choice." But Mother has her arsenal lined up and he has no chance. Poverty, education, and future growth are all eloquently cited by Mother and he finally capitulates. Arkansas is rejected and we are moving to Arizona. I guess they just started at the top of the list—Ari, Ark—and Arizona was the ticket. No one goes to visit Arizona, but we are moving anyway.

It's Bekins again! The church must have had a deal with Bekins because my mother *hates* Bekins. I hate them too. I don't know why, but my mother's opinion is good enough for me. Everything is packed up in boxes and barrels, the furniture loaded. "Bon voyage" is wished to all the relatives, though we are the ones going.

We pack up the Chevy. Trusty steed. Charlotte and I know the drill and are comfortable ensconced in the back seat. This time we're too old to be taken by our parents out to the car in our pajamas in the dead of night. I am seven and Charlotte is nine.

We have taken plenty of car trips in my young life, mostly inside Texas. Bay City to Houston. Bay City to Texas City to visit Uncle Amos and Aunt Sally. But this trip is going all the way out of Texas, across New Mexico, and into Arizona. I don't know how good your US geography is, but Texas is *very big*. The roads are now interstate highways, so we cruise along at a good clip of sixty miles per hour, but still, Daddy drives hard and all day long, and we're still in Texas. As my mother says, "The sun has riz, the sun has set, and we is still in Texas yet."

We stop at places of interest and national parks along the way. We camp overnight. Hotels are expensive. "We don't have money to throw around," my mother says. We must have been on a mission to get out of Texas because we don't stop anywhere of interest until we get to New Mexico. The Painted Desert. The Petrified Forest. She talks repeatedly of "being happy to leave all those cowboys behind." We are headed for Prescott, Arizona.

# seven

PRESCOTT IS A SMALL OLD TOWN. WHEN WE ARRIVE MOTHER SAYS, "We are going into the hotel downtown for breakfast." This in and of itself is remarkable. We are going out to eat! As usual, I'm hungry. My dinner the night before was sacrificed to satisfy the gods of car sickness. We ate sandwiches in the car so we didn't have to stop and because Daddy wanted to make it to Prescott this morning with one last push. But my stomach couldn't take the extra hours in the car. It's no wonder that I have grown into a lanky, scrawny kid. There are too many things I won't eat and enough tension internalized in my belly to make me reject whatever food is being offered, either before or after it goes in. Mixed-up food, mushy food, spicy food, anything with black pepper. They are all on the "I couldn't possibly eat that" list.

The hotel building is a square brick four-story structure. The lobby is massive with a large carved wooden front desk. We enter the restaurant and the first things I notice are the bar that stretches the length of the room and booths on the other side. Seated at our booth, which seems designed to seat a family of ten, my mother groans and says, "Oh Lord!" and drops her head into her hands. On the placemat a banner proclaims: "Prescott, Cowboy Capital of the World."

We order breakfast. I want bacon and toast with jelly and

grits. "We don't have grits," admonishes the waitress, "but we have potatoes." Potatoes are not a breakfast food. This is the first indication that we have landed in an alien world.

The next stop is the apartment where we will stay until our new house is finished. The church is building a house for the new priest, but it isn't finished yet and won't be for several months. The apartment we'll stay in is a duplex right next door to the church. Charlotte and I are to occupy the right side while Mother and Daddy live in the other. It's a strange setup and I don't like it. It's old, smells funny, and the bedroom has glass doors. There is a glass casement window over the front door designed for people to jump up and look in at you. The place is old and haunted, but I suppose it's better than camping without a bathroom. Plus, it's only temporary.

Charlotte is in fourth grade, and I'm in second now. My teacher is Miss Hall and no match for me. "I am sleeping in the bathtub as our furniture has not yet arrived," I tell her. She seems impressed by this, so we're off to a good start.

Charlotte and I spend weekends playing around the duplex. Mother is busy "making the place livable" with its dingy interior and leftover from "god knows who" furniture. Mr. Painter, as Charlotte and I name him, is at work painting the exterior. Charlotte and I are sifting sand through an old piece of window screen we found. Mr. Painter offers that we can put some of our sifted sand in his paint. There isn't much else to do. There's a tiger-striped kitty cat that shows up on our porch daily. We soon adopt her and name her Nosey.

Across the street is a vacant lot and Mother warns to "never cross the street." Being seven and obviously capable of making major decisions like this for myself, I decide to cross the street and explore. Almost immediately I discover a treasure: a small rifle, just my size. The bolt action kind they have in World War II movies. The bolt is frozen from lack of use and cleaning, it's covered in dirt, and the barrel is full of sand, but it's mine. "Losers weepers. Finders keepers."

I sneak back across the street undetected and proceed to play war. Charlotte has a poor attitude about my new find and is not at all interested in playing war. She's more inclined to continue the prince and princess drama, but this place is not at all suited to playing prince and princess. It's all dirt, no grass. Obviously more suitable for war. I am the hero of my drama, supported by my imaginary company of soldiers. Charlotte acquiesces to my choice for now and we proceed to sneak around the house in search of hapless German soldiers, dispatch them quickly, and revel in the glory of our heroics.

As dusk settles, Mr. Painter wraps up for the day and we're called in for dinner. I proudly display my new treasure, but Mother does not have the right amount of praise or enthusiasm. "Put that dirty thing out on the porch," she says, and I dutifully comply but with great reservation. A good soldier always has her rifle at hand, so much so I should sleep with it, but my mother is ignorant of this fact.

The next morning I run outside to reclaim my prize from the corner by the door where I left it for safekeeping, but it's gone! What a stupid idea to leave it on the porch! You can't leave a treasure of this magnitude unguarded. Seeing my gun, some thief in the night had crept onto our porch and stolen it.

"My gun is gone!" I cry to anyone who will listen. Mother is busy at the kitchen sink and doesn't even turn around to note my distress.

"It's probably just as well," she says.

I am bereft. To think, I had only one glorious day playing war with my rifle. This is the first betrayal. The first lie, but I don't know it yet. I am unaware of my mother's duplicity. *She* didn't like me having a gun. *She* took it and threw it away. She's content to let me believe a thief took it, but I will get smarter.

We finally move from the duplex to the new house. It's on Thumbutte Road with the actual butte not far behind our house. I think it's a dormant volcano—at least that's what it looks like. A large mass sticking straight up that one can imagine would spew fire and lava and then, in one glorious last gasp, blow its top, collapsing one side to explain its current shape. This gives me pause. *Has anyone checked it out to be sure it won't erupt again as I sleep, drowning me in molten lava?* Probably not, as parents don't have the foresight children do for pending disaster.

The house is a split-level ranch with an entry, bedrooms, a living room, a kitchen, and a dining room on the ground floor. Stairs lead down to a large family room with a fireplace. I am fond of the stairs but disappointed there's no banister for sliding.

I have my own bedroom. This is the first real separation from my sister, and I am quite pleased about it—but also afraid of the dark. I know well there *are* monsters who live in the dark, under the bed, and apparitions who travel through the house at night. No amount of parental admonishing or logic will dissuade me from what I know to be true. I *feel* them all around in the dark. They are monsters of ill will and I must stay vigilant and awake. The smallest amount of light in my bedroom is the vampire garlic to guard against their horror.

Bacon and toast with jelly is still the breakfast of choice. This is what my mother likes, and once again, she is correct. Mother sometimes makes eggs because that's what Daddy likes, but they are a soft, gooey mess that seems designed to make me gag. Being the era of "starving children in Africa," we're required to eat all the food provided, which is problematic where eggs or any other soft, sloppy mess is concerned. Stewed tomatoes come to mind. They make me gag.

Proving the theory of the collective consciousness, every kid knows the moves to survive the inedible food issue. The wipe your mouth with your napkin while spitting out the offending substance move. The fill your mouth then run to the bathroom and spit it in the toilet move. Charlotte, hater of all vegetables, has an impressive repertoire. She lines up her peas under her knife so they can't be seen. She once sacrificed half a potato skin by turning it upside down to create a cave under which to push all her lima beans. There are flaws in any approach, but I have to give her credit for sacrifice, inventiveness, and variety.

We take the school bus from the new house to our new school. This is a system invented by some Machiavellian-type grown-up. We are required to stand outside, in the snow, on the road, and wait for some indeterminate amount of time for the bus to arrive. There seems to be no real set time for when the bus will come, so if we're not out there waiting, it will just drive on by. If we are lucky enough to catch the bus, we board it with some disgruntled group of small humans such as ourselves but of suspect parentage and unknown origin. We are a mix of first to sixth graders, so imagine the hierarchy employed for seating and trading of or outright stealing of packed lunches.

We miss the bus regularly. At first Mother would throw us in the car and drive us to school, but she wearied of that quickly. She says we have to walk. I am sure she intends to teach us a lesson. "I don't know the way!" I cry the first time this happens. Charlotte apparently does, however, because Mother doesn't come to my rescue and we set off on one of many epic journeys to school.

The biggest problem with the walk isn't the boredom so much as being trapped with Charlotte, who still doesn't seem to like me much. Having to walk to school and inevitably arriving late has the desired effect, and I am now more willing to get out on the road and stand in the snow to catch the bus. Again this morning we are late and the bus drives by just as we are running out the front door. We don't turn back toward the house to see if Mother is inclined to drive us. We just head off down the road.

We don't talk, just walk, and that makes the time drag. I begin to play Twenty Questions and I Spy in my head, which really isn't any fun as I know the answers, but I don't know any games to play with just myself. I'm staring at the sky trying to create imaginary creatures out of the clouds when out of my peripheral vision I see Charlotte take a rather spectacular fall. In some scene straight out of vaudeville, she steps on a butter wrapper on the curb (probably margarine as no one eats real butter) and goes face down, legs flying out behind her, and bloodies her knee something ferocious. She limps to school, blood streaming down her leg and coagulating in her sock, and arrives in some state requiring advanced triage. I am merely hustled off to class without a second look or any attention at all.

My day is already compromised by the walk to school and Charlotte's fall and injury, and now I see the school janitor out at the flagpole. This being unfamiliar, I must investigate. I am fascinated by and very fond of the janitor. He wears a khaki shirt and pants with a black belt and shoes. He is a nice man, slightly tall, who always says "hi" and can regularly be seen pushing a long rectangular dust mop through the halls. He is lowering the flag.

"Why?" I ask.

"The president has been shot and killed," he says as the flag goes all the way down to half-mast. The janitor is crying. Other kids have left their games on the playground and gathered at the flagpole. We all begin to cry.

John Fitzgerald Kennedy is the man of the hour. He defeated the evil Nixon in a landslide victory and the country is headed for the Promised Land. President Kennedy is young and handsome, and his wife Jackie is beautiful with a French maiden name and is very exotic. He also has a not as handsome set of younger brothers, and my parents and the rest of the country seem very happy with the whole setup. The Cuban thing is over and the Russians have buckled about the nuclear missiles, so we're on a roll. We know we won the war, live in Camelot, and are safe from the Russians. We may not put all the facts together in a line, but we understand the magnitude of this tragedy.

At home the TV is on for the next several days as we watch the president get shot, the man arrested, the arrested man get shot, Jackie in her pink Chanel suit on the plane, Jackie with John-John and Caroline on the steps of the Capitol as John-John salutes his father, the riderless horse with the empty boots, the funeral, the flame at Arlington. We understand that all is lost and the fairy tales of our youth are gone. No more Pooh, no more Wind in the Willows, no more Camelot.

There is a pall over the country after the president is shot. We get Johnson but the system works. First man down, second man steps up. He's tall and not as handsome, his wife is homely and we long for Jackie, but if she can take it, we can, too, so everyone bucks up. The fact that Johnson is from Texas and known to my parents seems to make them okay with it, so I am okay with it, too, but it takes us all awhile to cheer up. Christmas doesn't have the same luster. No pony.

Nothing about second grade is hard, and there are plenty of outdoor adventures to fill my time. Recess and lunch are the highlight of my school day and I take full advantage. I am enthusiastic in whatever we are playing and regularly return to class bloody at the knees and elbows, which requires some sort of bandaging and even being sent to the nurse on a few occasions. The nurse eventually sends me to the school doctor for a "special evaluation." He's in some other office at school and sits with a clipboard in a chair, and there is a two-by-four on the floor. I am requested to perform a variety of tricks—walk the beam, spin around on the beam, and balance on my toes. He has obviously heard of the neighborhood circuses where we perform a variety of tricks, gymnastics (being my specialty), and magic acts and wants a private performance. Just when I am warming up to my best stuff, he laughs! I am humiliated and a bit pissed off, but he says, "There's nothing wrong with you," and sends me back to class.

So far I'd lived in Texas all my life, where every square inch that is not paved is covered in a heavy mat of Saint Augustine grass. The stuff is inches thick and practically bounces, so you can launch yourself across the yard or playground with little risk of injury. The playground in Prescott is packed, hard dirt with a dusting of gravel, so any errant move is bound to result in at least a scrape or scratch and, in my case, bloody knees and elbows.

There is a late spring snow in the mountains just north and we are going skiing. Everyone gets dressed up in their ski outfits that have been bought specifically for the occasion. Mother, Charlotte, and I all have black stretch ski pants from Sears and heavy wool sweaters knitted by my great-grandmother on my mother's side. We drive to somewhere near Flagstaff, where there is a log cabin lodge and two small hills. Mother rents me a pair of red skis, and I couldn't be happier with the selection. Red. I love red. Then I am turned loose on the hills with thirty seconds of instruction—something about how to snowplow to slow down, but I pay almost no attention.

The beginner hill has a rope tow, and the other hill has a lift where you put a disc under your butt and it carries you up. I head for the bunny slope and the rope tow. I have on red plastic-covered mittens that the rope tow shreds almost immediately, but I soon get the hang of letting the rope glide through my hands, then tighten my grip and the rope pulls me up the hill.

My first few attempts at dismount are disastrous. I fall down in the path of the lift, the rope drags across my legs, and I have to scramble and crawl, with skis attached, onto the hill. Once on the hill, I point my skis down and "ski" at breakneck speed toward the lodge. I have no interest in slowing down or learning how to stop. I throw myself sideways into the snow just before hitting the building. I will later finesse this move to throw myself down parallel to the entry to the rope tow. Glorious! What fun. I do this all day long. Up the rope tow. My dismount improves. Make my way to the center of the hill. Point my skis down and it's over in seconds. Thankfully, there is no one else on my hill. My mother and sister are on the big hill snowplowing back and forth. My father doesn't ski because of his back.

Eventually, my gloves are shredded, with bits of skin being removed with every pass, so I think to try the other lift. It seems straightforward. Grab the pole, sit down on the little seat, up you go. Someone probably tried to tell me what to do, but I didn't listen. I grab the pole, sit down on the seat, and I am not gloriously transported up the hill but unceremoniously land on my backside, stuck in the path of the lift with the following chairs knocking me in the back and head. The lift has to be stopped as I scramble off to the side. I am humiliated. This lack of listening to instruction, thinking I know how to do it, will haunt me for some time to come.

# eight

THE FOLLOWING SUMMER I PLAY COWBOYS AND INDIANS OUTSIDE by myself and occasionally prince and princess still with Charlotte. I'm not so big on playing prince and princess anymore, having graduated to cowboys. I have a cap gun with a holster that seals the deal. If I had a horse, life would be perfect, but I have evolved to imaginary friends for companionship. They let me be in charge, never argue about which way we are going to take the wagon train over the mountain, and never make me drink sun tea.

There is a stream behind our house—a little culvert for directing the water through the neighborhood—and when it rains, it runs. This particular afternoon it has rained enough through the night that the stream is running with a bit of volume. There is still a light drizzle and the stream seems like a great place to play. I set about making a dam. I imagine this dam will create a pool that we will swim in. I am joined by other kids from the neighborhood and our collective efforts are paying off. Like a family of beavers, we've got a couple of feet of water in our pond and it's starting to take up some real estate in the adjacent backyards. We take great pride in our efforts and engineering skills. Employing rocks and dirt, blocking the narrowest part of the channel, using a few logs for variety, our ingenuity is impressive.

Our project begins to draw attention. Most parents hadn't noticed anything as they were used to the kids being outside the house, out from underfoot and out of their hair. Especially on a rainy day, they are collectively relieved we are outside. Then some mother, looking out her back kitchen window, notices there are about twenty kids all gathered around an enormous and growing pond that is beginning to creep into yards and toward back doors. There must have been a flurry of phone calls as out of every house comes a mother or father, like some descending police force to break up the mob. No one remarks on our ingenuity. No one applauds our hours of effort in the rain. No. We are instructed to open the dam and let the water through before "it washes all our houses away."

I am in third grade now and seem to be the star of my class. I regularly win the spelling bee and read with the teacher at the back of the class on my own. The rest of the class is back to Dick and Jane, not having learned to read properly in the previous grades. So much for rejecting Arkansas based on the inadequate school system.

Having a few months of third grade under our belts by now and the playground pecking order established, my best friend is Becky Jones. We play horses at recess. We are dressed in short little dresses with ties around the waist, which work perfectly for playing horses. I untie my sash, and my "rider" takes hold of it and gallops me around the playground. There are also tetherball poles that enjoy a season of popularity. It's a stupid game where the players stand on opposing sides of the pole and try to get the ball, tied with a rope to the pole, past each other to wrap completely around the pole.

The best thing about my friend Becky is that she has real horses, or so she says. I am horse mad and wish for one every Christmas, knowing damn well I won't get one, but what is Santa for if not to wish for the impossible? I generally receive a model horse of some kind, which I proudly display on my windowsill.

Eventually, Becky invites me over to her house. I have visions of Roy Rogers or the Lone Ranger, where we will have guns and holsters and saddle up to ride the range all afternoon. No such fantasy materializes. We just walk around their barn and corral, pet the horses, then I go home. My fantasy collapsing because she wouldn't let me ride is the basis of a seething resentment that is to play out on the tetherball court.

Now it's my turn to invite Becky over to my house. The problem is, I lied and told her I have horses, too. This comes to no good as there are no horses. I make up a lie about the horses being in some other location, but it's an awkward and pivotal point in my life. I come to the realization that if you tell a lie, you have to back it up with more lies, and then to be found out is mortifying. I have a distant relationship with the truth. I am a big "storyteller," as my mother would say. I don't always mean to lie, but sometimes, when I tell stories of my adventures, there are opportunities to "embellish" the truth to improve the story, and this proves to be irresistible.

Becky's and my relationship deteriorates to the point that she is now leading a faction of girls, separate from my own, on the playground. This is the result of my resentment at not getting to ride her horses and her discovery that I am a stone-cold liar. Tetherball is the field of battle. Games become ruthless and mean, Becky and I vying for supremacy with our packs in head-to-head confrontation at the pole. I'm not happy, but I am determined to win. I know my reputation is at stake. Winning equals truth. I slander her on the playground. She is telling her newly formed faction that I am a liar, have no horses, and am not to be trusted.

Report cards from school are the measure of my worth. I am a kid who, up till now, had gotten all A's, B's here and there, and on the other side of the card where they marked your social skills—courteous, uses self-control, cooperates well, respects property—all E's for excellent. My report card from this period, however, has a U. Unsatisfactory in the category "Plays well with others."

My mind can't take it in. My eyes can't focus. *Unsatisfactory!?* How am I going to bring this horrible and offensive document home? I am a golden child. I am an overachiever. The former kindergarten princess. The leader on the playground. The spelling bee winner who reads with the teacher at the back of the room. This is not possible. There were no rewards for good report cards, just expectations.

What will mother say? Likely about the "starving children in Africa." It's one of her favorite themes when I have misbehaved or acted without thought. How I am privileged to have a home and food to eat. I've seen *National Geographic* and the pictures of mud hut villages and babies with distended bellies. I put myself in these scenes. Running naked on the African plains. Living in a mud hut where you don't have chores and your mother loves you very much. None of this dissuades me but the hunger gives me pause. I know hungry just a little, and what I know is enough to convince me that I am probably better off giving up my playground power struggle and trying to get along with Becky Jones. I try to act humble, grateful even.

Daddy says, "I am very disappointed in you, Emily." Mother requires an explanation of exactly what behavior would bring my teacher to give me a U in "Plays well with others." In my mind I am now standing naked in my mud hut village in Africa with my new humility, trying to get taken back into my family. I skirt around the truth, hemming and hawing about Becky having a horse and somehow alluding to it being her fault, preying on any possible guilt my parents might have for my not having a horse. None of it works and I am sent to my room.

# nine

THE U ON MY REPORT CARD HAS FADED FROM MY PARENTS' MEMORY and the holidays are here. At Thanksgiving we are having over for dinner the two families from the church who most befriended us. The Gagnons and their four kids, the McClouds and their six kids. Mother spends a lot of time during the days leading up to the feast worrying about "having fourteen people over for dinner."

We set up long tables and chairs borrowed from the church in the den downstairs. Mother drapes them with every white tablecloth we own. We use all of Great Grandmother's special china and our everyday dishes—every piece of silverware we own to set the table. At dinner, the grown-ups are at one end of the table and the kids at the other. I am seated on the border between and can hear most of the parents' conversation. Early in the dinner, they don't talk about anything interesting, but over pecan and pumpkin pie, the conversation drifts from general church goings-on to more specific talk of trouble at the church.

The rector wants Daddy fired, but the vestry, which includes Mr. Gagnon and McCloud, does not. I know the rector is the head priest that my dad was brought here to assist, and I know the vestry is a group of men at the church who help out with church business.

Between Thanksgiving and Christmas there is more serious talk between my parents, but I am too distracted with Santa Claus and what I might get for Christmas to pay it much mind. Right after Christmas, Daddy gets fired.

The house on Thumbutte always had an aura of tension; it never felt like "home," just the house we lived in. Maybe it has to do with the church and that we are outsiders. Maybe because the head guy never wanted my dad to come in the first place. Whatever the reasons, we are moving again. Tucson this time.

Bekins! My God, it's Bekins again. There are pieces of our furniture that have stickers on stickers. My mother packs all the same things she packed last time. We haven't been here long enough to use some of the things that are now going back into boxes.

It's another road trip in the Chevy, but this time straight south from northern Arizona and Prescott to southern Arizona and Tucson. It's only a five-hour drive and we get there by evening and check into a hotel for the night. We are to meet the Bekins truck at our new house in the morning.

We move into a rented house with green gravel in the front yard and another school at the end of the block. Everything is different here. They don't have grass. There are cacti everywhere, some of which will jump straight out and impale you with tiny stickers even if you don't touch them. It's hot. Not the Texas-you-could-drown-from-just-breathing kind of humid hot, but the suck-the-moisture-right-out-of-your-body dry hot.

I have to share a room with Charlotte again. The room is small and dark with long, narrow, high windows that run almost the entire length of the room. Our twin beds and a dresser fill the room with almost nowhere to play. I am disoriented, having been infected with the shame of Daddy being fired. We get the status of being the priest's family at church, so we also get to carry the rejection.

We have moved midyear and I am to finish third grade at a new school. Everyone else started the year together, where friends were made and alliances formed. I am odd man out. I have no group, no clan. I am alone. I cannot remember the name of my new teacher. She is old with gray hair piled on top of her head, very tall, and does not like me.

They do things differently at this school and I can't get the hang of it. I am not here. My mind is not in my head. I stand on the playground at lunchtime alone; I don't have or make any friends. I have always been popular at school and never have trouble making friends, but at this school I struggle. I'm tired. I don't have the energy for another school change, another reinvention of myself. I decide to sit this one out. Let the second half of third grade ride.

At this school, I am to leave my lunchbox on the porch outside after lunch and bring it in with me after lunch recess. Every day I forget. Every day I leave my lunchbox outside and the janitor brings it in to the teacher. Every day I am scolded by the teacher in front of the class. Every day I am humiliated. She's finally had enough and calls me up to her desk in front of the class and pins a note on my shirt that says, "I can't think."

I spend the rest of the day and many days after, as this solution is employed multiple times, trying to fold the note over by scrunching up my shoulder or leaning on it on my desk so no one could read the words. I remember nothing else of third grade.

Tucson sits in a valley between four mountain ranges. My daddy's new church sits just into the foothills and has a huge arched window at the back behind the altar that frames a large Saguaro cactus and Palo Verde tree. I can watch the seasons flow by and, during particularly boring parts of the service, watch a road runner stalking lizards or hummingbird territorial battles. The altar stands away from the back wall, and the priests stand behind it and face the congregation. The architect got it right on this one. God in all her glory.

We still have an issue being on time to church every Sunday. We live way across town and it takes a good half hour to get there. My mother's favored route is by way of River Road, which, as the name suggests, follows the path of the river or "wash"; it's a river when it rains and it's running, but water in the desert is seasonal and transient. The celebrated blue Chevy has been traded in for a used brown Oldsmobile station wagon that lacks the lightness of the Chevy. We fly down River Road, careening around corners, diving into stomach-churning dips, and flying over hills where the car occasionally leaves the ground. My mother has a lead foot, but we are still almost always late.

The new church is Spanish-style and my mother takes to this like she was born into the Mexican culture. She still wears her hair up in a twist, which has now morphed into the beehive hairdo popular of the era. To this she adds a lace mantilla, the Spanish equivalent of a veil. Like a hat for covering your head, which is expected for women. Not men, just women. Charlotte and I are given a children's variation of this to wear that looks like little lace hankies we bobby pin to our heads.

The entire setup of this church is spectacular. It's traditional Spanish architecture, with a white stucco interior and exterior. The adjacent buildings where we go to Sunday School have courtyards with olive trees and covered walkways around the courtyards to shield you from sun and rain as you walk from room to room. I never really got Sunday school. All the kids are escorted out of church just before the sermon to go to our designated classes. I guess they want us to get enough of the ceremony and mysteries they are selling but have determined that we're unable to sit quietly through the sermon. In Sunday school we are given lessons, stories, and art projects. I'm good with the stories but have absolutely no drawing ability. My rendition of Jesus on the cross is a combination of a body traced out of a book, stick legs and arms, and my freehand rendition of the head and crown of thorns. The piercing on his side where he is stabbed by the Roman soldiers is featured with a lot of blood there and coming from his head.

Tucson is sixty miles from Mexico and the border town of Nogales. Mother is in love with the Mexican culture and music. In Texas she had to seek out the Alonsos, but here in Arizona she has a lot more opportunity to use her Spanish, so we are destined to go. At first we just go to Nogales, but later on we will venture deeper into Mexico. I speak a smattering of Spanish (or so I think) from my mother continually speaking Spanish to us. She often threatens to drop me off in Mexico for two weeks, claiming I'll speak fluently when later retrieved.

Nogales is a typical border town with a multitude of stores and markets. We go in every store where my mother buys ceramic black angels and silver metal mirrors. She loves to bargain with the vendors to show off her Spanish. We buy *limones*, which, as the name suggests, are small Mexican limes that we squeeze in our iced tea. It is illegal to bring fruit across the border into the United States, but again, Mother knows more than the US Department of Agriculture, so we regularly smuggle the back-seat wheel wells full of *limones* across the border. Charlotte and I are instructed to put our feet over the contraband and sit well forward so the border agents can't see them. This is my first experience with criminal activity, which makes me nervous but it is also exciting.

Mexicans are a very sweet, polite, gentle people, and I find my ability to speak Spanish to be a big hit as it always elicits big smiles and a helpful attitude. When you ask directions in Nogales, the response is always "Just a few blocks further along the way you are going," but after several blocks and further directions of "just a few blocks further," you start to clue in. The people are too polite and nobody wants to give you the bad news—that your destination is three miles down the road and unless you are prepared to walk and arrive exhausted, dirty, and very sweaty, you better go back and get the car.

Since Daddy now has a new church and it's a "good job," my parents set about the task of buying a house. Charlotte and I are dragged along—old enough to be bored but not old enough to be trusted alone at home. The house Mother loves is $25,000, which is beyond the budget of $18,000 my parents set for the new house. The sellers belong to our church, so after some haggling, it is sold to my parents for $21,000. I think my father makes about $9,000 a year. It's enough to pay the mortgage and keep food on the table, but barely.

The new house feels big and fancy. It is a three-bedroom, two-bath ranch on a corner with a huge backyard. The front yard and driveway are gravel but the backyard is grass and has an above-ground pool. The sellers take the pool with them, but Mother promises we will get one as soon as we can afford it.

The neighbors across the street are the Molina family. Mother immediately speaks to them in Spanish, which I think insults Mrs. Molina as she speaks perfect English, but Mother is showing off. The Molinas own a Mexican restaurant in town, which we will eventually go to with church groups or on special occasions. They have three boys and Charlotte and I are quickly advised to close our bedroom curtains when getting undressed at night. It seems the boys are becoming curious about girls and Charlotte and I are putting on a show.

With a new house and a good job my parents should be entering a new phase of stability and happiness, but this is not how it works out. Daddy's back gives him pain, the reason for his inability to participate, and Mother continually exhausts herself trying to make us look middle class. She (with my help of course) digs a flower bed in the backyard, plants trees, reupholsters the living room furniture, and sews our clothes along with the daily chores of housework. I don't remember fighting between my parents at this time—more a growing sense of dread, darkness. Mother's attempts to make everything all right by making the house perfect don't work, but she will pass this skill down to me. If she can't find happiness in her relationship with Daddy, maybe she can create a sense of warmth and comfort in the beauty of our home. She puts great stock in the beauty of our home, but in the end, it's an empty shell.

Daddy is going to the hospital again. This time for back surgery to fix his pain. This is great news, as much of family life revolves around his pain. What he can and can't do. Where he can and can't go. There are jobs around the house that should be his, but he can't do them because of his back, so Mother takes them on and is often beginning to pass them along to me. Cutting the grass is my new chore.

We have good insurance because of the good job. Being in the hospital gets Daddy out of the house for a week, and the mood elevates. There is the hope that he will come back a changed man, ready to participate, shoulder his weight, and be husband to Mother instead of being the void that sucks me into his role.

His return is marked with much fanfare. Silence and deference for his recuperation are required. No running, no noise, Daddy may be sleeping. When he emerges from the bedroom, he seems changed. Happier. Not so much sitting around and moaning but still no real stepping up. He has pills now. Daddy has to take his pills for his back. Pain pills. His top drawer rattles like a snake when opened. Dozens of bottles laid on their side roll around the drawer. Darvon, Demerol, and Percodan are the new magic that make his life and ours tolerable.

# ten

I HAVE A NEW BEST FRIEND IN MY NEW NEIGHBORHOOD, PEGGY. She tells me about going to ballet class, so I want to go too. Mother surprisingly allows this, and Charlotte and I are soon part of a pack of girls from the neighborhood who carpool to ballet class.

We go once a week on Saturdays and the mothers alternate who is to drive. I have a very scratchy leotard from Sears that has a turtleneck and zips up the back. I guarantee you this offensive garment was on sale because no one wants an itchy leotard with a turtleneck and zipper, especially in Tucson. The ballet school is in a strip mall and has a small entry office, a dressing room behind a curtain, and a large rectangular studio with linoleum floors and bars on the two long walls. The teacher is a middle-aged woman with very long legs, pink tights, and ballet shoes. She wears a bandana wraparound top with a bare midriff, but she is so short-waisted that the bare part is barely a sliver of skin. There is also something odd about her back above one shoulder, which I cannot figure out. Her name is Maria and she leads us in exercises at the barre to music from dance records.

I am quite content to be with my new posse of friends and my new best friend. We do pliés (bend your knees), tendus (point your toes), ronds de jambe (make circles with your legs), grand battements (kick your leg high), then we go out in the middle of the floor and turn and leap. Sometimes we do cartwheels and backbends, at which I excel. Ballet class has become the highlight of my week and something I look forward to, so it immediately becomes a new leverage point for my mother. If you do/don't do such and such, "You aren't going to ballet class."

In ballet class, we are flowers and fairies. Jesters and gymnasts. The world of imagination is beautiful, but everything is a challenge and requires concentration. "Can you do this? Now try that." A turn, a leap—there is always more. Nothing is ever finished. It can always be higher, faster, longer, now all together in exact unison. There is joy in being part of something and submitting myself to the perfection of the group. The corps de ballet. It's in stark contrast to the singular, solitary world of my family existence. I look across at my friends as we work our regimentation. The uniformity is intoxicating. Everyone moving together, subjugated to the whole. All our arms and legs in exact unison. It's all clear and fair. If you step out of line or you're late, you can see it reflected in the mirror. No made-up mistakes or invented infractions. You either did the step or you didn't, and I have to be perfect because my mother has begun her sabotage. The next time it's Mother's turn to carpool, we are late or she's forgotten, and there are phone calls to get someone else's mother to drop everything and drive. I have a sense of shame as I walk to the car. I have not held up my end of the stick. I am colored by my mother's failure. I also know that my classes are not being paid for, or at least we are behind in paying our fees. My teacher runs this school but she also has a job working for the railroad. She works hard to keep the school going and her family fed. Mother doesn't work. The shame and feeling of "less than" is constant, but it must be compartmentalized. I have to survive. I put it away, but I know my teacher doesn't like me. Maybe she does, but in my mind, how could she?

Food has become an issue for me. We are poor but we don't look like it. We live in a nice house in a nice neighborhood, and my daddy has a good job. But the church barely pays enough to get by.

Mother buys everything on sale. I've been told the food budget is a dollar a day. We eat a lot of ground beef in some gastric variation popular in the '60s. There are no snacks in the house. No crackers or chips. There is a box of saltine crackers up with the puffed rice cereal box above the stove. Powdered milk, no soda, only occasionally Kool-Aid. No lunch meat for sandwiches. There is moldy cheese, which is scraped off with surgical precision, but you can still taste the mold. Dried-up raisins in a jar, pecans of somewhat dubious age (being the same pecans in the same jar for as long as I can remember).

We don't starve. When there is no bread, and Mother is out of the house, Charlotte teaches me to make "bread" by mixing up flour and water, rolling it out on a cookie sheet, and putting it in the oven. With enough margarine, it does fill your gut.

It's Saturday and I have spent the morning at ballet class, then home to do my chores. There was no oatmeal with raisins for breakfast today and there is no lunch. Breakfast is hit or miss. Is Mother up? Is she in the mood to make oatmeal? This depends on whether she is hungry or not.

After my chores I am out in the yard building my fort of old cinder blocks and carpet remnants left behind from the original construction of the house. By late afternoon I begin to feel the rumblings of hunger and the panic that accompanies it. It's always sudden and overwhelming. I can go hours without food, and do regularly, but there comes a point when my body quits and my brain becomes savage. I hit a wall and panic. All instinct. No other thought survives. It feels life-threatening. I need food *now*.

I go into the house and to my room. My touchstone. My safety. I regroup, make a plan, and wait for an opportunity when no one will be in or around the kitchen. I have skills. There is a new loaf of day-old bread in the bread box. I sneak in with practiced stealth, silently slide open the bread box, untwist the twist tie, and take two pieces of bread out of the middle of the loaf. I know I can't take any from the end. This is obvious and will be detected immediately. I take my booty from the center of the loaf, slide it under my shirt, then "fluff." This involves shaking the loaf back and forth until all the slices separate and begin to fill up the lost volume. It's a real skill to increase the volume without going so far as to show obvious gaps between slices. I twist up the end of the outer wrapper, reinstall the twist tie, and hightail it back to my room.

I close my bedroom door—this is suspicious in itself and could attract attention, but it's worth the risk. Mother could walk into my room unannounced at any moment. Even with the door closed, she will never consider knocking and just walk in. With the sound of the door opening, I'll have a few precious seconds to shove the bread under my pillow.

I sit at the head of my bed, retrieve the slices from under my shirt, and stuff them into my mouth one by one. The lack of any condiment—no butter, no jelly—results in a dry mouth, and chewing becomes an issue until the salivary glands kick in.

I'm a commando in my own house. Daring raids behind enemy lines (the kitchen) to rescue the concentration camp prisoners (bread) and return them to safety (my room). Awards are presented (the bread), accolades received (my blood sugar normalizes), and the hero can return to her humble life of building her fort until dinner.

# eleven

I AM IN THE FOURTH GRADE AND HAVE A MARVELOUS TEACHER, Miss Tynes. She is an older, slight woman with silver hair. She reads us stories about the Incas and their llamas, and there is "Painter of the Day," a much-coveted position where you get to do art all day. The only substantial drawback is that Miss Tynes has the habit of poking you in the little spot between your collarbone and shoulder when she speaks to you. I'm thinking this is to keep our attention so we focus on her when she speaks. She has long, bony fingers with big Mexican-style silver rings that clank when she pokes and speaks. If she has to talk to you for too long it wears a sore spot, so the best approach is to just agree to whatever she wants and get out as fast as you can.

I have a new best friend named Kimberly with Elizabeth Taylor looks, all long dark hair and blue eyes. We have the occasional sleepover and sing Broadway show tunes under the covers. "I Could Have Danced All Night" is a favorite because we both know all the words. I am popular on the playground, having started the school year with all the other kids. I try to get a game of "horses" going, but no one wears little dresses with ties in the back anymore. It's the '60s and we're all in A-line dresses or something approaching mod and Twiggy. We are too old for "horses."

There is a deep ravine (think ditch) at the back of the playground near the fence. I decide we are going to play war. I don't think it's fair to blame me completely for my bossiness. The girls ask me what we're going to play every day and I have to come up with something. Everyone is given a rank in our game of war. I am the admiral, of course, Kimberly is a captain, and everyone else is a private. War involves me telling the other girls to get in the ditch while I walk along the top with Kimberly. This game doesn't really have legs, as there is only one ditch with no opposing ditch to shoot at. If we had another ditch we could divide up and have a proper battle throwing dirt clods at each other, me deciding who gets hit and who's wounded or dead, but even I have to admit it's a pretty boring game just sitting in the ditch and me strutting along the top. The bell rings and we all rush inside. War was a bust.

It's fall, which means that Christmas, being the most fabulous time of year, will be here soon. The holiday season is my favorite, starting with the kickoff feast of Thanksgiving and ending with New Year's. The holidays bring food and company and presents.

Mother, the frustrated engineer, is not a cook. She *can* cook but really has very little interest other than the societally imposed idea of the perfect housewife presenting the perfect holiday dinner. She makes all the usual mid-1960s traditional favorites. Turkey, gravy (but she puts giblets in it for my father, which makes it horrible), stuffing, sweet potatoes, frozen green peas, pumpkin and pecan pies, and the pièce de résistance: Parker House rolls. These are yeast-rising rolls that make the whole house smell like heaven and taste like bread but better than any bread I ever had before. The preparation of the rolls starts a few days before the feast and involves a lot of mixing bowls, flour, yeast, and chemistry. I think my mother likes making the rolls because there is science involved. Rising yeast activated by boiling water. She is, for a moment, a chemist.

The dough has to be mixed and then placed in the refrigerator to rise. Once risen, it's removed and pounded down again, then the process gets repeated. Once the dough has risen enough times, it is placed in little mounds on a greased cookie sheet the day of the feast, allowed to rise for the last time, then placed in the oven just before it's time to sit down. I know Holy Communion as we have it at church every Sunday, but church has got nothing on the holy ritual of my mother's rolls coming out of the oven.

This year, it seems that the Parker House rolls push Mother over the edge. The sheer volume of dishes and preparation and the timing of the rolls, combined with the expectation of perfection, takes her down.

By midmorning the kitchen is a disaster zone with bowls and pans everywhere. The cutting board is dusted with flour and vegetable remnants. Mother has given up washing anything between different preparations; she just pushes things to the side or piles them in the sink. The turkey is in the oven, the turkey neck boiling on the stove for gravy. There's a pile of peeled and chopped sweet potatoes in a glass pan waiting on the caramel sauce that is about to boil over on the stove.

Charlotte and I are just finishing polishing the silver. I feel the crisis coming but can't intervene until it arrives. Many Thanksgiving and Christmas dinners have been ruined by Mother's meltdown in the kitchen, followed by a fight with my father because he is "not helping," which is quite true. He is relaxing in the living room in his green La-Z-Boy recliner. He's a soft target and no match for Mother in this condition.

I learn to let her blow up at my father, who doesn't respond or engage in the battle because he is high on pain pills. Her first strike is my cue to start washing pots, clear space, clean bowls, wipe counters, and generally clean and put things away to make order of the chaos. Sometimes this works and Thanksgiving goes on, generally because we are having company for dinner. Sometimes it doesn't.

We are nine and eleven years old and Charlotte and I are allowed to have a small glass of watered-down wine with dinner. The taste is not pleasant, but there is something about the stuff that I like. One of the benefits of pulling kitchen patrol duty on Thanksgiving is you get to finish up whatever wine is left in the glasses after dinner.

After dinner we are all stuffed to the gills. I have eaten my weight in turkey and cranberry sauce, but mainly it's Parker House rolls and butter. I'm just happy we pulled it off. Dinner made it to the table, a big beautiful brown turkey with stuffing bursting out of its insides, candied sweet potatoes with the caramel sauce rescued at the last minute from the stove, and token green beans that only grown-ups eat, as children know better than to waste valuable tummy space on vegetables at Thanksgiving. There's pumpkin pie and a plum pudding that Mother drowns in alcohol and lights on fire so it comes to the table in flames. It's all very fancy and beautiful—sparkling silver, fancy glasses, centerpiece flowers and candles—completely separate from the earlier chaos in the kitchen and Mother and Daddy's threat to burn the whole thing down.

Why do they do it? What's the point? Are they not capable of feeling the joy, and if that's the case, why do they lay out the magic carpet of what's to come, only to yank it away at the last minute? I am learning to manage Mother. I know her power to cast spells and create a wonderland during the holidays, but she doesn't know how to regulate, and her magic can turn. I never read a fairy tale in my books where the good witch and the bad witch were the same person, but that's how it is with her. Like Granny, she is a powerful wizard capable of casting great spells, but she also has a dark side.

Christmas is the next extravaganza. I still believe in Santa even though I know he's not real. My parents are still doing it all, so I maintain the fantasy in hope of possibly getting the elusive pony.

Christmas starts with tree shopping, a family affair. We go to every tree lot on our side of town. "I want a Douglas Fir, seven feet tall with no missing branches and not too wide at the base," my mother explains to the tree man when we arrive. That is the exact tree everyone wants, and it's $25, not the $10 my mother is willing to spend. She eventually makes a deal for two really bad trees that no one was going to buy, but she has a plan to strap them together to make one respectable tree.

Once the trees are home we take them in the yard and my father makes fresh cuts on the bottoms of each trunk. Then comes the challenge of strapping two trees together and fitting both trunks into a tree stand made for one, but Mother has a plan. First you start a fight with Daddy to get him out of the way so you can do it yourself without his interference. Then you elicit the help of your youngest child to stand inside the branches holding up the tree as you chop off with a hatchet bits of the trunk at the bottom until you can finally force both trees into the stand. She was right. The two trees together are lush and full, making one magnificent Christmas tree. I am learning her "magic." She casts no spells or incantations but has clever ideas she works to accomplish. I'm in awe of this accomplishment.

Then I am instructed to scramble to the bottom of the tree while she holds it upright to screw in the metal bolts at the bottom designed to keep one tree secure in the stand. I emerge covered in evergreen, scratches, and sap.

The living room furniture is rearranged, and the tree is given pride of place in a corner of the living room next to the dining room. All the Christmas boxes are pulled out of the storage closet in the carport. Once they're inside we are greeted by familiar ornaments: the balls with the chipping paint, the Santa drawing

Daddy made in school that I try to position toward the back of the tree, the red cardinal that's Mother's favorite, and the little toy trumpet Daddy insists on blowing every Christmas morning. Tinsel is still popular and I am presented with a box of it salvaged from all previous trees, making it a tangled mass that I am expected to comb through and hang on the tree. Many a lump of tinsel flung onto the tree by me gets returned with an admonishment: "Please hang the tinsel strand by strand, Emily. You can't just throw it on the branches."

There has already been another fight between my parents over the lights, their placement, and the frustration that they don't work.

"Try twisting all the bulbs in tightly again," suggests my father.

"That's not the problem, Parke. There must be a short in this string," is the aspiring engineer's response.

The words get nastier and the volume louder as each attempt to resuscitate the string of lights fails. Daddy leaves the field of battle (which was the point of the fight) and we are left to finish the job without him.

Mother takes us to midnight mass on Christmas Eve this year for the first time, which technically means we go to church and get to stay home on Christmas morning. Midnight mass is perfect. It doesn't start until 11:30 p.m., so the church is black dark and everything glitters in the candlelight. There is evergreen draped on any surface that will hold it and two full-size Christmas trees on either side of the altar. Red bows and ribbons on the trees and swag add to the festive atmosphere. The organist plays low, soft carols and we all take his cue to tone down our singing. Not the rowdy "Hark the Herald Angels Sing" of Christmas morning, more the sweetness of "Silent Night" in anticipation of the birth of Jesus.

I'm in a dress I don't like and never wear but it has a red top, so Mother decides it's suitable for church at Christmas. She's also decided to do my hair up fancy in two braided circles, one behind each ear, bobby pinned with some force into my head. I look like an alpine alien and have a headache from the bobby pins. At least my outfit doesn't involve scratchy petticoats, but the garter belts and stockings that have been added to my dress-up wardrobe threaten to pull my underpants down with each successive stand and kneel during the service.

The service is still overly long, and though I am wide awake from excitement at the beginning, I've begun to lag by the end. Finally the processional exit hymn, this time played by the organist with some gusto and volume designed to wake us all back up, then it's over.

We're not home until one in the morning, and though excited that it's Christmas Eve, I am tempered by the late hour and happy to go to bed.

I should sleep in the next morning, but the excitement of Christmas morning is irresistible and I rouse just after dawn. I go into Charlotte's room so we can fetch our stockings together but we're met with a new twist. Mother has taken the card table and wedged it wall-to-wall in the hallway so we can't get to the living room. Charlotte's opinion of this barricade is the same as mine. It's Mother's way of saying, "I'm tired and go back to sleep." Our father is at church, and she won't wake up till he gets back. I attempt a work-around by going out the sliding door from the master bathroom to the back door, which will get me into the living room —but it's locked. Thwarted, Charlotte reads a book and I spend a miserable morning thinking only of what's hiding in the living room and under the tree.

When the card table barricade is finally removed and we are let into the living room, there we find a Christmas unlike any other. Historically our stockings are filled with bottles of lotion, nail files, and other sundries we never get except on Christmas. This year they are barely acknowledged as there are two shiny new bikes! Charlotte's is grown-up size with saddlebag baskets on the back for books, and mine is a Stingray bicycle. A "girls" Huffy Stingray with a banana seat, high handlebars, and a white plastic basket on the front with pink and blue flowers. Yes, it's technically what I asked for. It was probably on sale at Sears, but what I wanted was the metallic-colored "boys" Stingray bike with *no* basket and *no* flowers. The cool one, not this grandma version, but it's a new bike and I'll take it as a win and see what I can do to make it cool.

There is an opulence to the bonanza under the tree. The volume of boxes under the tree makes it look like Christmas is going to be a joy. All brightly wrapped and bowed, but the packaging belies what is hiding inside, and it sure ain't a pony. I get underpants, nightgowns, a sweater, a Chinese purse from Granny, a card with a silver dollar from Grandma Smith, a box of material for a new dress with the pattern to make it from Mother ("I just couldn't get to it," she says), a book from a distant relative. I get everything I am going to get for the whole year at Christmas. This kills two birds with one stone. I have new underpants and my socks don't have holes.

This year is the best Christmas ever. There have been other pretty good years, like the year I got a "Chemlab" (which was a bitter disappointment as no matter what I mixed together, nothing blew up) and the year Charlotte got "Creepy Crawlers," a plug-in device to make bugs and spiders in a very hot metal form that no child should ever be allowed to play with. It made the entire house smell of burning rubber. To get anything is a win, so I pile my loot on my bed and admire the spoils. And I got a bike. A new bike, and that's big.

# twelve

SUMMER OF THE YEAR BETWEEN FOURTH AND FIFTH GRADES Charlotte goes to visit Granny and Pompy and I am being sent to summer camp for two weeks. I'm jealous that Charlotte gets to go visit them because I know they will go out to dinner, eat orange slices from the jar in the kitchen, play Parcheesi, and she will be the center of love and attention from Granny.

I have never been to camp. It's an unknown entity but I am told it's a YWCA camp an hour's drive outside of town and they have horses. My name is affixed to all my clothes, from shirts to underpants. I have a toothbrush case and am sent off with shorts and shirts sets to last.

The main bunkhouse is an old Spanish-style building with little rooms off the patio. My cabin is called Saguaro and I am in the next-to-youngest group. This does not bode well for world domination, but there are so many new things to do and new people to meet that I soon settle into the routine of archery, swimming, horseback riding, and crafts (yuck!). We line up for meals three times a day and receive a substantial tray of food. Mealtime is exciting, not only because of the volume and variety of food but because of Beaky Purse. She is the most popular girl at camp and laughs like a seal. I don't know why she is the best—she just is. We all want to look like her, act like her, laugh like her, and sit next to her. She stars as the male romantic lead in the end of the first week camp show, "Annie Get Your Gun," and she sings the song "The Girl That I Marry." I am transfixed, I am transformed, I am in love. I don't know I'm in love, I just know I have a huge secret.

At the end of the week they hold a Jymcana, which is an end-of-camp contest that features rodeo and sports events. I enter the pole bending, barrel races, swimming, and diving competitions.

When I show up for my first horseback riding class, I get assigned a horse that I will ride all week. My horse is named Captain. He's a bit small but friendly and doesn't try to rub me off into any cactus like other horses do. We trudge along trails through the desert and get to gallop in the wash. Galloping is the best. I am free and fast.

We are introduced to pole bending and barrel racing. One by one we are set out on a course of three barrels in a triangle in an open area. Everyone trots around by turn. My pony has other plans. It's my turn and I get ready to trot. I give a good kick, and Captain takes off as if possessed. Unexpected but thrilling, I hold on and lean into the turns. We are glorious. We are the best and there is much clapping and shouting as we cross the finish line. In my nine-year-old mind this is my accomplishment, but Captain knows it was all him. He's an old cattle-cutting workhorse and has skills I don't even know about. We round the barrels at a gallop, leaning into a good 45-degree angle. We fly through the poles. I see what he's doing and how we're going and I just hold on. He is magnificent.

Swimming is an altogether different situation. When we lived in Houston I was sent to the neighborhood pool to learn to swim, but the water was cold and my braids were shoved up inside a bathing cap, which made it too tight and gave me a headache. The teacher was an unhappy young girl on a summer job teaching kids to swim. I hated it and dreaded going. I like being in the pool but never mastered the turn-your-face-to-the-side-and-take-a-breath thing and I hate putting my face in the water. All I do is get a mouthful of water, so when they get around to the swimming events, my approach is much like skiing. Put your face in the water and just go as fast as you can until your lungs explode.

Diving is a skill I master at camp. I can do a reasonable jack-knife and manage a decent backflip. I am very fond of the back-flip. It begins with a serious walk down the board, at which point you turn around and balance at the end of the board on your toes. Let the tension build, get the audience invested, then push down and spring up into your flip. The beauty of my dive is somewhat marred by having to reach for my nose at the last minute to keep the water from going up it, but I've experienced the pain and brain hemorrhage of getting water with force shoved up my nose and feel there is no option but this aesthetic compromise.

Prizes are awarded at the end of the Jymcana, and this is the whole point, isn't it? We are cut-throat and serious competitors looking to win blue ribbons. My name is called and I go up in front of everyone (namely, Beaky Purse) to retrieve my award. On closer examination, I realize that my medallion with the red, white, and blue ribbons trailing is actually an empty and washed jelly tin from breakfast, with a ribbon attached and my place written in block magic marker.

Archery was another big camp activity, though not part of the Jymcana. There is no head-to-head competition. It's all about accuracy and accumulating points. I quickly discover that my excellent eyesight serves me well. There is a drawback, though, as I have elbows that hyperextend, and when drawing back my bow and releasing my arrow, that hyperextended elbow is going to get a very painful strafing by the bowstring. But archery awards little pins for achieving a certain number of points at each distance, and I am all about the prizes!

I am at camp for two weeks and Mother comes to visit on the Sunday of the first weekend. She shows up late, and I am immediately instructed to go and change my clothes. I have been wearing my one and only pair of cutoffs and the same shirt for the entire week (with the exception of when we go riding and have to wear jeans). It is my best and coolest outfit because all the cool kids wear cutoffs. I dutifully comply and put on the blue shorts with the daisy and the matching daisy shirt that my mother made. We walk around and I proudly introduce her to Captain, show her the archery field, and display my Jymcana awards.

As soon as she leaves I race back to the cabin to change back into my cutoffs. They're gone! I can't find them anywhere. I search both sides of the cabin and through everyone's luggage, but they are nowhere to be found. My social status immediately plummets in my mind. How will Beaky Purse recognize me as someone she wants to sit next to her at lunch if I'm not in cutoffs? It takes a moment to dawn on me that my mother was the only person who could have taken them, all because she wants me to wear matching shorts and shirts. The fury inside is deep. Another betrayal.

Archery strangely transfers to home life. The same woman who proves herself to be untrustworthy and deceitful, who steals rifles and cutoffs, comes home from the Goodwill store with a used bow for me. I am also gifted a quiver and half a dozen metal-tipped arrows. I get a bale of straw to shoot at. I don't know why I have the sudden favor of having money spent in my direction, but I don't look a gift horse . . .

My bow being from the Goodwill means it isn't as good as the ones at camp, and to shoot any real distance I have to arch my shot to reach the target. This has the unfortunate effect of occasionally going over the fence into the Bockers' yard. I can climb the fence to retrieve my arrows, but this isn't as easy as it sounds. We don't share a fence. The Bockers' fence is three feet from ours, creating a dead zone in between. This is neutral territory and you count your lucky stars if your arrow ends up here, as having to forage in their actual yard is worthy of any Nazi commando raid.

The Bockers are a "don't say hello" couple who live next door. They aren't friendly and yell at us for stealing the cumquats from their tree when the branches are on our side of the fence, making them clearly ours. They are older and don't have kids, so this makes them suspect from the start.

Seeing Mr. Bocker standing at the back door, clutching a fistful of my arrows and talking to Mother, is cause for paralysis. I know it's dangerous to arch my arrows. I know they have a dog, or someone could be in the yard, but these consequences don't mean that I stop arching my arrow in the direction of their yard and shooting. I get a "talking to" and my bow and arrows are confiscated for a week. Shooting in the backyard is really losing its luster anyway.

The neighborhood in Tucson is much the same as Bay City. Suburban ranch-style houses and everyone has kids, except the Bockers. Bicycles are the major mode of transportation and freedom for every kid. We ride our bikes everywhere. To school, to visit friends, to the park, out into the desert, everywhere.

I have my Stingray and am still working on a plan to make it cooler. I take it out into the desert and throw it around in the dirt in an effort to dislodge the horrible girlie basket with the flowers, but we make things to last in this country, and no amount of pounding or scraping will dislodge it.

Eventually I realize I will have to use tools to remove it and come up with a different lie than the one originally planned: "It just snapped off when I fell." Now I will have to say, "It was stolen at school," which is a much weaker lie, as who will believe anyone wanted to steal a white plastic basket with pink and blue flowers?

Consequences. I have to think these things through. The consequences of removing the basket are that I will be cooler, but I will have no way to carry my notebook or books to school.

I start to marry my current favorite activities: bicycle riding and archery. Taking my bow and arrows out of the yard is the solution to Mr. Bocker. I can hang my quiver of arrows on a belt and wear my bow across my body. I start out trying to ride with no hands and shoot, but that just results in some nasty crashes ending up in creosote bushes and the dirt. I had hoped to shoot and ride, like Native Americans attacking the fort on horseback. I shoot at horned toads and lizards, but even at very close range I can't ever hit anything. I eventually stop my bike and aim my arrow straight down at some hapless horned toad, inches from his body, but he scampers away just as I release my arrow.

My escapades apparently are of some note to the other kids in the neighborhood, and I am soon in a pack of boys. We are all on our Stingray bikes with bows and arrows. We ride around the desert shooting at anything that moves but soon get bored of this game as none of us can hit anything and end up in somebody's front yard with the idea of playing heads up. Heads up is a game where you throw something up in the air and everybody freezes and waits in place to see if they get hit. Whoever gets hit is out. We all take our bow and arrows and shoot straight up, freezing in our spots. Those are the rules.

The mom of the boy whose yard we are playing in comes out and tells us all to go home. Most of the games we play eventually evolve to the point that they push into areas of danger. Heads up is supposed to be played with balls, not arrows. I have the image of an arrow going straight down into someone's head (not mine). Consequences. This is why we have parents.

# thirteen

AT NINE, I THINK, I FEEL, I AM FULLY FORMED. I GO TO SCHOOL, I go to camp, I ride my bike. I have a life of my own beyond my parents. I wake up with ideas of what to do that day. Build a fort, ride my bike, go to a friend's house. This is where the conflict begins. Mother also has plans. "Let's dig the garden today. Let's go on the roof and service the swamp cooler." Sure, when I was younger this sounded like great fun, but now it isn't what I want. I want adventures away from my mother.

There's a list of chores on the bulletin board in the kitchen for Charlotte and me to do daily when we get home from school. Monday: dust or vacuum. Tuesday: dump the trash or sweep the carport, etc. This is augmented with special projects. I mow the lawn as my father can't because of his back. I enjoy mowing the lawn. I enjoy the grown-up responsibility and machinery of it, but I'm also very conscious of the dangers of cutting off my toes. I am a good worker. Whatever task is set I take to with gusto. I enjoy seeing the house all clean and shiny from my dusting, vacuuming, and sweeping. I am proud of the fresh-cut lawn and that fabulous smell. I give it my all and the feeling of accomplishment is real. It puffs me up.

I am a good kid. I bring home ribbons from camp, I do well in school, I do my chores. And yet, my mother is increasingly unhappy with me. My newfound desire for independence is not popular.

"Can I go to Karen's house today? I can walk and we aren't meeting until noon." It's Saturday. There's no reason for her to say no.

Mother says, "Fine, as soon as you finish all your chores."

No problem, but she has added a supplemental list of major proportions. I see it. I see it all now. The stolen rifle, the missing cutoffs, and now the monumental list of chores. Magic Mommy was just an illusion. There is no straightforward conversation like, "I don't want you to have a gun," or "Those cutoffs are filthy," or "I don't like Karen, so I don't want you to go to her house." It's all underhanded and deceitful. I'm not stupid, even if I'm only nine. It's all about keeping me bound to her and doing what she wants. I'm not allowed to have ideas and adventures that don't involve *her*!

The list today involves helping her service the swamp cooler on the roof. This involves cleaning the water reservoir at the bottom to remove all the rust, grime, and any green junk growing in the water. Remove the old straw pads, replace the pads with new ones, make sure the little pump works, and check that all the hoses pumping water to the pads are clear and flowing freely. This takes forever as Mother seems to be intentionally moving in slow motion. She suddenly needs tools we haven't brought so I make multiple trips up and down the ladder to fetch this and that from the toolbox in the laundry room.

Mow the lawn. I pray the mower starts and has enough gas. I get lucky on both counts and mow at warp speed with no delays due to having to involve Mother. Mow the outside of the yard first, continue around the perimeter until it narrows and becomes two distinct but separate areas. Then mow the first area until complete, then switch to the second. Turn the mower off, having double-checked the yard in case I missed any spots. I don't want to have to restart the mower and risk it not starting. Put the mower away.

Sweep the back patio, which means moving all the patio furniture, then sweep the garage, front porch, walkway, and sidewalk. Iron six shirts and hankies for my father. I am obsessed, moving from each task with deliberate speed and coordinated effort. No wasted movement. I don't even mind; it becomes a game.

Out the side gate and into the kitchen closet to get the broom. Not through the house, as this route is longer. Mother has left so the car is gone. Lucky break for me so I don't have to move the car to sweep the carport. Start at the back wall, edge carefully against the house, long hard strokes getting as much efficiency as possible out of each stroke. Up to the front door and sweep the porch then down the walkway and finish on the sidewalk. In the house, through the kitchen door to put the broom away, and straight into the adjacent laundry room. Six shirts to iron. Collars first, then sleeves, slide the front of the shirt onto the little end of the board and press, shift the shirt toward the back and press, don't forget the back placket, back around to the other side of the front, carefully between each button, and I've got one shirt done. Repeat times five. Finish with the hankies so my brain can rest and I can plan the rest of my day with Karen.

Mother pulls into the carport as I put the ironing board and iron away. Board against the wall, iron on the shelf. "I've finished," I announce. "I'm going to go to Karen's now, okay?"

"No, it's three o'clock and too late to go now," she says.

It's not just the injustice of today, the effort and concentration it took to get everything done, but the gathering weight of her daily infractions. Her micromanagement of me. The rage inside me is overwhelming. I have worked so hard to get everything done. We had a deal! The deceit, the lies, the betrayal. This was her plan all along. To keep me from going to Karen's house.

Having been so hyperfocused on my goal, not a movement wasted, not a moment's rest allowed, full of the adrenaline of my efforts, I explode. I run out the sliding glass door to the yard, race across the grass, and vault the fence. This is a six-foot redwood fence and maybe I hit the intermediate cross piece of the framing on the way up, but fueled by my fury, I took it at a run and go straight over with a Spiderman landing on the back side. We live on the corner, so I am on the side of the road and take off at a dead run to Karen's house.

Karen is Jewish, which makes her different from other kids, but I like this. We are best friends. Her parents are cool. Karen's room is painted fluorescent green, and she has albums by Santana and the Moody Blues. She burns incense in her room, plays any music she wants, and wears any clothes she wants. I am confused by the discord she has with her parents because they seem like heaven to me. They're cool, she's cool, and I'm not. I'm a refugee.

Dinner at their house is an extravaganza. There is a pot roast with potatoes, corn on the cob, salad, and a whole stack of bread if you're still hungry. There is as much food to eat as you want. Karen is silent and sullen, but I am a chatterbox of gratitude and wish to be accepted. At my house there is only the plate of food provided for any given meal. There is no "more" and there is no bread except what you can steal.

I've run away from home and I'm not going back. Karen's mom says I can spend the night. I know there are phone calls between Karen's mom and mine. Like treaty negotiations, her mom plays my Kissinger. I don't know what is said, but I am reassured that going home the next morning is safe and there will be no repercussions. Ha! I've won for now, but I'm becoming aware that a darkness has descended on my world. An undercurrent of evil. A veil of shadows. Everything is not what it seemed. Life has become a mystery that I do not understand, nor do I understand where it came from. It just descended, like a mist that seeped under the doors and gassed everyone.

It is strange to have gone from treasured child to enemy in my own home. I am hers and she is mine. It is a duet choreographed for just us. My father and sister are not involved in our dance. I have become the partner of choice. My every move and word are scrutinized. I still bring home the prizes. I built the Panama Canal and win first prize at the science fair, for God's sake, but I am still at fault. Seems I have also developed "a tone."

There is a growing distance between my parents. Silence where there used to be sound. Calling, laughing, giggling, and teasing are no more. In its place is a sense of strangulation in the air interrupted by outbursts of my mother's fury. Like a landmine buried in the road, it explodes unexpectedly with carnage in the house and blood on the walls. They start to quarrel, generally around some special occasion, event, or celebration, and then it's a full-blown battle. Doors are slammed, lipstick on the bedroom mirror, holes in the bathroom door. Charlotte and I retreat behind a closed door to her room. The raised voices, horrible words, fractions of sentences overheard make your blood run cold.

Charlotte can't take it and sends me out to intervene. It's my job and I know it. I open the door, cross the hall, knock on my parents' door, and hear nothing but silence. I open the door. They are wrestling on the floor, my mother in her slip, my father in his T-shirt and boxers. The room is chaos, though not much is out of place. "I'll kill you," scrawled in lipstick across the mirror. "You have to stop," is all I say, and somehow the spell is broken. I walk out and close the door behind me. No more fighting. Silence.

I don't tell Charlotte what I saw. I don't think she could take it. I can't take it. This is when the family meetings start, coincidentally after each big fight, but they always seem to focus on my "behavior." *My* behavior? Charlotte is never chastised except for minor infractions. Her ability to do her chores is the predominant complaint, and with this criticism I must agree. She has a lackadaisical attitude toward housework in general, but this seems only a ploy to have something to say to her to cover the multitude of aspersions cast in my direction. My attitude, my "tone," and my disrespect of parental authority are recurring themes. The only incident in recent memory that even merits being called out is the day I ran away to Karen's house.

They sit side by side on the couch, calling each other "dear" or by their first names.

"Well, I think her attitude lately has been very poor, Parke," Mother says.

"Yes, I agree, Binny," is Daddy's reply.

Then I am addressed directly with some vaguely remembered incident of "back talk" or disobeying. "You are on restriction for a week. This means no friends after school, no extracurricular activities, no bike riding, no going to the park. Just school and straight home."

Every meeting is the same, and they seem to be called after every big fight where I have to go break things up. My parents might give it a day or two between the fight and the meeting. The fight seems to exhaust their fury. They get it all out, feel better, patch things up, then turn their focus to me.

Restriction isolates me at home, and when I am alone for any long period of time I retreat into fantasy. My teddy bears and dolls bear the brunt of this incarceration. There are battles of epic proportions waged in my room. In one particularly bad fight "Big Teddy" almost had his leg torn off. My Aunt Jemima doll has severe burns on her legs. After the battle a triage is set up to treat the wounded. Toothpaste salve for Jemima's legs, ace bandages and toilet paper to wrap the other wounds. I have also become quite fond of bandaging myself and limping around the house using a cane my father got after one of his back surgeries.

We are all wounded, but we are brave. Teddy recovers, though his leg gash has to be sewn up. Jemima doesn't cry.

There's a photograph in the family photo album of me playing in my bedroom. I have a Madam Alexander Jackie Kennedy doll—no Barbies for me as Mother says they are junk. I am sitting at the bottom of the tall secretary desk in my room, the kind with a glass cabinet above, a fold-down desk in the middle where I am supposed to do my homework but never do, and three dresser drawers below. I have developed a game where I tie a string around the scroll work at the top of the chest, put the string around Jackie's neck, wedge a large but thin children's storybook into the slightly open lower drawer, and stand Jackie on the book. Then I slam the drawer shut, the book falls, and Jackie hangs. Possibly I have not previously mentioned how much my mother looks like Jackie Kennedy. The hair is different, but there's a similarity in that both are dark-haired, brown-eyed beauties.

# fourteen

I'M IN FIFTH GRADE NOW AND HAVE A NEW BEST FRIEND. KAREN IS in a different class, so my new friend is named Becky (again). She is what my mother would call "trashy," but I think she's cool and we are instant best friends.

Boys have become a thing. I haven't noticed them much before now, but Becky comes to me with earth-shaking information: "Corey Lieber wants to give you his ring!" I'm not even sure I know who Corey is, but the offer of a ring can't be easily dismissed. Becky points him out. He is dark-haired and has big blue eyes, but he's short. Handsome indeed, but the short thing gives me pause. It's a cruel trick of nature that girls grow faster than boys when your boyfriend is supposed to be taller than you are. But the ring! I can't resist and once it is delivered, I am overjoyed and Corey seems taller. The ring is silver plastic and has a flat black "stone" with a silver C. I have to put tape around the band to make it fit, but I have a ring! I've never had a ring before. I have a boyfriend. I've never had a boyfriend before. Fifth grade is getting off to a rollicking start.

Our teacher, Miss Roy, is tall and thin and a bit pinched. She reads us stories when we come in after lunch, but everything else is just work and math. There is no "Painter of the Day," but also no poking. Experience with my parents has taught me to pay attention to grown-ups and their moods. Grown-up moods rule the world.

If they are happy, your chances for a good day are much improved. If they are unhappy, you learn to prepare. Miss Roy never breaks a smile unless Mr. Tuttle, the sixth-grade teacher, is around. Then she is all aflutter like a big gawky bird.

Somehow the ring from Corey has hit her radar. Teachers have radars, especially for things they disapprove of, and I get the sense that Miss Roy does not approve of me "going steady" with Corey. It feels like she is jealous and wants Corey to herself. This is a consequence I had not anticipated, but still, the ring! I also transgress in another area. I take a dozen or so of the little pieces of paper that are used to check out books from the library, the ones where you write your name, the date, and when you checked out the book. These are supposed to stay in the loaned books on the inside the front cover, dated and stamped again once they're returned.

I am using the blank library checkout chits to make an address book. Technically I did "steal" these little pieces of paper to staple a dozen or so together to write names, addresses, and phone numbers on. Very grown-up stuff, an address book. Kind of clever, I think. Miss Roy, however, walks by my desk right at the moment I am admiring my new prize. She demands I hand it over. *Make your own!* I think, but it's gone.

I shouldn't be surprised when I am called to the principal's office. This is big stuff. Only the bad boys ever get called to the principal's office, and this usually implies expulsion or at least "swats." Upon entering this place of death and doom, I am faced with my mother sitting across the desk from the principal. My mother! I go unconscious, leave my body. I cannot imagine what is about to transpire, but it can't be good.

The principal explains to Mother that I have been accused of stealing and produces my little homemade address book, which she hands to her for examination. This is where it gets good because Mother smiles and says, "Well, this seems harmless," and hands back the little book. She is obviously amused at my crime, even seems proud of me and stands to leave, thanking the principal profusely for her time. I am hugged and kissed in farewell and told to return to my class. I reenter my body and a state of consciousness. Magic Mommy has returned to save the day!

I walk back to class in a state of triumph, the sound of trumpets heralding my return. I have defeated the Bird! The tall, gawky, unhappy bird. "Take that, Miss Roy!" You are no match for my mother and never will be. I am the golden child again. For now at least.

There is another fight. This one is a doozie that ends with Daddy being locked out of the house in his boxers and undershirt. Not to be thwarted, he gets into the backyard through the side gate and attempts to break in through the bedroom window, reaching his arms through the gap he's managed to open. Mother is fending him off with a knitting needle, stabbing his arms as they flail. His forearms have little holes that are bleeding down his arms. I am on patrol, moving between the bedroom and Mother, then Daddy and the bloody scene in the backyard. On one circuit of my patrol a police cruiser turns the corner and pulls into our driveway. I see them pause as they read the black and white printed name on the mailbox: "The Reverend Francis Parke Smith." I escort the officers through the gate and into the yard where the scene is playing out. I stand behind the newly planted olive tree and watch through the branches as Daddy halts his attack, Mother drops her weapon, and the discussion begins. My father is offered first aid for his injuries and then escorted to the cruiser and they drive away.

I feel a sense of relief at my father being removed from the house. The current situation is resolved, but the larger family picture is revealed to be more damaged than I had previously known. Mother moves up the food chain. She reigned victorious in the fight and Daddy is now vanquished. But we are all confused, Mother, Charlotte, and me. It's good to have a clear winner, good to know where everyone stands, but the family is now oddly reordered. We all know that Mother is in charge inside our family, but we'd always kept up the public illusion. Daddy, head of household, then wife and children in descending order. After today it's getting harder to maintain the illusion. Especially for me not to stray outside my bounds.

My father's return to the house is mysterious. He just appears the next day, probably while we are at school. Nobody tells us anything. Mother tries to alleviate the tension by showing affection and saying "dear" and "darling," but my fear of them is growing.

The following Saturday another family meeting is held and I am again the focus. My attitude, my "tone," my disrespect. This is delivered by the underwear bandit and the knitting needle warrior. How do I take these people seriously? The meeting escalates. I am on restriction, again, for two weeks this time, but with no actual incident cited, no concrete evidence other than the sin of being witness to the last battle. I am guilty of seeing through their veneer, escorting the police, helping clean up the house. I'm not taking it well and talk back, argue, demand evidence of my crime. I am threatened with being taken to juvenile hall and, in my fury, I accept. Fine. Get me out of this nuthouse.

"Juvie," as it is referred to on the playground, is where all the really bad boys in school go. The ones who take drugs and do actual crimes: smoke pot, steal bikes, that kind of stuff. Not girls, and definitely not the kids of a Magic Mommy and God's ordained priest. It is a long drive to juvenile hall and when we finally arrive, we're escorted into an office where a man behind a desk fills out forms and talks to my parents about me. I slump in my chair with my bad attitude. They talk like I'm not there.

Mother does most of the talking, but Daddy throws in a few comments here and there. "She's just incorrigible, doesn't mind, has a bad attitude when asked to do anything." Yes me, the kid with A's and B's on her report card, science fair winner, grass-mowing, chore-doing horror of a child.

I sit in my chair, swinging my feet in disinterest and begin to play the scenario out in my head. My parents leave, and I am left behind in this strange place with strange people and probably bad children. I will be given some horrible uniform to wear, assigned a bunkbed in an open dormitory of hooligans who will attack me in my sleep. I will have to fight for my food and won't be allowed to brush my teeth, as I have not brought a toothbrush. Maybe I am looking for a way to capitulate this standoff. The dormitory, the hooligans, all of it seems like a survivable adventure, but not being able to brush my teeth is a brutal punishment I won't survive, so I decide to become conciliatory. Yes, I will behave. No, I won't talk back. My parents shake hands with the form-filling man and we go home.

Faced with a constant barrage of misinformation, I begin to compartmentalize my brain. *This* is what I see and feel. *That* is what I am told by the parental units. I am a child and my world is informed by the instruction of my parents, teachers, and grown-ups in general, but I am also not stupid. The things they tell me and the things I see and what they do are in constant conflict. I am conditioned to believe them, so what they tell me has to be considered. I am bad, I lack respect, I can't think.

Back to the bears. The external expressions of the battle going on in my head. Back to my bike to physicalize the growing rage. It comes out of my body, but the siren song still sings in my head. I carry this weight all day long. It plays on repeat, grooving the record that will play in my head for years to come.

When I get home from school after long days of learning new

stuff and playing hard with my friends, I know I'll find my mother either heavily involved in some new project or prostrate on her bed weeping. "What's wrong?" I will ask, but there is no response. There is no middle ground, no ordinary days, only the extreme highs or "the blues." She has either reinvented the wheel or is in such a deep depression it feels life-threatening. If she's involved in a project, I am elicited to help; if it's "the blues," I am dragged into her misery. Her world, my world, our world, revolves around her. How she feels dominates life. You can try to fix it, you can try to anticipate; your efforts never hit pay dirt, but you have to try. Do all your chores, bring home a good report card, "behave," be cheerful, tell stories from the day's adventures, but it's never enough to bring her out of her black hole, and she isn't happy until she has dragged me in with her. Charlotte retreats to her room and her books, my father disappears with his pills, and I am left as sentry. It's family trickle-down economics. Daddy's not here, Charlotte has vanished. Someone has to watch her, and I, having elected myself the hero child, have inherited this role.

Today, however, Mother is neither involved in a project nor laid out on the bed. Instead, there's a police car in the driveway and she's seated inside. I could have done without this scene. My mother won't look at me or speak. My father is talking to a man in a suit and then the police car holding my mother drives away. Daddy takes us into the house to explain. "Mommy is very tired and needs some time away. She is going to a hospital to get better." I am fully aware that they are taking her to the funny farm.

Several weeks go by before we visit her. The funny farm is not the farm of rolling hills and white cross-rail fences of my imagination but an anonymous-looking brick building with a large, empty lobby. A lady in a white coat with a clipboard comes out to greet us and we are escorted through large double doors into a wide hallway with rooms on either side. The lady slows at an open door and gently knocks. "Virginia, your family is here to see you," she says cheerily to my mother inside. I am excited at the prospect of seeing her and I'm sure she will be very happy to see us. She isn't. She won't look at me or talk to me. Her sewing machine is set up in her room and she spends the whole time we are there sewing in silence. I employ my tried-and-true arsenal of winners. Tell funny stories I am sure she will love. Dance about. Nothing. She is enclosed in her own madness. I don't mean crazy so much as fury. I can feel the rage inside her. We are rejected as a group, which seems unfair. I have always sided with her against my father at any opportunity, but now I seem to be guilty by association. We are free, she is incarcerated.

This place is full of women. There are no men except the men in white jackets, trousers, and shoes who work there. It's full of women like my mother who didn't do anything wrong other than admit to being unhappy and wanting more. This seems to be enough of a crime against the norm that they lock you up for it. You are supposed to be happy with the lot you are left in life. Your family, your children, your home. This is your world. Even I know this Groundhog Day life of a housewife is not enough for my mother. She needs to move mountains, build bridges, and conquer the world, and even if she failed, at least she would have had the adventure of trying. Without goals or meaningful problems to solve, the women in this place have taken their energy and creativity and turned it against themselves. Their minds constantly question their reality, they punish themselves for their lack of satisfaction, and they go mad. They get shock treatment or are prescribed little blue and yellow pills that scramble their brains. They talk to the doctors who try to explain everything away and help them back into the little box that is killing them.

After a month or so Mother comes home, but she isn't the

same. I'd take the version hyperfocused on me or putting me on restriction over this strange version of my mother. She's locked inside herself like a time bomb. Living with unexploded ordinance requires constant vigilance about what you say or where you walk. It's a dichotomy for me. I feel for her and understand that she's stuck, but I don't know how to help her. I have the limited resources of a child, and I'm also angry about the past injustices. Being put on restriction, the constant scolding, my "tone," the feeling that everything I do is bad. But I know I'm a good kid.

I imagine that if I had other parents my life would be much improved. I try people out in my mind. My ballet teacher? No, she's not fond of me. My gym teacher? That has possibilities, so I spend time in my imagination with that scenario: the love I would be shown, the food we would eat, the laughing at the dinner table, how I would be given lunch money, new shoes, and a new dress for school. Life would be grand.

To go along with this idea, I develop a darker companion fantasy that involves a machete knife my father brought home from a fishing trip. It's rough and scary and sharp and my father makes a big deal of it when he sharpens it. My fantasy has developed into a simple scenario: In the middle of the night, fetch the knife from its drawer in the kitchen and sneak into my parents' bedroom when they're sleeping; plunge the machete into their hearts. My mother first, then my father. There is no "after" to this scenario. Just the doing of it. I feel bad for thinking it, but that doesn't make me stop imagining how life would be if they weren't around.

I don't want them dead. I don't want other parents. I just want the pain and confusion to stop. I don't want to feel this rage, but there is only so much room in me for thoughts and feelings. Every time they twist my world with their rage or their illusion of our family, I have to block out natural parts of me to carry their weight. They are so dishonest with themselves, each other, and with Charlotte and me. They twist and distort themselves and have become monsters—and they know it. They know it because I know it. I am becoming a baby monster. There is a twisting in me I can't deny. My insides and my outsides don't match. What's going on inside my skin sack is not what I show the world.

Karen and I aren't in the same class in school this year, but we still hang out and go to the park after school. The park is a big recreation center behind my house with multiple baseball fields, an Olympic-size swimming pool, swing sets and teeter-totters, old adobe ruins, and even a museum. The ruins are what's left of Fort Lowell, an old cavalry fort from before Arizona was a state. We play and ride our bikes amongst the crumbling walls. A metal roof is eventually built to cover the ruins and protect the adobe from the weather, but kids regularly carve their initials or other equally important messages on its walls.

Karen brings cigarettes today and we both light up. I know I am doing it wrong as soon as I see the look on Karen's face. She is way cooler than me and has begun to dress in jeans and surfer shirts. Not so much Beach Boys surfer shirts but more hippie kind of stuff that I can only aspire to. I have a book of matches and strike them as we walk along, letting them fly in the wind and land on the still-dead Bermuda grass of the ball fields. Walk, strike, let fly until I have emptied the whole pack. We don't have much else to do. We can only smoke so much and walk so far, so I fill my time with pyrotechnics.

As we reach the water fountain by the pool, the one under the cottonwood tree, a gang of boys on their Stingrays come careening around the corner, surround us, and skid to a halt, all excited and hollering. I can't figure out what they're talking about, but up comes a man dressed in a park ranger outfit, followed by another rather out-of-breath man dressed like a janitor from school. As Karen and I turn to see what's going on, I see the blackened char on the ball field behind us, little rows of flame not yet extinguished and all the sprinklers waving their water in the wind. The entire baseball field of grass is on fire. Slowly I put two and two together and a thought enters my mind that maybe my game of matches is to blame for this disaster.

I am a good kid, though, so I couldn't possibly have done this. Maybe it was Karen because she is definitely bad and a hippie and plays rock music. I am a good kid who is not allowed to wear jeans to school, even on "rodeo day." My defensive, compartmentalized brain employs an old strategy: deny, deny, deny.

"I don't know what you're talking about" and "I don't even have any matches" escape from my lips when confronted. Never mind walk, strike, let fly. The commotion doesn't last long because the sprinklers have saved the day and all that's left is a charred outfield. The men go away and the boys ride off.

"It's not like I tried to set the grass on fire," I say to Karen. It was an accident but a very foreseeable one, even to me. Consequences. Life is full of them, but I seem to just "do" and think about that later, if at all.

Daddy smokes and I start stealing cigarettes from him. Only one at a time, as I am sure more will be missed. He smokes True cigarettes and they don't feel like smoking at all. Karen has Marlboros, so those are the cool ones to have.

I have a babysitting job across the street for two horrible little boys. Their family is obviously rich, as they have a kitchen full of snacks, the parents are both fat, and even the little boys are chubby. I eat my way through the evening, devouring every kind of snack they have while I watch television. This is what passes for babysitting.

I don't like this family, but I get fifty cents an hour and they tend to stay out late, so I generally make a good haul for the evening. They even sometimes give me a tip or round up to the nearest dollar. The parents smoke and have a carton of cigarettes in the cabinet in the kitchen. They leave open packs of smokes around the house when they go out so I can take a few from each pack to smoke through the evening, spread my pilfering around, and not be noticed. I stockpile enough to get me through to the next babysitting gig.

I still don't get the thrill of smoking but stay at it with dogged determination. It tastes nasty and smells even worse, but my efforts pay off one night. I am in the living room of their house, brown shag carpet, beige and brown couches, and chairs upholstered in a coarse fabric. Brown paneling on the wall where the fireplace is. The TV is under the front picture window, giving it pride of place with all the furniture surrounding it. I am walking from the living room into the kitchen for my next round of snacks when it happens. I inhale by accident. Bam! That's it! I did it! I finally figured it out. I do it again quickly to see if I can replicate the feeling and huzzah! The smack in the back of my throat, the dizzy feeling in my head. I knew there was something more to this. I smoke three cigarettes in a row to make sure I've mastered the task. I am instantly addicted.

# fifteen

SIXTH GRADE IS ALL ABOUT TRYING TO FIT IN. I START OUT ON A ROLL, getting the cute blonde boy for my boyfriend. He is the cutest, most popular boy in class and everyone calls him "Humpy." There are a lot of H+Es carved into trees and benches around the playground. He doesn't give me a ring, and I'm not even sure how he became my boyfriend. It's not like I ever talk to him, but it's a thing.

My new best friend this year is Debbie. She is definitely rich because she has a house with a pool and wears a different outfit almost every day. I have five acceptable outfits that I rotate.

It doesn't take long before Debbie steals my boyfriend and it's now H+D. Amazing how you can turn an E into a D without much effort. Humpy didn't break up with me as far as I know—I was just suddenly on the outs and Debbie was the new girl. Our friendship suffers but I totally get it. I can't compete. She is cute, has clothes, has Capezio shoes, wears little bows in her hair, and talks to the boys. She also wears a bra. I don't wear a bra. Bra strap snapping has become a thing and I am embarrassed anytime a boy goes for mine and comes up empty. Other girls, like Debbie, have the little beginnings of boobs, barely anything to speak of, but they have bras! Some of them even get their period, which is whispered about in the girls' bathroom. I have no bra, no boobs, no period. It's all these deficits that prevent me from competing. I retreat from the field of battle and surrender Humpy and #1 girl status to Debbie Lee.

It's a regular day sitting at my desk doing my work when Mother appears at my classroom door. My heart stops. She pokes her head in, then retreats and flings the door open wide and walks in. In unison my classmates gasp. I told you she was pretty, but I wonder if you appreciate how pretty you have to be to make a room full of sixth graders gasp. She's tall, thin, and dark hair with big eyes. I inherited the big eyes with batwing eyelashes and heavy brows. She's wearing the deep purple dress handed down from Granny that she cut down for herself, black pumps and stockings, and cuts a striking figure. I think she got dressed that morning and, seeing the result, decided to add a stop at my school and charge up a few elementary schoolers.

I am immediately horrified. I know why she's here. Socks! Every morning I take my socks off and stash them behind the trash can in the alley because no self-respecting sixth-grade girl wears socks to school anymore. I am sure my mother is there to inspect my feet, discover my crime, and haul me away in front of God and everyone. Instead, she heads straight for Mr. Tuttle. My teacher is a tall man with dark hair, sweat stains under his arms, and dried spit collecting in the corners of his mouth. Mother comes in with all the confidence of a woman who knows she has already conquered the room. Mr. Tuttle doesn't know what to do with himself. He's so excited he starts to stutter and hyperventilate. There is a brief conversation, and just as quickly she is gone. With a quick wave in my direction, she's out the door. Mr. Tuttle never tells me anything regarding this visit.

The summer between sixth grade and junior high school, *Gone With the Wind* is playing at one of the movie theaters in town and I have been invited to go by one of my school chums. Mother not only approves of this outing but has volunteered to drive us and says I will need a dollar for popcorn as the movie is three and a half hours long with a much-needed intermission.

I am not rich or Southern and didn't grow up on a plantation, but if ever I met a heroine I could relate to, it's Scarlett O'Hara. They just couldn't keep that woman down! Betrayed by the love of her life, the anemic Ashley Wilkes, she survives the Civil War, midwifes her romantic nemesis in childbirth, kills a robber, saves the family and their home, rebuilds her fortune, and marries two men she doesn't love in the process—the first for revenge, the second to survive. Finally finding a seemingly appropriate match in Rhett Butler, she's then betrayed by miscommunication and misplaced jealousy. Through it all she yearns for Ashley, only to finally realize that he deeply loves Melanie. Oh, and don't I feel for her on the romantic side too? Will she ever find love? Will she ever find a man whose ego isn't threatened by her? She's stunningly beautiful, smart, clever, fearless, determined, unbound by social order and convention, successful, and rich. Is there anything not to like about this woman? Okay, she's a terrible flirt, a little manipulative, known to lie when it suits her, stubborn as a mule, arrogant, and completely self-centered, but at twelve years old, these negative qualities don't register with me. She gets shit done and nobody helps her, but she just keeps going, just keeps trying. Scarlett will have a lasting impact well beyond the movie theater.

# sixteen

JUNIOR HIGH IS A DIFFERENT SCHOOL AND I HAVE TO WALK THE OTHER way from home and much farther, but the best part is that Karen has to walk past my house on the way to school, so she stops and picks me up every morning. It's like our friendship just needed a new hook to hang on, and walking to school was it. We don't mingle in school, but the walk to and from school and home every day deepens our bond.

Karen is my best friend, but I wouldn't tell you that if you asked me. I'd say it was Dianne or Barbara, but that wouldn't be true. Those are just the girls I hang out with at school, trying to fit in. The girls I have in class. The girls I eat lunch with. My compartmentalized brain has created a compartmentalized life.

Karen knows everything about me like no one else does. She knows I don't have clothes to wear to school. Yes, I am covered with fabric and I do my best, but I wear my sister's hand-me-downs or what my mother sews or what my relatives send for Christmas. She knows all about my parents, all about the fighting, the police, Mother at the funny farm. She knows every time I am on restriction because I can't go to the park on those days.

I know everything about Karen too. Her parents both work. Her dad is a sergeant in the army, and they go to the PX for their food. I went with them once and it was like all the stores put together. You can get food and shoes, clothes, cigarettes, booze, hats, shovels, and all really cheap. This is probably why they have so much food and are my "run away from home" destination of choice. She is as unhappy at home as I am, and I have sympathy but don't really understand it. She seems to have all the things I long for: food, clothes, music, freedom. It all looks good to me from the outside, but she fights with her parents all the time like I do.

She is my rock, my sanity, my touchstone. No matter what happens Karen will always be there in the morning to walk me to school and in the afternoon to walk me home. Unlike me, Karen is cool. She wears jeans and T-shirts every day. I'm still not allowed to wear jeans to school or at all. Karen has bell bottoms, a leather fringed vest that she got for Chanukah, a leather shoulder bag with fringe, and a seemingly never-ending supply of T-shirts. I don't know why she puts up with me, but I am grateful for her association. I work hard to deserve her attention by telling stories that I hope will entertain and maintain my value. On the way home from school every day we stop at the Circle K for snacks. I rarely have money, so I have begun to steal from my parents, usually from my father's change purse. He keeps it in a little drawer in the center of his chest of drawers, which is just inside the bedroom door. You can slip in, silently slide the drawer open, snatch a quarter off the top, and be out in seconds.

Karen is teaching me the fine art of shoplifting. You put your notebook down on the top of the ice cream cabinet, slide the door open, rummage around like you're looking for something, slip a long ice pop inside your notebook, remark, "No, they don't have any," then close the door and walk out.

They keep the cigarettes, the most prized item in the store, above the candy section next to the register. I imagine they do that to keep an eye on them, but they are no match for the hordes of junior high schoolers that descend en masse. Candy bars and cigarettes disappear by the handful. Down our pants, in our pockets, inside notebooks, slipped into purses. Anyone paying attention would see the nerves and fear emanating from me. I broadcast my terror. If I am caught and my parents called, I can't even imagine the consequences, but I'm always hungry and I need cigarettes. My addiction to cigarettes has created a growing need, and I'm high from the thrill of stealing. This is life on the edge with Karen, and I can't back down. I can't be afraid. I have to measure up.

Gym class is my new favorite, and my gym teacher is the new light of my life. Not the older chubby one but the tall, dark-haired, pretty one. I get very nervous around her but can't wait to get to her class every day. I have a posse of girls in gym class—Anne, Kim, Annette—the girls who play sports well and take things seriously. Softball or kickball, I don't care what we're playing. I want to win. Pay attention, do your best, that's all anyone is asking of you, but there are always girls who close their eyes when the ball comes their way or can't run for shit.

In the spring our class starts to prepare for the Presidential Physical Fitness badge. There's a list of athletic events we have to master to get the award. Chin-ups, sit-ups, throwing a softball, broad jump, running the 440-yard dash. Things like that. I think I am a top athlete because I've seen the Jim Thorpe movie and I want to be just like him. He was poor and didn't have shoes, but he made the Olympic team and won the decathlon. I want to be Jim.

I'm thin, reasonably athletic, and enthusiastic, so I assume I'll do well. Sit-ups prove to be my first challenge. I have a natural sway to my back that makes bending forward the way you need to for sit-ups unnatural for me. The other girls in my posse whip off the fifty sit-ups with no problem, but I struggle. The last ten are by sheer force of will and hip flexors, not abs, but I get my fifty within the time limit. Next are chin-ups. I've never done a chin-up but assume I will be able to, no problem. When I get to the bar, I hang like a helpless flounder. I am horrified, but we only have to do ten. With youth and determination, I eventually make it, but the older, chubby teacher is supervising today and almost defeats me, disqualifying one of my chin-ups as not going high enough. She must know I hate her. Hate her for not being the other teacher.

Softball throw is pretty easy for me, but Anne is the best. I like Anne, so I let this go. I run the fastest time for the 440-yard dash practice. It's a cruel event. You have to run as fast as you can until your heart explodes out of your chest and you can no longer breathe or feel your legs. But I am first, and there's a brief moment in the sun with my teacher.

Beth is a new girl who arrives just as the Presidential Physical Fitness challenges begin. She hasn't trained with the rest of us and yet she seems to breeze through all her events. She whips off her sit-ups, has arms to do her chin-ups, and can throw a softball very well (but not as far as Anne, thank God). The 440 will be our final event, the pièce de résistance.

We line up at the starting line. I know my heart will explode, my lungs will fail, and my legs will go numb, but I am ready. Off we go, charging around the field. I am in front and imaging my glory at the end with a laurel wreath on my head held "shoulder high" at my victory. I charge down the first straightaway making sure I am in front and destined for victory. But at the first turn I can no longer get enough air. I can either run or breathe, but I can't do both. My legs begin to falter, but I am an object set in motion, and by sheer force of will I remain in motion. I make the next turn and see the finish line in the distance, and the potential for glory spurs my every step. Then there is Beth. Coming up beside me fast and beginning to pass. I have nothing. We are in the home stretch and my dream of victory dies right there on the playground as we pass the softball backstop. Beth wins and falls into the arms of our teacher. I stumble across the finish line in second place. All my glory gone, no laurel wreath or attention from the teacher.

Our gym class is full of the girls at school who are the most talented in sports. There are to be tryouts for the softball team and the posse all make it. Anne will pitch, Kim is the catcher, Annette is shortstop, and I play first base. We start playing against other schools and then there is a tournament for the city championship. We do well (Anne is a really good pitcher) and get all the way to the final game, but there's a last-minute change-up. Beth will play first base and I will be moved to left field. Left field?! Outfield is where you put the girls who can't play. I am humiliated. Plus, it's Beth. Fucking Beth who ruined my life in the 440.

The city championship game will be played on our home field against Marana Junior High. The day of the game, I am nervous but know my team is good and I'm sure we will win. Why am I always so sure we will win? Maybe I read *The Little Engine That Could* too many times as a child. I think I can, I think I can, I think I can.

The Marana team shows up and they are almost all Hispanic and Black girls who are a foot taller, bigger, and stronger than we are. If it had been left up to me, we probably wouldn't have bothered to take the field. We don't have any Black kids in our school. Tucson is segregated in the way that towns are segregated, with the new suburbia being all white, the south side Black, and the barrio Mexican.

The game is vomit-inducing. Anne is so brave on the pitcher's mound. Beth is flawless at first base. Annette is deadly at shortstop. Kim catches a perfect game. We are ahead by one run. I haven't scored a single run. I'm lucky not to have thrown up with my nerves so on edge. I've spent the game standing in left field praying the ball never makes it out of the infield, but as the gods are fickle, my turn comes on the last out.

They have a girl on base, there are two outs, and the last batter is big and powerful-looking, and I am sure she will hit a home run over my head and win the game. I watch like a spectator as Anne faces her down, throwing strike after strike. The batter fights her off with multiple foul balls that only add to my tension. Then that sound. The high-pitched "ping" of the ball being hit hard and straight by a metal bat. I wake from my stupor, realizing the ball has been hit high in the air toward left field. Toward me! Will this be my hour of redemption for coming in second in the 440? Will I catch the last out that wins the game and make our teacher love me, or will I add to my list of failures and drop the ball? I search the sky, see the ball, extend my glove, and catch it. It's an out-of-body experience. All I know is that I caught the ball and we won. I never moved my feet because I was paralyzed. The ball was hit straight to me, and I was where I was supposed to be. As I said, the gods are fickle.

# seventeen

WE ARE GOING ON A SUMMER VACATION TO MEXICO TO A PLACE called Chino Bay. We have a new station wagon, a beige Plymouth that my father has to have but my mother doesn't want as we "can't afford it." The Oldsmobile finally died. Mother regularly "fixed" it by pouring Pepsi over the battery contacts, then hitting it with a hammer until the car started. Magic Mommy. This is white magic. Nothing is explained. Just look, listen, and learn.

We stop at the border in Nogales. You have to get a visa to go deeper than the border town into Mexico, and my parents will have to buy Mexican car insurance before we can drive across the border, or that's how I understand it. Charlotte and I sit in the very back in a seat that faces backward. The fascination with this doesn't last longer than the trip because it makes me car sick to sit facing the cars coming up behind us. I have to sit too close to Charlotte, and looking at where we've been is not as much fun as where we're going. This is a new modern adaptation of the station wagon that goes along with all the space-age styling and buttons. There are push buttons for everything, like the radio and the AC that barely works against the Arizona heat.

We park and Mother and Daddy walk into the office to get the visa and insurance. As they walk past the car Charlotte whispers, "I think Mom's pregnant."

"*What?!*" I gasp.

She says, "Look at her belly. She's definitely pregnant." I argue against this point as I know at least that your parents have to like each other to get pregnant, but they *are* going through a strange new lovey-dovey period. All holding hands and "dears" and "darlings."

I study my mother and have to admit Charlotte has a point. She always has a belly though she is thin, but something has changed. Charlotte says not to say anything. I am gratified to be drawn into her confidence and readily agree.

We camp on the beach at Chino Bay. We have an old army surplus tent whose only function is to gather heat during the day and restrict any breeze at night. The wind blows nonstop, and there is sand in every square inch of the tent, our food, our hair, and every orifice of my body. The beach is fine but it's too windy. The surf is too rough to be any fun. I am sunburnt, hot, sand-infested, and not having the fun vacation at the beach I imagined. Poverty has its consequences.

Mother at some point reveals that she is indeed pregnant. Like I can't plainly see it once she puts on her bathing suit. Charlotte is vindicated in her observations (which I find very impressive), but I am still confused. I am twelve, Charlotte is fourteen. I know pregnant means a baby is coming, but I'm not sure how this all goes together. We are a nuclear family of four, so how will this new baby fit in? Will it be a boy or a girl? Where will it sit? What will its name be? I cannot imagine any of it, so I just dismiss it from my imagination. For now.

We are in the dog days of August in Arizona, monsoon season, where the rains roll in like putting the lid on a terrarium. Everyone lives with swamp coolers, which are perfect in the dry heat, but once the humidity shows up we are always sweaty and don't sleep.

You can smell it before you feel it and feel it before you see it.

First you smell the rain, a damp odor that gives the desert smell a richness of the creosote and cottonwoods that the dry air never reveals. Then you feel the breeze and humidity. The breeze is a welcome relief from the heat, but the humidity changes the dryness to an unfamiliar closeness. Then the clouds come. Tucson sits in a valley between four mountain ranges, and the wind brings the dark clouds that roll in like a cap over the valley.

It's like a sorcerer casting spells. The smell, the wind, the clouds. Then the sky goes dark, thunder rumbles, and you see lightning in the distance. The energy begins to build and then suddenly—it pours. There is nothing subtle about rain in the desert. Its very existence is revered, discussed, celebrated, reported, and feared. Feared by grown-ups who know better, but for us kids, it's the most exciting thing that happens all summer. We leap onto our bikes and ride to the dry washes to wait for the water. If you happen to be exploring in the wash when the rain hits, you have been given sufficient warning to get out, so no one would feel sorry for you if you have to scramble up the bank to save yourself.

Tucson has a population of about a quarter of a million people. Some will cast that number higher, saying we are nearing half a million, but they are exaggerating with the cowboys who were swaggering around town when Princess Margaret came to visit. We don't have money to build bridges, so they just pave down through the riverbeds. Since it doesn't rain all that often I guess the logic is sound, but it makes for poor choices and exciting water rescues.

The water comes quickly. Locals run out to the store only to be faced by a flooded wash on their way home. They try to convince themselves that it isn't that deep and that they can surely make it, even though the evidence of many a stranded motorist marooned atop their cars should tell them otherwise.

Having discarded our bicycles, we line the banks and wait

for events to unfold. We provide experienced advice *not* to try to cross as the water is too deep, but we are children and readily ignored. Off they go, driving through the riverbed on its perilous little ribbon of asphalt laid down over the sand. It's early yet, so most make it across, but as the volume of water increases some hapless motorist is the unfortunate recipient of today's "You are going to be on the six o'clock news" prize.

Speaking of water, Mother announces that hers has broken. I know this is the harbinger of "The Baby" and imagine scenes of rushing about the house gathering suitcases and toothbrushes and the mad dash to the hospital, just like in the movies. But Mother calmly empties the dishwasher, makes her bed, and performs other mundane tasks of tidying around the house as Charlotte and I hyperventilate and hover nearby. It's August so we are home from school. Daddy eventually shows up from work and the two of them calmly get in the car, tell us to be good, and leave for the hospital. It all seems very anticlimactic to me. Daddy eventually comes home late that evening with the news that we have a new little sister.

Melanie Rose Randolph Smith is born at 5:00 p.m. at Saint Joseph's Hospital and brought home the next morning. My mother is in her fancy pink bathrobe (which she made) carrying my new little sister. I catch her in the hall as she heads for the bedroom, my arms outstretched to be given the new prize, but I am immediately rebuffed, with "Go wash your hands." My mother, the bacteriologist who barely scrapes the mold off of the cheese and blows dirt off your picnic sandwich, is now requiring a new level of hygiene heretofore unknown in our house.

The world has tilted, the axis is bent, and we are now a family of five, not four. There are now three girls, not two. I am the middle child, no longer the youngest.

Melanie is tiny, pink, adorable, and generally a good baby. She doesn't cry more than a baby seemingly should, but my contact, at first, is limited, as she is in a bassinet in my parents' bedroom and my mother keeps her mostly to herself. I'm not sure what I am more jealous of—Melanie, who's getting all my mother's attention, or my mother, who's spending all her time with Melanie.

A new red recliner is purchased and installed in my parents' bedroom for nursing. The purchase of a brand-new piece of furniture is remarkable enough, but the nursing seems archaic. I know about nursing, but in the movies and on TV babies are fed from a bottle. How typical of Mother to do things differently.

There are a slew of "firsts." The first diaper I ever change. How such stink and putrid excrement could come out of such a perfect pink body is a disappointing revelation. First smile. Oh, what we won't all do for that smile. First vomit over the back of your shoulder, accompanied by a belching sound that belongs to a demon. First crying fit that goes on for hours and no amount of rocking, cuddling, or singing can soothe. I am her slave. I will do anything to have her and hold her. I sing every foolish song I ever learned to her. "Rings on her fingers, bells on her toes. Elephants to ride upon my little Irish Rose. So come to my nabob for next Saint Patrick's day. Be Mistress Mumbo Jumbo Jigaboo J. O'Shea."

# eighteen

SEPTEMBER COMES QUICKLY AND WE ARE BACK IN SCHOOL. THE new baby is six weeks old and has brought a joy and lightness to our home, and my parents are often ensconced in their bedroom alone with her with the door closed. But it's not like it was before. This isn't the closed door of before, a harbinger of a coming storm. Rather, it's an energy of "We are together with the new baby, and you will have to earn your way in."

Melanie is the new prize that my mother doles out for good behavior. "Are your chores done?" "Do you have homework?"

Her every move and progress is worthy of note. She rolls over, she is smiling, she eats mushed-up green beans, she is sitting, she is standing. We are all enthralled. I rush home every day to play with her. My mother is no longer depressed or crying on the bed.

Mother takes to sewing again. Little pink nighties with rosebuds embroidered on the collars, baby blankets to wrap and swaddle Melanie in. I had no idea until Melanie arrived how messy and dirty babies are. The vomit and poop are relentless and uncontainable. We have a diaper service, which seems very fancy to me because it's something that costs money. Wet diapers are just tossed in the bin, but dirty diapers have to be dipped in the toilet repeatedly until the majority of the poop comes off. This has the common and unfortunate result of producing the dry heaves if not all-out vomit. "Oh, isn't she adorable."

When Melanie is about a year old, a crib is brought down from the deep, dark recesses of the storage room out in the carport. I am in the eighth grade now and have my *Sergeant Pepper* album and flowers I cut out of a shopping bag from Foley's scotch-taped to my bedroom walls. The crib and a dresser are moved into my room. At first I am annoyed at the invasion of my sanctuary without so much as a how-do-you-do, but I am so in love with this baby that I don't mind. Except when she cries and no amount of holding or rocking or singing or any other distraction I can think of will soothe her. But I hang in. I have to show that I am up to the task or they will take her away.

Melanie and I develop a dance all our own. She wakes up early in the morning and, in a ritual designed to wake a sleeping teenager, throws her pacifier out of the crib, then calls for me to fetch it. "Ummm. Ummm."

My mother has designed a system—elastic through the pacifier, which is then looped around Melanie's wrist. This is to keep the pacifier attached to her so that we're not always looking for where she dropped it but also so she can always find it and soothe herself when needed. Once awakened from my teenage sleep coma, I fetch the pacifier and loop it back to her wrist and stumble back to bed. Repeat. She pulls the pacifier off her wrist, throws it out of the crib, then whimpers "Ummm Ummm" until I wake up. This little duet is repeated until I retrieve her from her crib and bring her to my bed. It was never about the pacifier, and eventually I abandon step one and just go straight to step two. I may be half asleep, but having learned this pas de deux, I now skip straight to the coda.

Melanie's first word is "Um." My mother tries to make this "Mom," but we know better. The little call in the early dawn hours to be fetched from her crib is "Ummmmm," which morphs eventually into "Ummy." Emily. We are besties and that's just how it is. Finally, someone to love. She is pure, innocent, and not yet polluted by the dark forces. We have a love bubble all our own. Maybe part of it is because I know the performance of love that has become my mother. There are great shows of love and affection, yes, but I also know the underlying darkness. The betrayal that can come at any moment. I will protect Melanie.

Melanie and I play various games that entail crawling around the living room. "Pacifier keep-away" is a favorite and elicits squeals of delight as the pacifier is detached from her wrist and hurled across the room. The chase is on. Who will get to it first? I can win this game every time if I choose to but am impressed by her determination and allow her to just barely beat me. This elicits a delightful squeal of joy.

Airplane is another favorite. I lay on my back, take her hands, put my feet on her belly, then lift her into the air, producing the accompanying sounds of propellers and zooming about the sky. More gratifying squealing, and we play this game until I am exhausted, as Melanie never tires of it. Our repertoire includes elephant rides on my back (which must be accompanied by singing), pony trots on my knees, swinging statue in the yard. Hours of it.

I don't really think of her as a baby anymore, more like a really short young human. She walks and talks now, has opinions, is developing likes and dislikes. What she wants to wear, what she wants to eat. It's interesting to see her grow and develop. She surprises me with her stubbornness and sometimes makes me laugh when she gets frustrated. We interact like equals, but I obviously have more ability, so I am conscious of my status as role model. Her new catchphrase is, "I want to do what Ummy do's."

Junior high is pretty much a bust. I'm not popular, and no grown-up fawns over me and my long eyelashes the way they did when I was young. I float around the edges of things. I have friends but I only put in the required energy to fit in. I participate in sports and ballet but always feel different and not quite good enough, though at the same time, I seem to think I am a star. I have no concrete evidence for this, but living with my devastating insecurities requires balancing an overinflated ego to survive. Any movie with a hero or heroine who overcomes great odds to win the day is assimilated into my personality. I am Vivien Leigh in *Gone With the Wind*, Bette Davis in *Now, Voyager*, Scout in *To Kill a Mockingbird*. I become them and they bolster my self-esteem. Walking around with these conflicting sentiments ping-ponging through my brain is exhausting. Karen is my only constant. We go to the park and smoke.

I have a crush on Craig, the most popular boy in school. He is a more advanced version of Humpy: khaki slacks with matching three-tone elastic belt, brown and beige saddle shoes, and a short-sleeved button-down shirt. Very preppy and very handsome. All the cool boys wear English Leather cologne.

But Craig is paired with Shelly, the most popular girl in school who, like Debbie in sixth grade, has great clothes and Capezio shoes. I am still rotating the same five dresses and the three Parcheesi dresses from my Granny last year. I do get a boyfriend, but it's not Craig. It's like we are lined up in order of popularity, girls on one side, boys on the other, and you get the boy across from you who matches your ranking in popularity. I get Frankie.

Frankie is adorable. Dark hair and dark eyes. He wears the correct preppy outfit and cologne. Problem is, I am slightly taller and going through a growth spurt. I spend all of eighth grade slouching over onto one hip trying to be shorter than Frankie. I get invited to a party and Frankie and I make out under a tree in the backyard (my first make out) and I get four tiny hickeys on my neck like he was sucking through a gap in his front teeth. I still don't get the boy thing entirely. I want a boyfriend because it's what you are supposed to want, but once I get one, I don't know what to do with him. Lying under a tree in the backyard getting hickeys isn't the thrill it should be.

But I have Karen and I have Melanie. These are my two main relationships as they cannot be interrupted by being on restriction, which is still a regular occurrence. Karen will always be there to walk to school with and Melanie will always be at home to love.

Things have been better for everyone since Melanie was born—Mother is happier having produced this adorable child, Daddy is out of Mother's crosshairs, and Charlotte uses her presence as a screen to shield against any disapproval—but I don't fare as well. I still have a "tone," and adding to this how obvious it is that Melanie loves me best, Mother has a new resentment to mitigate. Any infraction results in Melanie being taken away from me as punishment, except when it suits Mother for me to take care of her.

# nineteen

MY BALLET SCHOOL IS KIND OF FUNKY, BUT I THINK THAT'S WHY I GO. It's one place where I feel like I fit in. If it was too fancy, I couldn't go. Plus, a fancy teacher wouldn't put up with my mother never paying the bill on time. My friends are there and we bond during carpool as much as in class. My mother regularly flakes out on her carpool shifts, so I get something else to feel like shit about, but I love going to class, so I shove this feeling down to deal with another time.

I'm not very good. Natalie, with the red hair and the mom who always pays her bill on time and shows up for carpool, is the star of our class. She seems to effortlessly do all the exercises and combinations while I work like the devil to not much effect. But I can jump. Boy can I jump. The floor of the studio is linoleum over concrete, not the wood floor you see in all the posters of Margot Fonteyn and Rudolf Nureyev, but still, I can hover and fly. It feels like I bounce off the floor and hang in the air. I get high from it. I am fully in my body. My body feels like a toy I play with. Can I do this? Can I do that? Yes, I can. Watch.

I also go to Pony Club because of my lifelong love of horses. The people who own the farm and run the club are members of our church, and I am there on scholarship. I am given hand-me-down boots and jodhpur pants from Jay, the daughter of the owners. She is also my teacher and makes me freeze inside when she's around, and if she speaks to me my ears ring.

The horse I ride every week is Miss Moffat, a Welsh pony with an infection in her hoof I am supposed to take care of and manage. I have no idea what I'm doing. I curry, brush, and pick out hooves, but I'm never sure if I'm doing it right or how much is good enough. I put on bridles and saddles and walk my horse to the ring. We ride around the ring and trot and post. It never seems right. We canter and I am supposed to make the lead leg of the horse be on the outside. I give the proper instructions to Miss Moffat but can never tell if she's doing it. I'm a bust.

I participate in the horse show in the spring. Mother makes me a beautiful royal blue jacket and paisley cravat. I wear my borrowed boots, jodhpurs, and hard hat. I win seventh place in the walk/trot class but it's just not enough. I'm just not enough. Even for Jay, it's just not enough. During my Pony Club days I also go to Junior Assembly. This is where you wear a dress and learn how to sit properly with your ankles crossed, hands in your lap, and dance with boys. We learn to foxtrot, waltz, all the old-fashioned formal dances.

Pony Club is from nine to eleven on Saturday mornings. Junior Assembly is at noon. The problem is logistics. Mother is always late picking me up from Pony Club, and the Junior Assembly carpool is usually already there, sitting in front of the house, or they've given up and left, so Mother has to drive me. I rush into the house and throw on a dress, stockings, and shoes without a moment to even wash my hands, much less shower.

I smell like a horse. There is dirt under my fingernails. God knows what I am wearing, but it isn't good. Boys ask me to dance before they get a chance to take in the whole picture. Dirty hands, smells like horse. If I were them, I'd ask Debbie or Sheila to dance over me any day.

On the morning that turns out to be my last day at Pony Club, we are going to jump. This sounds good and I am excited. Jay comes over to me to check my saddle before I go. She is singing the latest David Cassidy hit, "I Think I Love You," and I get nauseous and have bees in my head. I don't hear a word of instruction, just *I think I love you* in my mind.

"Okay, go!"

I am to clear a little cavalletti, a low jump about twelve inches off the ground. I am to approach at a trot and Miss Moffat will jump over.

"Don't worry," Jay instructs. "Just let her do all the work. She knows how." I'm not there, I'm not on the horse, and then I am on the ground. Miss Moffat jumped over but I did not. I fell off somewhere in the process and am now in Jay's arms being checked for injury.

Mother tells me I have to choose. Ballet or Pony Club, I can't do both. I choose ballet. Pony Club is for girls with families and money, not girls on scholarship with bees in their head. It's during this period that Mother starts telling me, "You are a privileged character. You get all the opportunities in life, and because of this, you owe something back to the world."

Okay, I hear ya, Mother, but it doesn't fit with how I *feel*. I don't feel privileged. I feel like an outsider looking in on almost every situation I am in. I was on scholarship at Pony Club, you don't pay on time for ballet class. I smelled like a horse at formal, fancy Junior Assembly. My clothes are old and stained. I don't invite anyone over because I never know what's going to be happening in the house. I show up late everywhere I go if you're driving. You sometimes forget me altogether, which is really embarrassing when it's carpool. But somehow, I am still enthusiastic about all the things I'm doing, so I'm not going to let you ruin everything and drag me down.

Daddy has been fired again from his job at the church—the good job. There is talk of his not raising enough money from the parishioners. There is some woman who works at the church named Jean who he says has it out for him, but this time is not like all the other times he's been fired. No Bekins, no transfer to another town. This time it's just fired and you're on your own, buddy. I don't know what this means, but I know it feels like the bottom has fallen out. The tension in the house is suffocating, but we pretend it isn't there. I have an even greater sense of insecurity.

Being disconnected from the church is a blow. My pride in my father being a priest has been the only thing I could ever hang my hat on with him. That he must be good. That he must be special. Now he's just the guy who can't do stuff and fights with my mother. We are cut adrift with no church. No place to go where I am "the preacher's kid, a PK." We're not special.

Because of Daddy's new unemployment, Mother has decided to go back to work and gets a job at Tucson Medical Center in the Bacteriology Lab. This sounds promising and I am proud of her. Bacteriology. Even the word seems important. I know she has a degree, and working at the hospital sounds impressive. Yes. We are a team! Daddy is down but not out. He is looking for work, and Mother has stepped into the gap. We're not finished yet!

My father gets some work doing services on Sunday at a little church on the bad side of town. Nothing permanent but something. Mother is telling tales at the dinner table of the mean lady who runs the lab at the hospital "who doesn't know what she's doing." She is very animated and puffed up at her new employment status. My father starts driving a cab at night. He counts quarters at the table in the morning from tips and tells stories of drunks and loose women he picks up. Men with no prospects. Women of low morals who fall against him and try to put lipstick on his collar. It sounds very dangerous.

The world has tilted again, but we have not completely spun out of the solar system.

# twenty

MELANIE IS TWO. SHE WALKS AND HAS LITTLE WHITE HIGH-TOPS THAT she is very fond of. "Shoe" was her first word after "Um." It's my parents' anniversary and they are going out. Pink carnations have been produced by my father and they are dressed up fancy. It must be a significant anniversary as their "going out" is a rare occurrence. The family going out at all is rare, with the occasional foray to the drive-in movies being the exception. But they are going out alone to dinner. Charlotte and I will babysit Melanie, which doesn't involve much because Melanie pretty much spends all her time with me, whether my parents are home or not.

We almost never get to watch TV. TV is considered "junk" with a few exceptions: *The Carol Burnett Show, Masterpiece Theater, Sixty Minutes.* After they leave the house Charlotte and I grab Melanie and race for the television but are not surprised to discover Mother has removed the power cord from the back of the TV. Clever mothers breed clever children, so Charlotte and I set about searching for the cord's hiding place. Having stowed it in her underwear drawer (the usual spot), I wonder if it wasn't all a setup for us to find it and then be in even more trouble for having gone through her drawers.

Now we have a more complex problem to solve. When they come home, Mother's first move will be to place her hand on the top of the TV to feel for warmth. Having been busted for this a few times, I guess this is why the battle has escalated to removing the power cord. But Charlotte is not to be thwarted. She removes ice trays from the freezer and places them on top of the television. Brilliant!

I have to wonder what goes on in Mother's mind to engage in this kind of battle with her own children. What great harm will come to us if we watch a few hours of unsupervised television while they're gone? I hate the feeling of "badness" for disobeying her, but I see what we are doing as normal in the world around me. It's what my friends are doing and what we see on television. Everyone watches TV. How does she not see that we will risk fire and electrocution to try to be normal like everyone else? Why does she hate us and what have we done?

My parents' return from going out prompts the usual rituals. They say hello, ask us what we did while they were gone. The hand makes its way to the top of the TV, but something is off. They depart to their bedroom and close the door, which is never a good sign. Charlotte and I retreat to our rooms wondering how the movie we were watching ended.

First we hear the muffled voices, then louder, then the bedroom door is flung open and my father rushes out of the house, gets in his car, and drives off. Charlotte and I stay in our rooms.

The reverend returns a half hour later but leaves the VW running in the driveway—not his usual parking spot on the side of the carport. He comes in and the fight continues but is no longer contained in their bedroom. There is shouting, hitting, pushing, horrible words, and my father storms out the back door without closing it. Mother rushes to lock and deadbolt it behind him. He gets in his car, revs the engine (which doesn't have the desired effect due to being a Volkswagen), and drives up onto the front yard toward the front door. I can see the headlight coming at us through the glass pane in the door. He sits there for several minutes, seemingly deciding if he really is going to drive through the front door into the house, then reverses and drives away. I don't know where he is going. Mother tells us to get some PJs and a change of clothes. I fetch Melanie from her crib and we go across the street to the Molina's house to seek refuge for the night.

I float above the scene, having left my body somewhere mid-fight. I now occupy only a small part of my brain, the part required to form one-word-syllable responses to questions asked or kindnesses given. "Yes, no, thank you." "Yes, I'd like a blanket. No, I don't need anything else. Thank you for taking us in."

In the morning we are all dressed, teeth brushed, and ready to go home. We leave with a lot of "thank yous" and walk across the street to our back door. The VW is parked behind the station wagon, blocking it from leaving. As we approach the back door, a pink carnation with a meticulously tied noose around it is hanging from a thumbtack. My mother doesn't remove it but fumbles with the keys. She opens the door and we stand, framed in the back doorway.

We are just about to step into the house when the louver doors from the kitchen into the front entry hall are kicked open to reveal my father in his boxers and T-shirt with his fancy satin robe and slippers (which he only wears at Christmas), sitting on the kitchen stool with his deer hunting rifle across his lap. He cocks the rifle, meticulously sliding the bolt back then forward, and begins to lift the gun, pointing it in our direction. Not a word is said, not a sound made. We back away from the door and retreat across the street to the safety of the Molina's.

Daddy moves out of the house. Mother tells us he is gone and goes on to the next thing she is doing. This all takes place under cover of darkness or when we are at school because after the big fight and the gun, it seems they just can't take it anymore. The rage on my father's face, the cool hatred as he sat on the stool pointing the gun at us, obviously very proud of himself and his ambush, isn't lost on me. I don't know my father's side because he doesn't talk to us, but maybe it isn't only my mother he hates. Maybe it's us too. Maybe if it wasn't for us he could be off doing something else instead of being tied to this family, this house, and my mother. These are all things I should not be thinking about. I have enough trouble remembering my schoolwork or figuring out what to wear to school.

With my father absent, I move up the ladder into full-blown paramour to my mother. There is no more pretense of asking my father to do things or help her with things. I am Mother's choice, and though it doesn't make sense, even to me, I am generally enthusiastic. I like going up on the roof to fix the swamp cooler. I like running the little rented backhoe to dig the garden. I like setting up the Doughboy pool in the backyard and learning how to make the pump work and how to clean it out and put in fresh diatomaceous earth.

This may be why I am also the target of her rage. I'm just there. She has transferred her frustrations with life and with my father to me as I now occupy his place. It seems these feelings explode out of her like Old Faithful at Yellowstone.

The structure of the nuclear family has had a core meltdown. Dinner isn't a regular occurrence. The rhythm of my father coming home from work seems to have freed Mother from this tedium, but that's okay because Charlotte and I have found other ships to sail. Charlotte is heavily involved in the school newspaper. I have my team sport, and we are both going to ballet class several times a week.

The dichotomy of this is that I know I still need to take care of Mother. I have to watch her as much as possible to make sure she is okay. She has become even more central to my survival as I no longer have a father and I also have a tiny little sister who I don't trust her with. When Charlotte and I were small, Mother forgot us at the grocery store. She only came back after going all the way home and the lady who did our ironing asked where we were. I once sat for hours on the steps of a strange school in Bay City after being locked out of the building after summer craft camp. All the other kids got picked up and the teachers had left.

Mother's behavior is terrifying. She weaves through traffic with the attitude that everyone should look out for her. She doesn't obey the speed limit or lane lines or use her turn signal. She will sit down on the floor of the grocery store suddenly, go into the bank and lay down on the couch because she is suddenly tired. It's a terrifying existence, and though I need to watch her, I also want to be as far away from her as possible. With Melanie. I need to take Melanie with me.

# twenty-one

MY BALLET TEACHER, MARIA, IS A STRANGER TO ME. I GO TO CLASS several times a week, but after five years of this, I still don't really know her. She prefers the girls whose families pay their bills, and you can't really blame her. She has famous ballet-star friends who sometimes come to visit and teach us special classes. There is a poster of George Zoritch on the wall in the studio. His picture is beyond physically magnificent, and now he is coming to visit Maria and will teach us class.

Mr. Zoritch has some kind of foreign accent and a rather large belly for such a big ballet star, but I overlook this due to the poster of him in his prime on the wall. He was young and handsome with very long legs, a V-shaped torso topped with broad shoulders, arms held high, his head turned in profile. He makes fun of me for constantly tugging at my leotard, but you would, too, if you had to wear a turtleneck leotard from Sears.

In the spring of my sophomore year, Maria takes us to an audition for a scholarship to San Francisco Ballet School's summer session. She knows Mr. Christianson, the director of the school, who is coming to town to give the audition. There are six of us from the school who go, and it seems like all the kids from all the other schools are there too. In a small town like Tucson there is great rivalry between ballet schools. The only other school I know is Mrs. Fritchey's, and we hate them. They do everything wrong

(Maria tells us) and we think they are not as good as we are. There have been attempts to join the whole ballet community together to create a company and even a combined show where all the schools put their egos aside for the greater good, but it didn't go well.

Eight weeks after the audition, I get a letter in the mail telling me I got a scholarship. Well knock me down and slap me silly. Me? A scholarship?! I find this unbelievable, but I am very proud. Even Mother seems enthusiastic.

The plan is we will all drive to San Francisco in July, Mother, Charlotte, Melanie, and I, stay with Uncle Amos (from Daddy's seminary days and Texas), then drive into town to the convent where I am to stay. We've been given a list of places where I can stay and Mother of course picked the one associated with a church. Did she notice the location? It's a block from the corner of Haight and Ashbury where I will get felt up by some man in the grocery store.

The convent is a massive white building on a corner run by the nuns. I am moved into my room, and everyone leaves with promises of seeing me in August.

It's July and I have packed all my summer clothes. I didn't know and no one thought to tell me that San Francisco in July is windy, gray, cold, and rainy. Then of course there is the famous fog. The convent is perched on a hill above the city and I watch the cold damp fog roll in every night. I do not leave my heart.

It takes us three buses to get to the ballet school and I am lost most of the time. Thank God there are other girls who seem to know their way around. We have ballet, point, pas de deux, and character classes. There are a lot of very skinny, very pretty, very talented girls in my class, but I am not one of them. I am also skinny and pretty, but I'm not talented. I work hard, and as usual I'm enthusiastic and display my jumping ability to its best advantage, but ballet for girls is all about poise, grace, and very long legs. Enthusiasm will not cover up for my lack of hyperextended knees.

There are twelve of us in the summer scholarship program staying at the convent. The nuns prowl around at all hours and look at us as if we are always doing something wrong. Sometimes we are, like smoking cigarettes out the windows of our rooms or stealing food from the kitchen, but mostly, we go to class all day and then gather in the large corner room that is occupied by five girls. My room is a ten-by-ten cell that I share with another girl. Two single beds shoved against opposing walls with a sink, a little dresser, and a window overlooking the city. You can barely walk between the beds, and I'm sure it was designed for one nun, but the convent is cashing in on the ballet-school bonanza. There can't be a lot of ways for a convent to make money.

There are ladies who sit on the couch in the TV room holding hands. They seem to live there, too, but not on our floor. One of them threw a cereal box and screamed at one of the girls at breakfast this morning. This gains them their required space and we no longer watch TV. We just talk and smoke in our rooms and are on the constant hunt for food.

At the end of the summer session, we are all called out of class one by one into the office. We're given a basic rundown of what they think we're good at and if we qualify to go to the school full time or come back next summer. I'm not asked to return next summer, but there's no surprise here. Some girls come back into class crying, but they're silly. Look in the mirror. The walls are covered with them. Do you look like the girls in the ballet posters? Is the teacher paying extra attention to you in class every day? No. We all know who the best students are. Still, I had an adventure, spent a month away from home, and got to see some more of the world, some of which is exciting and some just strange.

I have always had jobs, around the house and otherwise,

chores, babysitting, and now my mother has come up with a new plan. I am to work at the Molina's restaurant as a busboy. I am a girl of course, and bussing tables is traditionally work for boys, but I am looking forward to the prospect of being out of the house, earning money, and doing something different.

On my first day at the restaurant I am given a metal cart to push around and retrieve dishes from the dirty tables, then wipe the tables all down and reorganize the condiments. Put the dirty glasses on the top of the cart, dishes on the bottom, and silverware in the little tray. If you've ever been to a traditional Mexican restaurant, you know that the plates are large and heavy. The food is also heavy. Enchiladas, rice, and beans all seem to weigh an enormous amount, so I am grateful for folks who eat all their food.

I work three nights a week and I'm a girl on a mission. Give me a goal and I am on it. I'm fast and I'm good. I speed through the restaurant, clearing and wiping down tables. The waitresses who were at first skeptical of a girl doing this traditionally boy job are soon my biggest fans. I am invited to sit at the waitresses' table in the corner by the kitchen. They smoke cigarettes, fill out the checks for the tables, and rest. They are glorious creatures. All loud with big hair. We laugh and complain to each other, make fun of the regulars (but not in a mean way), and generally make the heavy work of waiting tables a good time.

Mary is the head waitress. She has worked at the restaurant for years and many patrons ask to sit in her section and hail her by name as they come in the door. "Mary, is your station full?" She's loud and makes fun of the patrons and their orders. "Chimichangas again, George?" she chides, but she handles a seemingly huge number of tables and delivers food with precision. No asking who ordered the chimichanga because she knows.

After just a few shifts, I am treated as an equal by the waitresses, though they are many years older than I am. I smoke and no one, not even Mr. Molina who lives across the street and knows I'm only fifteen, says a word. I am allowed to drink as much Coke and eat as much food as I like. I am paid by the restaurant hourly and the waitresses also throw me tips, especially if I really hustle, which I always do. Food, soda, cigarettes, liberation, and money—I have found an amazing life.

I try to make friends with the boys in the dishwashing room. I don't know if it's our age difference or that I'm a girl, but they regard me with suspicion and hold me at arm's length. They are friendly but they don't warm to me like the waitresses do. I bring my cart of dishes to the back of the restaurant and heave the loaded tub onto their stainless steel counter. They retrieve the plates, scrape and spray off the beans and rice, and stack them in the green plastic trays to send through the Hobart dishwasher. Glasses are dumped of their Coke and iced tea and loaded onto another green tray with little cubbies that perfectly fit their size and shape. Silverware is dumped into an open tray, sprayed down, and sent through. The dish room is a room of spraying water and catapulted food particles. Not the kind of place you linger.

I have nothing to do with the kitchen or food preparation. I only pass through on my way to the dishwashing room. There are little old grandmas seated on milk crates mashing beans in five-gallon buckets. A boy about my age sending head after head of lettuce through a machine that shreds it. Sweaty men at the stove making enchiladas, tacos, and the cheese crisp of local Tucson fame. I love seeing all the magic behind the scenes.

Mother has to drive me to and from work every night. She comes in to wait for me to finish and flirts with Mr. Molina, and I suspect this is why she is willing to take me and pick me up. She needs attention. It's embarrassing to watch as her flirting is so obvious. With my father out of the picture I guess she's looking for an alternate source. I am sufficient for chores but don't fill the need for male attention. She's still very pretty and needs to feel that power.

Tonight on the drive home she's in a mood. She didn't come in to flirt and I am again the target of her frustrations. In the car she spits, "You smell like cigarettes!" I don't respond. Of course I smell like cigarettes. I would smell like cigarettes even if I wasn't smoking because I sit with the waitresses who chain smoke and leave cigarettes constantly burning in the ashtray so they can get a quick drag as they pass by the table on the way to the kitchen. I smell like cigarettes, sweat, the entire kitchen, and all the food that is cooked and served, but she has found a fault to exploit.

I'm sitting in the front seat next to her in the Skylark and she grabs my purse. Tareyton 100s. Busted. She throws my purse across me, out my open window, then pushes me, as if to shove me out of the car. I grab the door handle in the melee, the door opens, and the asphalt is visible as we speed toward home.

Finding myself leaning out of the open car door, clutching the door handle as the asphalt whizzes by, saved only by my seat belt, is a new terror. Something breaks in my brain. I am not safe. I am going to fall out of the car and onto the road. My mother is trying to kill me.

This is the first time I've felt real violence toward me from my mother. I have seen her violence toward my father and his toward her, but her rage was mostly internal, constantly simmering under the surface. Toward me it was packaged in modern parental discipline. "I've had enough out of you, young lady. Restriction for a week!" The result of some "tone" or failure to instantly comply, or God help you if you argue. We were spanked when we were little, and she graduated to the hairbrush as we got older. A few were broken on my backside, but never did I feel like major bodily harm was imminent.

I don't fall out, but it's close. We're about a half mile from the house when she pulls over. I hike back, searching in the dark for my purse. Once located, I dodge traffic, careful to snatch everything that scattered, and walk back home.

My job at Molina's doesn't last much longer as school starts soon. But the experience has bolstered me. I can survive in the world without her. My growing independence emboldens me.

# twenty-two

FRESHMAN YEAR OF HIGH SCHOOL IS A BLUR. THERE ARE TOO MANY fights with Mother about where I am going, what I am doing, what I am wearing, how I speak, what I say. Everything I do is wrong. I live in fear of her, with too many threats to my overall safety for me to stay in my body. I barely manage to get up in the morning and get to school. I'm rehearsing with the Tucson Civic Ballet for Swan Lake (I am a swan in the corps de ballet) six to ten o'clock, five nights a week, and don't get home until after ten thirty, at which point I am beyond starving, having eaten Jell-O for lunch and nothing more. I am grateful if there is an overcooked, dried, and shriveled dinner waiting for me in the oven, or I forage for something to eat, then do whatever homework has to be turned in the next day. I don't study. Studying is for girls who have time and I don't.

In the morning I regularly sleep through my alarm and wake to the sound of Karen's parents pulling into the driveway waiting to drive Charlotte and me to school. My mother doesn't work, doesn't get up or make us breakfast, and doesn't drive us to school. When I'm lucky she sprays me with water from a squirt bottle to get me out of bed and hands me a carob and wheat germ shake as I walk out the door.

My school is very large. There are seven hundred kids in my graduating class, and just getting from Spanish to biology can be daunting. No time to mess around. You've got six minutes and you'd better hustle. Walt Disney designed our school and it shows. There is a round theater in the front of the building and curved walls as you enter the front doors. Big open hallways with stairs up and stairs down to get from here to there. My locker is strategically placed near the front door and Spanish class. Central locker location is best because I don't want to have to carry a whole morning's worth of books *and* go to the science building.

My sophomore year I make a new friend. Her name is Mary Kay (MK) and we meet in English class. I don't know why we click. She's tall with long hair and she's very, very smart. I like smart girls and I think we bond over dysfunctional families. Her father is a doctor who got addicted to pills and had an affair with his nurse. So stereotypical. He divorced MK's mother and married the nurse. Her mom moved out with the five daughters while he kept the family home with the pool and moved in his new family.

MK played volleyball on the freshman team and is trying out again this year. I tag along to tryouts and discover a lot of my old junior high softball team is there. Apparently most of them played as freshman. Kim, Anne, Annette, even Beth. They are all there and it feels like old home week. I make the junior varsity team. They all make varsity but still treat me like an equal. We work out and practice together, so it's only for games against other schools that I am separated.

Our coach's name is Mary but we all call her Miss Hines. She's totally boss and I like her, but I'm also afraid of her. Because I'm only JV, I do my darndest to overachieve and stand out, and after a few weeks I get promoted to the varsity team.

MK is five-foot-ten and a spiker on the team. That means the setter sets the ball at the net for her to spike and kill. I am only five-six, but I can jump. I don't want to be a setter because, frankly, I don't like setting and would probably mess it up. I can bump the ball from the back row, and I move around and hustle well, but setting the ball with your fingers is not for me.

Being only a sophomore and it being my first year on the team, I don't play much. MK plays a lot. We have one girl, Mary Beth, who is the star and Miss Hines's favorite. She's tall, pretty, and can spike the ball hard and straight down. Juanita and Terry are the main setters, with Anne, Kim, and Annette rotating in. I have the annoying habit of either mistiming my jump or jumping too far under the ball to be a very effective spiker, so I mostly rotate in for back-row work, but I'm happy just to be there.

Practices are long and hard. Miss Hines takes her volleyball team very seriously and so do we. The very first day of practice, she works us hard. Squat thrusts. We do a lot of squat thrusts. I feel I breeze through. Hey, I go to ballet class, I'm in shape. The next day I can barely walk.

I have never been so sore in my life. I stagger around school straight-legged in an effort not to have to bend my knees and engage my quadriceps. You can identify the volleyball team that day as the staggering zombies roaming the halls, late to every class and moaning in real pain if we are forced to go down stairs. You can hear us in the bathroom as our legs fail and we fall the last six inches to the toilet seat. It's not pretty but we are bonded by our pain and misery. Proud of our wounds and the dedication required to get them. Miss Hines laughs at us and gives no quarter.

We are given laps to run around the gym for missing during serving practice. My serve is pretty good, so I don't have to do many laps. One of coach's favorite back-row drills is to stand on a table on the other side of the net and hit balls down to us to dig like the opposing team had just hit a good spike and we hadn't effectively blocked the ball at the net. She hits hard. Looks this way, then hits that way. Whack! Straight into your chest! Whack!

Head height and you duck if you're lucky. "Protect your ugly," is her favorite catcall.

We are good (I use the word "we" broadly here) and have made it to the state championship. It's a heady affair with special practices, notes sent from the coach to us in class, and articles in the school paper. We travel as a team by van to Marcos De Niza High School in Tempe. It's a single-elimination, win-or-go-home, tournament. There are eight teams representing the best from various regions of the state. It's nerve-wracking, but the stars play their hearts out and we progress game by game to the finals. Mary Beth is on, and Juanita captains us along with encouragement and scolds where required. I play for a rotation or two but never in the front row. I "protect my ugly" but that's about all.

We win the game and the championship! I almost throw up with excitement, then realize I haven't eaten all day. Mother has driven all the way to Tempe to watch the tournament and I am proud but also terrified she will do something weird to draw attention, but I have my team. The van ride home is joyous with lots of singing and chants of "S-P-R-I-T!" Our chant was meant to be S-P-I-R-I-T, but that didn't work with the cadence of the cheer. It was our chant, our team, and we won, so say what you will, it was perfect!

Having had experience at the Molina's restaurant busing tables, Mother's new idea is to send me to El Taco, the fast-food restaurant on the corner, for my summer job. It's walking distance so she won't have to drive me, and that suits us both just fine. I am supposed to be fifteen and some months to be legal to work, but Mom says to just lie. I do and they don't check, so I'm in. I regularly burn the beans and eat my weight in tacos. I probably cost them more in food and damage than I ever earn in work.

Grateful to be out of the house and earning money again, I love going to work and seeing my new pals. Apparently the owners regularly sit across the street with binoculars to spy on us to be sure we are working and not stealing from them. This is a story, and a good one, from Sue my coworker. Why don't they just come in and see what we're up to? Grown-ups are weird.

Everything about my job is great until the day a boy I know from junior high drives up to the window where I'm working and I am suddenly mortified. I go from happy camper to ashamed and embarrassed. I can see he is embarrassed for me too. He's ordering from El Taco in his own car. I'm slinging tacos at a fast-food joint and I have to give my check to my mom when I get home. He was a boy who wasn't cool enough in junior high for me to like, and now I'm the bullet he dodged.

Having regular access to food is a blessing and a curse. You can't smell El Taco all day and then really want to eat the stuff. I'm still skinny but have developed the required dancer mentality that I am fat and must not eat. My morning routine is to stand in first position, heels together, toes out and see if my inner thighs touch. Disaster looms if they do and I can only eat a very small amount that day. A whole summer of this is enough so I'm relieved that school starts soon.

# twenty-three

ONCE JUNIOR YEAR STARTS I FIRMLY DECIDE I WANT TO BE A DANCER, and being the heyday of George Balanchine, who set the standard at New York City Ballet under his dictatorship, all girls are required to be very young and excessively skinny with the bones in their chest showing. I eat no breakfast (the carob and wheat germ shake is awful and regularly poured out), Jell-O for lunch, and the occasional candy bar when desperate. I play volleyball for half the year, go to ballet class every night, and in the fall and spring rehearse after class with the Civic Ballet. Nutcracker season starts in November, and we are in full swing.

It's my third year in the corps de ballet and I am to be a snowflake in the first act and a flower in the second. I love being in the corps. It's all teamwork and precision. The whole point is the uniformity, all the dancers moving as one. It's beautiful when you see sixteen or twenty-four or thirty-two girls (depending on the size of the company) in complete unison. Every head, hand, shoulder, foot in exactly the same place, at exactly the same time, and I find it intoxicating to be part of it. You give up your individuality and are subjected to the whole because the combination of you all is far greater than any individual. Yes, there are stars and solos, but I really love the corps.

Then there is always that one girl, the one who thinks she's a star trying to punch above her weight, who wants to stand out by overdoing an arm or jumping the beat, and all she does is ruin the corps. This year, that girl is Kirsten. I routinely glare at her from the back row (I'd have to be behind her to see the infraction) and pray she's going to get a "talking to" from the director, but for the most part I am in heaven. "The Waltz of the Snowflakes" is fun because we flit about being snowflakes and then there's the big finale where they shake the snow bag and it starts to snow on stage. Stage snow is made of little pieces of paper in a long bag the length of the stage. On cue, the stagehand pulls the rope and shakes the bag back and forth to make it "snow." The snow is swept up after every performance and returned to the bag.

As in regular outdoor snow and ice, stage snow can be precarious. We are in pointe shoes, those little pink shoes with the ends made of cardboard and glue, made to be hard enough to stand on your toes, but not so hard that you can't bend your foot, or that you sound like a Heffalump running across the stage. This can make for some unsure footing in itself, but add a bunch of paper strewn all over the floor and things happen. Plus, we never rehearse with the snow until we get to the theater. We know about it, but when it finally happens in the performance, it's like driving around a racetrack when it begins to rain. First, your vision is obscured by the falling snow, then it begins to stick to your sweaty skin and get in your eyes and mouth. With experience you learn not to look up or open your mouth, but it's one of those sadistic things about ballet that nobody tells you about. In a world where "break a leg" translates to "good luck," I don't think they forgot.

Then there's the slip factor. Now it's paper, not ice, but dancing on pointe is precarious enough and we are just a civic ballet company. Girls slip and slide, little drifts form that get kicked around. It really is like a car race. Everyone waiting to see if there will be a crash.

By the end of the run of performances, the snow has been swept and returned to the bag enough times that it begins to accumulate little extras. Dirt, dust bunnies, rosin from the stage floor, bobby pins, the earring that Beth lost at the Saturday matinee, a loose piece of satin from a shoe that wasn't correctly darned—all of it rains down with the snow. We hear the hard metal objects as they hit the stage, especially the earring. It's a game of soccer with the earring as we try to kick it either upstage and out of the way (never varying from the choreography, mind you) or into the orchestra pit (sorry orchestra, but we're up here fighting for our little snowflake lives).

Somebody always slips. Maybe not a big slip, maybe you don't even notice from the audience, but we do and the tension mounts. Then it happens. Little miss "I Want to be a star and will do anything I can to stand out" hits the earring and down she goes. Not just down, but on her butt in a vaudeville-worthy clown fall. It couldn't have happened to a nicer girl.

Mother tells me that Daddy is in the hospital and we are going to visit. There's no asking me if I want to go. It's not worth a fight, though, and I'm curious. He's been out of the house for ten months. I don't count them; I just enjoy the relative calm of no one pointing guns at me and not having to call the police.

The VA Hospital is way over on the other side of town, and Melanie and I snuggle in the front seat while Mother does her version of driving. Once there we don't go inside but over to a shady area in front of the building, where I see my father sitting in his typical uniform of boxers and T-shirt, with the addition of the fancy Christmas robe and slippers. His legs are crossed and he's smoking and man does he look mad! We just got there, so I don't think the mad is about us, but maybe he hates us? This was true the last time I saw him.

Mother goes over and they speak for quite a while. Melanie and I sit on a bench far enough away that we can't hear what is said, but I can see clearly. There is no warmth emanating from this man. No love, just rage. I glance over a few times, but honestly I don't even want to look at him or feel his energy. I'm never called over to speak or say hello. Nothing is explained to me as to why we are there. I just sit like backup, Mother's personal Secret Service agent guarding against disaster. Not close enough to invade their privacy but close enough to respond in an emergency.

Before I know it we're back home. Still nothing explained. Is he there for another back surgery? Are they speaking regularly? Is he coming home soon? What the fuck is going on? Nothing. Just silence and bad driving.

This is the kind of thing that fucks me up. My brain wants information. I don't walk down roads with no idea where I'm going. I have a destination and a reason for going there. I either know the way or I'm with someone who does or has a map. I know enough to know that this is a game my mother plays. The game is called withholding, and she is a champion. Information is power. If I knew what was going on I might do something, or think something, or say something, or have an opinion. These options are off the table. Removed before they can even be considered. I retreat into Melanie. She plays with my hair. We chatter. It's comforting for us both. If I can feel their angst, surely she can too. Lord knows what her mind does with it. She's only three years old.

# twenty-four

CHARLOTTE IS GEARING UP FOR COLLEGE AND LOOKING AT SCHOOLS. ONE of the leading contenders is the University of the South in Sewanee, Tennessee. If you're in the know, you just call it Sewanee. Our daddy went to school there, which is surprising, as it's all stone buildings with ivy-covered walls and very snotty, but he was an only child, spoiled beyond belief by his mother, probably to make up for his alcoholic father. It's so elite you've never heard of it. I guess regular kids like my sister go there, but it's also favored by the ultra-wealthy Southern gentry. The people who go there are so rich that they wear shirts with frayed collars and drive old BMWs just to show how much they don't care about money. You have to have a lot of it to not care so much.

Charlotte flies there to look at the school and comes home with tales of being in love with the guy assigned to show her around. There are lots of late-night phone calls and she is all atwitter. He's the new love of her life and she has to go there.

She fills out masses of forms and applications. Submits grade transcripts and applies for student aid. Mother helps her through this process and only at the very end begins to waffle. Now the terror campaign begins. "Maybe you should just go to the U of A here in town and transfer to Sewanee next year," she says.

Charlotte musters all the game she's got. No emotion. No fighting or breaking down. Don't react. I'd be having a fit, exploding, over the back fence, but she's got advanced moves. Perfect behavior. Not a move out of place that can be faulted. Mother baits, she weaves. Mother threatens, she leaves the room without a word. It's very crafty stuff. I'd never manage it.

The acceptance letter comes and Charlotte can't contain her glee. Mother leads with "lack of funds" and that there will "have to be financial aid." Charlotte counters with financial aid acceptance and loan forms. I think she's making progress, but there is always the old faithful "because I said so" lurking in Mother's back pocket.

Eventually, her wardrobe is assembled (involving a lot of sewing) and her bags are packed. Into a trunk go sheets, pillows, and blankets, and then she's out the door and onto an airplane. When faced with her actual departure I'm surprised at my feeling. I never thought she'd make it. I didn't think Mother would let her go, and I have to face the loss. Charlotte never was my best friend or gave me much notice beyond the prince and princess days, but at least she was there. The constant in my life since birth. Mother and Daddy had proven to be fleeting, variable, but Charlotte was reliable. Now she's gone and my world tilts. The axis resets and rotation starts again. I have Melanie. We are best pals.

I sort of have a boyfriend now. His name is Marshall and we go on dates to the movies and concerts when I am allowed. He called to ask me out five times before I could go. He had to call and ask MK if it was really true that I was on restriction every time he called and she confirmed that yes, indeed, I have spent most of my life being grounded. I'm still allowed to play volleyball and go to ballet when I'm grounded, but not to the park, to a party, or on a date. In other words, I'm grounded against fun.

Our first date is right after the first of the year and we go to an Alice Cooper concert. Marshall picks me up and Mother flirts outrageously with him as he stands nervously in the front entry hall. I have spent the last two hours trying to get dressed but I know what I'm going to wear. Influenced completely by Mother, I have on a store-bought long-sleeve blue-checked shirt with white collar and cuffs, blue polyester pants that I made, and wedge cork sandals, an outfit she would have worn. My hair is loose down my back. I'm just coming into my own in the looks department: big eyes, long eyelashes, and dark, bushy eyebrows that I have to cut to keep from taking over my face. From the look on Marshall's face he is either very happy to see me or relieved to be rescued from my mother. He walks me out to the car and opens my car door. Conversation on the way is a bit sparse as I don't know how to be me yet. It's my first concert and I take in the scene as we enter: an enormous venue with seating on three sides, everyone, including Marshall, dressed in jeans and T-shirts, not like me, dressed like my mother.

Once seated, Marshall pulls out a pan of brownies he made at home, transported in a small brown bag, and a small bottle of alcohol to spike his Coke. Oh, thank God, food, because I've been at class and rehearsal all day and haven't eaten a bite, so I'm starved. Marshall offers and I greedily scarf down a few brownies and wash them down with his Coke. The concert starts and we sit through the heavy metal assault of Alice Cooper. I don't realize until the lights come up that I'm stoned and tipsy. I ate at least half the pan of brownies, which Marshall then explains to me contained a "four finger lid" of pot. I have sat stupefied in my seat for the past hour and a half.

I have never been high before, and this is quite the indoctrination. Marshall steers us toward the exit and his car. I don't know where I am or what I'm doing. I'm feeling quite out of control and advise Marshall on every stop sign, traffic light, and other car on the road all the way home. He's finally had enough and raises his voice to me. "I know! The light is still half a mile away!" Well, I just wanted to be sure he saw them.

He walks me to the door and we are both relieved that I am home. He kisses me sweetly, though it's clear he can't wait to get back into his car. I navigate the back door with my keys to find Mother sitting at the dining room table reading the newspaper, waiting up for me. "How was the concert?" she asks. I have no idea. I sat like a zombie stoned out of my mind while Alice Cooper screamed and railed "School's Out." Had I not been stoned, I probably would have spent the evening in the girl's bathroom to escape the musical onslaught.

"It was great," I reply, then immediately say I'm exhausted and going to bed to escape any further inquiry.

# twenty-five

"DADDY IS MOVING HOME." THAT'S ALL MOTHER SAYS. "DADDY IS moving back tomorrow." Then she says something about him only taking aspirin for his pain. I know that Daddy's pain meds cost a lot ("as much as the mortgage," she once said), and I know he has a drawer full of pills, but I don't understand that he's a drug addict and that's why he was at the VA and looked like a wild animal when we went to visit.

Daddy has lived in constant pain for a decade, and in the '60s, they hand out pain pills like candy. He's eaten them like candy. Now they've taken away all his drugs and given him aspirin. I also don't know that Daddy's father was an alcoholic. Neither of my parents drink, with the exception of a glass of wine on holidays, but his addictive genetics have caught up with him. But I don't know this. I only know that the asshole who is pretentious and pious when not coming to blows with my mother is moving home.

I see his car in the driveway when I get home from rehearsal, but thankfully it's ten o'clock. They're in their room, and I don't have to interact. It's back to "dears" and "darlings" in the morning, and I get out of the house as soon as possible.

Nobody talks to me. I've seen this performance before and know it doesn't last. Going to the VA notwithstanding, I've seen the eight miraculous back surgeries to fix Daddy's pain and those didn't work either. I've seen my mother go into the nuthouse twice and come out worse than before, so I'm just waiting for the crash.

Daddy has a new job with Big Brothers of America, and everyone (except me) is all excited. I'm getting ready to launch so I just want him to be back to take care of Mother and Melanie so I can leave next year. I don't care what his new job is. Besides, I will never get over the guy on the stool with the rifle, so I'm not up for this show they're putting on. And I know it's just a show.

He gets to wear his old preacher outfit, the black suit with the rabat and clerical collar, to his new job. I guess the higher-ups at Big Brothers like the idea of a preacher working there. The outfit always engendered a sense of reverence and respect from people, and that's exactly what it's designed for.

My job as paramour to my mother is officially ended (unless there's something heavy to be lifted), and they are back to the Reverend and Mrs. Parke Smith deal. He may not have his own church, but they can't take his priest status away. I am home as little as possible, with acceptable school activities and ballet, but still I can't stay off the radar. I seem to be a bonding force for them. Something they can agree on, and they agree I am bad.

Christmas has come and gone. Nutcracker is over, Daddy's back in the house, and we settle into the drudgery of winter. Winter in Arizona isn't much more than struggling to figure out how to get dressed because it's darned cold in the morning then in the eighties midday and you're sweating in your sweater.

Granny and Pompy are coming to visit. This is big news. Charlotte and I both went to Houston to visit them after we moved to Tucson. We'd alternated summers since our early teens, but they've never come to visit us in Arizona before. There will be a reprieve for me with witnesses in the house.

Mother's big concession with Charlotte going off to college and Daddy moving home is that I will move into Charlotte's old room and Melanie gets my old room to herself. Mother has been gifted Great Grandmother's guest room furniture (Granny didn't want it) with two beautiful four-poster twin beds with matching lowboy and highboy dressers. They are beautiful but take up the entire room. Granny and Pompy will stay in this room with the good furniture and Melanie will bunk with me while they're here.

Granny and Pompy never really liked my father. With his working-class Galveston roots, they were always against the marriage. The only saving grace was that Daddy was going to be a priest in the Episcopal Church. We went to Houston the first Christmas Daddy was out of the house, and apparently Pompy offered to support us all for a year if Mother divorced my father. That was his solution. No big deal, right? To support a mother who's never really worked and her three kids. My grandparents are what nice Episcopalians would call "well-to-do." You don't say rich as that would be tacky, so it's not really a stretch for them to give my mother enough money for a year, but it's always been clear that they all hate each other. She resents the hell out of them for whatever it is she never got from them, and they, in turn, disapprove of her.

With Granny and Pompy in the house, I hang out with them as much as possible. I show off and gripe about my parents, and Granny can't help but show her hand (which is most unusual as she is a magnolia of great skill) and agree with me about my father. He's useless, weak, never was much of a prospect, so here we are. "I told you so."

Daddy is having a new issue. Some sort of pain in his throat and esophagus, so Mother takes him to multiple doctors while Granny and Pompy are visiting. This produces a lot of knowing criticism from my grandmother. "Hypochondriac, weak, always something," and I play right along, making fun of him behind his back. His new pain produces a lot of different opinions from various doctors. Esophageal hernia, indigestion, and finally that it is psychosomatic and he should go to the nuthouse.

Somehow, during all these goings-on, I manage to get on restriction again. It's another living room couch family meeting, this time for the benefit of my grandparents so they can see what magnificent, progressive parents I have. The performance is so nauseating to me that when I pass my father in the hall the next morning, I turn my face to the wall so as not to look at him. You're the guy with the rifle, right? You're the guy who was gonna drive through the front door. You're the guy who doesn't take care of me or my sisters or my mother, but now you're back and I'm supposed to be all respectful? Not on your fucking life, buster.

As soon as I get home from school that day, the phone rings and it's my grandmother. They have moved on to the Inn on the Desert, a fancy Tucson hotel befitting of my grandparents. Eisenhower stayed there, so I guess it's good enough for them. Granny says I am to go immediately to Saint Joseph's Hospital and meet my mother. My father is in the hospital. I got my license this year, so I am to drive my father's car. Something big is up. I can feel it.

When I get to the hospital, my mother is sitting, looking very small in a large waiting area just outside my father's room. I join her at a round table. "Your father's had a heart attack," she says to her folded hands on the table. I can see people running in and out of Daddy's room. As the door opens and closes, I see the end of his bed and his feet bouncing up and down. I know this must be the result of a defibrillator machine they're using to try to restart his heart. I've seen it on TV. This is bad. Then I feel him. Nothing physical, but a sense of him, his spirit floating just below the tile ceiling. He says, "I'm sorry, but I can't stay." His heart is broken and I broke it. What a rotten kid to turn your face away from your father when he's trying so hard. He couldn't take it anymore so he's leaving, and it's your fault.

Mother and I are ushered into a little room off the waiting area. It feels like an unused storage room and has pegboard walls and nowhere to sit. We are standing alone until Dr. Nash, the neurosurgeon, and Dr. Carol, the cardiologist, come in. They both attended Daddy's old church, the good job, so I know these men. They'd been referred to in conversations regarding my father's multiple back surgeries over the years.

Doctor Carol says, "Binny, I'm sorry. He's gone."

# twenty-six

MY FATHER IS DEAD. I DRIVE MY MOTHER HOME FROM THE HOSPITAL. It's February 5th and pouring rain. Melanie is at home with my grandparents babysitting. Mother goes straight to my sister, kneels down, and says, "Your daddy died." Melanie takes her little fist and delivers a roundhouse right straight to my mother's face. Pretty much my reaction, too, Mel. Just when it looked like they were going to get it together. Just when it looked like we had a shot at happy, he split.

I don't really blame him. I watched my father suffer with his pain all my life. It was constant. Even with the pills he hurt all the time. From my selfish kid point of view it ruined my life because he wasn't doing his life, but I felt for the guy. He couldn't do fun stuff, my mother resented him not being there for her, and then he got hooked on drugs. I just didn't have any sympathy when the pain got directed my way or when my father's pain consumed him and became him. I hated his pain and eventually him.

I used to rub his back and comb his hair to try to make him feel better. I'd happily do his jobs and try to take up the slack, but I just wasn't big enough to fix it. I didn't have enough to give. I was just a kid.

I can't sleep that night, so I stand at the open window of my room and smoke. My mother opens the door and in an oh-so-un-typical response says, "I can't believe you're doing that when it killed your father," then closes the door and goes back to her room.

I can't cry. I can't feel anything. Or, I feel everything all at once. Loss, regret, anger, humiliation, shame—there isn't a negative emotion I don't have and they're all fighting to get out, so they trample each other in the doorway and die. The loss of my father is tragic, liberating, and terrifying. Who will take care of my mother? I'm consumed with regret at how I turned away from him the last moment I saw him alive. Anger that now I really have been left to take care of what's left of my family. Humiliation and shame at having laughed and made fun of him with Granny when it turns out the whole time he was having a heart attack. What a rotten kid. They were right. I am a stinking, rotten kid.

My mother is a zombie. Melanie just cries. Charlotte is home from Sewanee. People bring food. All kinds of food. Our refrigerator is stuffed like at the holidays. My ballet teacher brings a standing rib roast. I'm shocked she knows where we live, and it's strange to see her standing at our back door in her street clothes. I'd never seen a standing rib roast before in my life. The Molinas bring tamales. Everyone brings something and I'm supposed to be present for awkward conversations and say thank you when people say they're so sorry. I don't know how to say anything else. I could never say to anyone, "We had a very conflicted relationship because of his pain, his violence, then abandoning us and his focus with my mother on making me the family scapegoat, but yeah, I'm sorry he's dead too."

My grandparents go back to Houston, not staying for the funeral. I think Granny was humiliated by her behavior and how things played out and couldn't face it. It's just as well.

Mother, Charlotte, Melanie, and I go to the undertaker to arrange for the funeral. We sit at a desk with a smarmy man who is trying very hard to sell my mother a mahogany coffin for $5,000.

My father is dead and we don't have any money and she's already told him this, but he keeps saying things like, "It's a way to show your beloved how much they meant to you."

I want to launch across the desk and tear his throat out. He's humiliating my mother, but she's standing her ground. "What's the cheapest thing you have?" she keeps asking. Finally, he capitulates under her resistance and reveals that Daddy can be buried in a plywood box generally used for shipping bodies. Since his coffin will be draped with the heavily embroidered cloth befitting a priest of the church and then cremated, my mother settles on this solution.

Daddy's funeral is held in the little church on the wrong side of town where he had been celebrating mass. I am grateful that the little church is full. Mother is in fine form in her dark purple dress and black mantilla. Charlotte wears Daddy's favorite dress with the red apples on it and I wear the darkest thing I can find. It's a navy blue and white print dress that is old and doesn't fit me anymore. It's way too short and I spend most of the service pulling it down in the back every time we kneel down and stand up. You do a lot of that during the Service for the Dead.

As the service progresses, my heart finally opens and I begin to weep uncontrollably. Church is what I most associate with love for my father. Being proud of him, proud that he's my dad. Doing fun stuff at the church, being a preacher's kid, stealing unconsecrated communion wafers in the sacristy, trying on his fancy priest getup, singing really loud because who's gonna say anything to the preacher's kid, ya know.

A single thought plagues me: *I killed my father*. I turned away from him the last moment I saw him. How selfish. How mean. How lacking in any compassion. It feels like a setup. How was I to know this was my last moment with my father? How was I to know this was the last straw? That I would break his heart and now he has to go. There is no love. I'm a rotten kid. As William

Shakespeare once wrote: "How sharper than a serpent's tooth it is to have a thankless child."

Having your father die when you're a junior in high school is a thing. Everybody knows and some kids say they're sorry, but for the most part you just get a wide berth. Creative writing is my first period class, and with my penchant for oversleeping and being late, I don't get to school on time. Combine this with the deep, dark thoughts in my head, and I struggle with writing anything creatively. My teacher is young and pretty and my best current candidate for a crush. I think she knows and doesn't like it. All my writing comes back with major red pencil marks for structure, punctuation, and spelling. *Give a girl a break, will ya? My dad just died, I'm slightly dyslexic, and I thought this was creative writing.*

I ditch first period a lot. Mother threw me the keys to my father's car my first day back at school. That was a shocker but goes right along with the Daddy replacement theory. Being able to drive myself gives me a lot of freedom. I can smoke in the car because my father smoked in the car, so who's gonna know. Given that I often don't wake up, or I'm at least late, it's not surprising that I ditch first period. A lot of times I just drive around and smoke.

I eventually get called to the Dean's office, and like a repeat of fifth grade, there sits my mother. The Dean says something about me missing first period a lot and hands my mother a manila folder full of all my forged excuses. "Please excuse Emily for missing first period. She had a doctor's appointment." I'm not sure what my other excuses were, but I didn't care, so I'd say anything.

Mother barely moves. She takes the folder from the Dean and without looking at the notes, closes it and says, "Yes, those are all my notes and my signature." If I wasn't so depressed I'd have been more relieved, but I don't care. Kick me out, expel me, put me on restriction, I don't care. *My father's dead and I don't know what the fuck is going on!*

# twenty-seven

BALLET HAS BECOME MY REFUGE FROM THE WORLD AND REALITY. IT takes all my concentration and energy to do the moves and remember the combinations. There is no room in my brain or body for dead fathers or crazy mothers. I spend my time either trying to master some impossible physical task or becoming a nymph or a fairy.

Last year I was a swan in Swan Lake, a snowflake, a flower in "The Waltz of the Flowers"—your basic corps de ballet stuff, nothing fancy. This year the girl who was supposed to dance the Sugar Plum Fairy is sick and I am tapped for the role. This is even more amazing, as the director of the company, Mr. France, is the head of a rival studio and there were other girls from his studio who should have been chosen. I am shocked and not especially pleased. It's too much pressure. It's the starring role. The grand pas de deux. I've never even had a solo part and now I'm leapfrogging to the top. At rehearsal I feel like everyone is judging me and thinking, *That should be Kim.* But Kim is in the hospital with anorexia. She even outdoes me at being skinny. I am too fat: 105 pounds at five-foot-six and not good enough.

Ballet is a vicious sport. Nothing is ever good enough. It can always be higher, longer, faster, more. Jump higher, hold the pose longer, beat faster, turn more. This applies to every move you make, but I think that's part of why I love it. My ballet teacher once said that Natalie or Charlotte or Barbara could be professional dancers, but not me. My knees don't hyperextend and in the ballet world we see this as "bowlegged," a cause for instant rejection. What a horrible thing to say to a kid. Tell me I can't and I'll show you I can. My rebellious nature kicks into high gear. I am immediately determined to be a dancer. Final decision.

Mr. France (Richard) is my sugar plum cavalier. An old Broadway dancer, he and his wife moved to Tucson and set up shop after they retired from "The Great White Way." They're pretty glamorous with the Broadway résumé.

First, I have to learn the pas de deux and the variation. Ballet has a traditional setup for the main event. The pas de deux, the male variation, the female variation, then the coda. This all seems only fair to me as the pas de deux is much harder for the girl, so she should get a chance to rest before her solo.

I work way too hard *all the time,* driven by my sense of not being good enough. Every step, every move, gets maximum effort. There is no nuance to my dancing, just blunt force and will. My friend Natalie with the red hair from my studio did the same part last year and was magnificent. I watched from the wings as she breezed through the grand pas de deux. Everything seemed effortless, like she was laughing at us with how easy it was.

Richard rehearses the pas de deux while smoking a cigarette, which gives me the feeling he doesn't take it seriously and I don't need to worry. The cigarette moves from hand to hand as we progress and to his mouth when he needs both hands. It's like he's too cool to care, or maybe this is how they do it on Broadway. Truth is he doesn't have that much to do other than hold my hand and a few lifts. Mostly he stands around with one leg stretched out, toe pointed, as I do something I find insanely hard. Held extensions, rotating held extensions, etc. He's just there to showcase the ballerina, and this you can do with a lit cigarette in your mouth.

Karen invites me to a party the night before the performance, and though it's a very poor choice, I'm thrilled to go. Mostly because Karen invited me to something. She offers me tea when I get there, which I find odd because Karen isn't the hostess type. She returns with a little white pill, not the glass of iced tea I was expecting, but I am trying too hard to be too cool, so I take it. Karen tells me later that it's THC, which I know is a drug. I wake up the next morning having passed out. It's dawn by the time I drive home. This is not how you should spend the night before the big game.

After a shower and a nap at home, I'm getting myself ready for the show. I walk through the living room to find Melanie doing all the steps to "The March of the Wooden Soldiers." Mother has *The Nutcracker* playing on the stereo and Melanie is dancing her heart out. It amazes me to watch her correctly perform every step and turn. She often comes with me to rehearsals, so I guess it isn't surprising, but I hadn't realized how much she absorbed. I wonder if she can do "The Waltz of the Flowers" or maybe even the pas de deux?

Backstage at the theater downtown I have my own dressing room because I have the star part. This sounds glamorous, but really it's isolating and I long for the camaraderie of the corps de ballet. All my friends getting dressed together, putting on and borrowing each other's makeup, teaching each other how to put on false eyelashes and affix tiaras. All important life skills for a budding ballerina. Instead, I am alone in my head with my nerves. A delivery of flowers shows up at my dressing room door with a note from my ballet teacher. "Knock 'em dead kid. I know you can!" I am floored and thrilled. Maria acknowledges my existence and is rooting for me! Maybe I can do this!

Getting the main ballerina part means I get the best costume. Two-tone pink tutu, maroon V-shaped panel down the front, paler pink on the rest of the bodice, and the tutu itself, all scattered with sequins so I sparkle. My hair is pulled back tight in a classic ballerina bun with a sparkling tiara. Pink tights, pointe shoes. I love the outfit. I look like a fairy princess but feel like I'm entering my worst nightmare. Richard is in a maroon cavalier jacket that matches the panel on my bodice, white tights, and ballet flats.

The pas de deux is hard. It's all slow, held leg extensions and balances which should look effortless as I am a fairy. Project the illusion of floating and grace. I'd rather be jumping. How did I end up here? My insecurities dog my every step. Two tracks that constantly run in my brain: *I am the star. I'm not good enough.*

There is a photograph my mother took of Richard and me from the dress rehearsal because she is of course there. It's magnificent. We look fabulous. We're in a "fish dive." We execute everything perfectly. He's in a small lunge on his right leg, his left arm extended to the side. I bourrée up to him from behind, take his arm, do a pique en dedans turn. He reaches around my waist with his left arm as I am turning and throws me forward over his left knee as he steps back. It's probably the fanciest move of the whole performance, but I find it really easy. It looks fabulous. Then he brings me up into a front attitude and I step around him upstage to do it again. It's a real crowd-pleaser. Without the photograph I wonder if I would believe I had really done all this. Been the enchanted fairy.

After the pas de deux, I exit stage right, do a quick vomit in the fire bucket, and pull myself together for my variation. The sugar plum fairy variation is all little fast footwork on pointe and I hate it. I was so bad at it in rehearsals that they sent me back to Maria for her to try to fix it, to no avail. A lot of my problem is that nobody breaks down the steps or counts to the music. They just throw it out there and I'm supposed to understand the intricacies and timing by osmosis. I don't. To me, music is the why and wherefore of dancing. It's a feeling of being transported when you are in sync with and dancing to the music. You and the music become one. Well, I'm not one with the music. My apologies to Tchaikovsky. I mash through it, finding spots to come together at significant points, but mostly it feels like a mechanical exercise. No joy.

After my variation we get through the coda, then the curtain calls and it's all over. This next part I am good at. Standing around backstage in my tutu and tiara getting flowers and being congratulated for a great performance. Granny and Pompy are here. Friends from school are here. Mother runs around basking in my glory and taking pictures. Everyone says I was great. Even Natalie, who is home for Christmas, says I was good. Dancers are very kind to each other. They know how hard it can be. How hard it is to be onstage, risk it all, and come out the other end. There are no "do-overs" in dancing, no stopping, no "Excuse me that got messed up and we're going to start over." Nope, never done. Deal with it. Movies and TV can be perfect, but live performance, that's where the thrills are.

# twenty-eight

I HAVE DONE EXTRA CLASSES IN SCHOOL EVERY YEAR AND SUMMER school for three years, so I graduate midyear of my senior year. I am already too old to dance professionally, as I should have reached my dancer prime at age fifteen, ready to take on a job with a ballet company. I am seventeen, though the bones in my chest do show. Thank you again, Mr. Balanchine.

I should be taking off for New York City to seek my fame and fortune, but I have no ability to do that. Even if I had the resolve I am still trapped in "what a rotten person I am" in my brain, and fighting this off flatlines me. I'm always driving. Always moving forward. There's always a goal, but I have nothing. I am numb. Plus, there is the matter of my mother being insane and Melanie. I cannot leave them. Mother has to be watched. Melanie has to be protected and taken care of.

Mother steps in with another one of her unfulfilled fantasies. I am to go to Texas Christian University because it's college and I should get a "good education." They have a dance department and, most importantly, my mother has fond memories of her life as a child in Fort Worth where TCU is located. Perfect!

We drive to Texas over Christmas break after *The Nutcracker.* Charlotte is home from Sewanee, so we all take off on a road trip to see the school. Arizona then New Mexico and into Texas. We have previously established the fact that Texas is big and it takes forever to get across the state. We stop for the night somewhere just outside Midland/Odessa. Mother is planning for an early start and a short jaunt into Fort Worth in the morning. I see nothing. The campus is huge and overwhelming and not where I want to be, but Mother seems pleased. It is decided that this is where I will go come the spring term in January.

We are on our return trip from Fort Worth to Tucson. It's December and a storm has rolled in, making driving conditions treacherous. You don't really associate Texas with harsh winter weather, but this storm is freezing cold, rain and snow, ice on the road, and everyone going twenty-five miles per hour. About ninety miles down the highway, as the storm gets worse and worse, we start trying to get off the road and into some hotel for the night. All the truckers and anyone else with any sense are already off the road and hunkered down. We try every exit, but all the hotels are full. No room at the inn.

We press on and are pretty much alone on the road. Just over a rise, we hit some black ice and the Skylark starts to fishtail. Mother does her best; for all her bad driving habits, she actually does have some knowledge and skill, but no amount of steering into the skid is helping. The car is just sliding down the hill by itself. She eventually loses control as we hit the flat part of the highway and do a double donut down the middle of the road. Thank God there wasn't anyone else around or we'd have taken them out like pinballs. We spin around twice, straight down the middle of the highway, and end up on the shoulder. Once we stop, I grab the flashlight from the glove compartment, jump out of the car, and run around checking all the tires. I don't know why or what I am checking for—I just have to do something. Once everyone's blood pressure comes down, Mother gets some traction with the gravel on the shoulder and we slide off at the very next exit. Eastland, Texas.

Eastland is what my mother would describe as "a wide place in the road." We pull up to a large white building that proudly says, "Hotel, No Vacancy." We all get out and walk into the lobby. Mother pleads her case. "We need a place to stay for the night. I have my three girls with me and we almost just wrecked out there alone on the highway."

"Sorry, all full up," says the lady behind the desk.

"Well then, we will sleep here in the chairs in the lobby because we'll freeze to death in the car and we have nowhere else to go."

At this point the lady behind the desk takes a beat, realizes there is a state of emergency and we are probably the last car off the highway. "Well, the top floor of the hotel is unused. It's a mess and no one has stayed up there for years, but I can give you some clean sheets and towels and you can probably make do up there. There is no heat but there is hot water."

"Thank you," is all my mother says.

We are escorted up by the janitor. He has to unlock the fourth floor on the elevator and then other doors between the elevator and where we are to stay. It's a large room, very dark, with all kinds of furniture and mattresses strewn about the floor and covered in years' worth of dust. But we are out of the storm, it's ours, and we are grateful.

Charlotte turns on the bathtub and it takes about as long for the brown water to clear the pipes as it does for the hot water to come. We arrange mattresses in a little family clump on the floor just outside the bathroom and begin to settle in. Warmed by a bath and snuggled into our beds, we aren't really bothered by the family of mice, having had reservations, being somewhat perturbed at our presence. Live and let live.

Dawn breaks the next morning. We have slept like the grateful not to be dead on the highway. Starving, we get another bath, put our yesterday clothes back on, and head down the elevator.

Luggage was not a consideration last night, though I do remember somehow brushing my teeth. Mother again speaks to the lady behind the desk. She complains that the lady charged us for the room, but hey, how much chance do they have to make any money in Eastland, Texas?

The nice lady tells us there is a diner next door. If Eastland is a wide place in the road, then this "diner" is a forgotten hallway. Long and narrow with a small counter and two booths. We sit at one of the booths and order everything on the menu: eggs, bacon, toast, pancakes, and grits. I eat like a hog. We all do. I swear it's the best food I've ever eaten. The storm has passed. We get in the car and get back on the road.

# twenty-nine

TWO WEEKS LATER, MOTHER, MELANIE, AND I ARE BACK ON THE ROAD to Texas to deliver me to TCU. Charlotte is back in Sewanee. I am sure she has gotten the better end of the college deal, but I am not as invested.

Texas Christian University. The name embodies nothing I want. I don't want to be in Texas. I am not a Christian, being on the outs with God as I see no guiding or omnipotent hand influencing my life. I don't want to be at university. I want to be dancing somewhere, somehow.

My roommate in my dorm is Cynthia. She is rich, chubby, and has lots of clothes but seems reasonably friendly in a kind of fake Southern way where people say, "Bless your heart," which means you're a loser and they don't want anything to do with you.

Mother takes me shopping for things for my room. I get a big roll of red carpet for the door room floor. Cynthia contributes a light blue and navy bedspread for my bed. The result is visually jarring, as is almost everything else I encounter.

Mom and Melanie take off back to Tucson. Kissing them goodbye I am suddenly faced with the fact that I am abandoning Melanie to Mother. I can see it on her face. She's only five years old and has a steely determination beyond her years, but I can see a sadness around the edges of her eyes and mouth. There is nothing to do but go on with the plan. Being the baby of the family has been good for her so far, but the reality of the years ahead of her, alone with Mother, might be sinking in.

I am left to navigate this new world, register for classes, pay my tuition, and learn the lay of the land. The campus is big, and by coming in midyear I have no organized orientation, no idea where my classes are, or even where the cafeteria is. Thankfully there are some nice girls who take me under their wing. Janet and Leslie live in the room next door, and Lynn lives in another room but always seems to be in their room. They take me to the cafeteria, get me a map of the campus, and invite me to their room to play cards and listen to Marvin Gaye, Diana Ross, and Stevie Wonder records. I begin to settle in.

The dance department is in the arts building all the way across campus. I am nervous and excited to take my first class. I'm majoring in dance, so I have one ballet class every day and modern dance class twice a week. It doesn't seem like much of a schedule. I also have to take American history, psychology, and religion. What a lineup. We'll study the same American history I have studied since first grade, but now we'll just do it in a semester. Psychology is in a huge lecture hall being taught by a young man not much older than me, and the class focuses on child development. I don't care at what age children develop depth perception and won't crawl across a piece of glass over a steep drop.

Religion. Oh, joy! Let's talk about religion. I can tell you a few things about religion! Still, it becomes my favorite class. Even more than ballet. Religion is a class of about forty students, taught by a man who explains and breaks down the religions of the world, their origins, and how they influence people and cultures. Hindus, Buddhists, Muslims, Sikhs, Confucianism, Catholicism, Protestants, and Lutherans. He makes the world make sense. I learn to think in his class. I begin to see and understand the world around me based on the environment, culture, and religion.

Ballet class is another matter. My teacher is Wayne, a tall man with skinny legs, balding on top, with the rest of his hair down to his shoulders, which he sometimes wears in a ponytail. I show up for class on my first day and stand at the barre. He doesn't even say hello or acknowledge my existence. He seems to revel in making up combinations at the barre for no other purpose than to make them hard and complicated. Just like third grade, I have shown up midyear. Everyone else has been here for a semester, they all know each other, have no use for me, and I hate it. I had dreams of dancing, but this is a slog.

Everything is confusing; he teaches Cecchetti style, which is Italian and all wrong. I was taught Royal Ballet style, which is all logic and precision. The Italians are not at all logical or precise. He doesn't like me. I don't like him.

I have never taken a modern dance class in my life, but I'm game. I get to dance barefoot and they don't do pointe work. Our teacher is the skinniest woman I have ever seen. She wears black leotards and tights and has long dark hair that she wears down, then throws up in a messy bun sometimes. We are instructed to stand parallel. Wrong. We are to "contract," or pull our stomachs in and make them hollow. Wrong. Flex our feet. Wrong. I don't get it. It's not pretty. It feels strange and I get the sense that my poor attitude and ability translate broadly to the teacher and my fellow students.

I go to my classes but it's nothing I enjoy or know how to work at. Except for my religion class. Without that I don't think I'd be able to stay. I can't find any value in either my dance or psychology or American history classes. It feels like marking time. Ticking boxes to get a degree, and the life I have in mind, that of a professional dancer, doesn't need a degree. At no audition you ever go to are they going to say, "Oh great. You have a BA in dance." Nope.

Cynthia and I settle into a routine of avoiding each other as much as possible. I don't know anything about her other than she's from Tyler, Texas, and her parents have lots of money. I get back to my room to regularly find new outfits for Cynthia laid out on her bed, apparently bought by her mom. There are always three of them, the exact same outfit in three different sizes. Cynthia's closet is organized the same way. By size. All the same outfits in three different sizes. The one she is, the one she aspires to, and the fallback position.

I work evenings at the dorm snack bar, which is a table in a closet with a selection of Hostess cupcakes, snowballs, pies, Snickers and Milky Way bars, and Dr Pepper and Mr. Pib soft drinks. I have a cash box to make change and keep the money and a book to read to pass the time. It's humiliating to work at the snack bar. Mostly because the girls who come to the snack bar don't talk to me, just grab their sugar and go. I can tell they're embarrassed for me and want to be sure I don't try to talk to them or be their friend.

One day two girls I don't know stop by the room and inquire if I want to be in their sorority. They scare me. They have a lot of hair, show a lot of teeth, and have long fingernails. And they wear pearls. I take one look at them and I'm sure I don't want whatever they're selling, which must be a little shocking to them. When I tell Cynthia this story, she chastises me for turning down such an opportunity. I think Cynthia wants desperately to be in a sorority.

Janet and Lynn next door are dating football players, and when the guys are over I have to leave. Their football boyfriends are Black and enormous. They fill the room when they come in. They're having sex in their room, which I find shocking. I've never had sex, much less wanted to. I don't get the big thrill. I had a boyfriend in high school and we made out, but it wasn't anything I really wanted to do. I know it's what you're supposed to do, but I have never felt the tingle in my toes or butterflies in my tummy for a boy. I'm afraid I'm broken or crazy. Just like my parents. I know there is something wrong with me, and I do my best to hide it.

One morning before classes, Janet is running down the hall naked from the shower. "I have crabs! I have crabs!" She was in the bathroom looking in the mirror after her shower and saw something moving in her eyebrow. Upon closer examination she saw it was a tiny crab. I know you get crabs from sex, but how you get them in your eyebrows is a mystery to me. I have led a rather sheltered life, but based on this additional information, I'm pretty sure sex is not for me.

At spring break, I fly back to Tucson feeling very grown-up. I've been away at school, living my own life, and I've learned a few things about the world. Some of it interesting, but a lot of it I could do without. I don't like the school and I don't like most of the people. The undercurrent of racism is pervasive, and I hate my dance classes. I tell my mother I will go back and finish the semester, but after that, I'm out of there. I'm either going to New York or to London. New York City is the dance capital of the world, and my former ballet teacher taught from the syllabus of the Royal Academy of Dancing in London. Somehow I convince Mother of my plan. I go back, finish my classes, get my credits, pack my stuff, wish a fond farewell to Cynthia, and get the hell out. I ship my trunk home. The carpet, which is now filthy, is sacrificed to Cynthia and her slovenly ways.

# thirty

HOME FOR THE SUMMER, I HANG OUT WITH MK AGAIN. SHE SHOULD be in university this coming fall but doesn't have the money to go. She's supporting herself working at Coco's Famous Hamburgers and doing okay. I have to get a summer job, so I go apply and get hired. Another girl from our high school, Jane Rhea, also works there with MK and they share a little apartment. We form a pack.

Our graduation ceremony will be held at the football stadium tonight and MK is going to be celebrated as class valedictorian. We are going together but I will sit in the stands and not participate as I technically graduated midyear. MK will give a speech and receive an award, and everyone will get their diplomas and switch their tassels. I'll sit in the stands with the relatives, all cheering wildly as their children officially graduate and the parents express their wild relief at having survived the teenage years and being on the verge of fledging their flock.

I bid my mother goodbye and tell her, "I won't be too late." Mother responds with, "Be home by ten o'clock." *Are you out of your mind?* It's my high school graduation night! True, I am not participating in the ceremony, but I'm going to salvage as much of it as I can by going to a party and staying out late to celebrate. Like everybody else. Like MK, whose mother won't say a word if she comes home at dawn because she knows she's a good kid. I explode in the driveway. I have learned a few things from my mother, and the use of rage is apparently a transferable skill. I attempt to offer logic: "I've been living on my own at school, it's my graduation for Christ's sake, and I'm working tomorrow so I can't stay out too late." She stands firm in her ridiculous decision with a kind of glee, knowing she's forcing me into a corner I can't retreat from. "Be home by ten."

The explosion erupts before I even know what's happening. "You motherfucking whore!" I scream from the driveway for the neighborhood to hear. MK is witness to the dynamic between us and is cowed back into her El Camino. I get in the car and we drive off in silence. I am ashamed by my words. MK is embarrassed for me and would probably like to drop me by the side of the road until she can shake the debris of the scene from her mind.

After the ceremony, we go to a party, but it's all very anticlimactic as I am not a part of what everyone else went through. You can't go backward to fit in. I've been away, and my old friends seem small and unremarkable.

MK drives me home and I arrive at exactly the prescribed hour: ten o'clock. The back door is bolted shut and the house completely dark. I knock, but there is no response. I stand humiliated in the glare of the El Camino's headlights as MK waits to see me safely inside. I suppose I can sleep in the yard, but I have to work tomorrow. My uniform and my things are inside. I wait like the pathetic child I am, knocking and calling to my mother to be let in. This is the punishment for my words and her demonstrating power over me. I tell MK to go, but she won't. I walk back and forth from the car to the back door.

After about ten minutes, Mother appears at the door. An apparition in darkness. I can't really see her, just the vague image of her body at the door in her nightgown. She says nothing, just stands there. I begin to apologize and explain how frustrated I was. How unfair she was being. How I have been living on my own with no one to micromanage my time. After what she decides has been a sufficient amount of time and contrition, I hear the sound of the bolt being slid back and she walks away. She doesn't unlock the door; I do that with my key. She has retreated to her room and closed the door.

Being just hired at Coco's and low man on the totem pole, I have to open the restaurant every morning. I have to be at work at 5:30 a.m., which means getting up before dawn and navigating the dark, quiet house. I saw *The Exorcist* last year and it scared the shit out of me, so every morning I imagine the devil lurking in the dark waiting to possess my soul on the way down the hall to the bathroom. It's a lot to go through to go work at a glorified diner.

At Coco's, we are taught some modification of French service. Serve from the right, clear from the left, glasses on the right, never pour a coffee cup on the table, always pick it up to pour. It's all an expansion of what I was taught by my grandmother and mother in terms of how to set and lay a table properly. I'm feeling very accomplished and making money.

My bosses are Alan and Neil. Alan is handsome, short, slightly balding, and the big boss. Neil has red hair and isn't as handsome, though he's taller than Alan. They're both nice guys. They flirt and fool around with all the waitresses and we have a good time even though we work hard.

When I get to work, I go about setting up—making coffee, filling creamers and jelly jars, and distributing them around the restaurant. I open the doors at 6:00 a.m. sharp and the regulars file in with their newspapers and go to their regular spots. I know who wants coffee, cream, orange or tomato juice, and most of their orders. They are all men. Men in short-sleeve button-down shirts and khaki pants. The middle management guys. They sit in the stations of the girls they have crushes on. They aren't aggressive or bothersome. Just nice, respectful, and good tippers.

One morning, just as I'm starting the jellies, I look over at the big glass window to the office and see Neil sitting at his desk. He already has a pale complexion, but this morning he seems even paler than usual. Almost translucent. When I focus and really take in the scene, I see a man standing next to him in the shadows holding a big silver gun to his head. I turn away, set down the jelly jar I'm holding, put my hands flat on the table in front of me, and pee my pants. I am wearing the regulation peasant blouse, dirndl skirt, pantyhose, and white nurse shoes. The pee runs down my legs, inside my pantyhose, and into my shoes. It can't be more than a few seconds when I hear the back door slam and Neil emerges from his office. For some reason I run to the front door, the pee squishing in my shoes. The door is still locked, but I open it and step out, looking for the robber. Neil shows up behind me, has locked the back door, pulls me back inside, and relocks the front door. He calls the police, who respond quickly. They know we have good coffee and breakfast. They talk to Neil for some time, then come to question me. I tell them my story, including peeing my pantyhose. Problem is, I am not a good witness. I don't remember ever seeing the man. I just saw the big silver gun and turned away. Neil sends me home to change but says I have to come back to work the lunch shift. *Really?* I risk life and limb in a robbery and I have to come back to work lunch? I want to point out that the pee in my shoes hasn't quite dried yet, but I don't bother. I just get on with it.

Charlotte is home from Sewanee for the summer and brings a sense of normalcy to our lives. A missing piece of the puzzle of our fractured family. But she is different and more separate too. She's been living her own life and is now influenced by the people she hangs out with at school. She talks about the SAEs, a boys' fraternity at school. She's in love with some new boy. She plays Motown music, wears topsiders, and has even developed a drawl. Very

Southern. More sophisticated and worldly. She tells me that Mother is regularly sneaking out the back gate at night. How does she know these things? I've been here for months and have never noticed this. Maybe it's because I sneak out every night to smoke in the little hidden side yard beside the house. Mother and I are both sneaking around. It would be funny if we ran into each other in the backyard, she on her way out the back gate, me on my way to the side yard.

Tonight Charlotte follows Mother out the back gate (her stealth game is impressive), through the apartment building behind our house, and to the park, where she sees a turquoise and white Chevy parked next to the swings. There's a man waiting there and Mother joins him. This is enough for Charlotte, and she returns to recount her story to me. Her suspicions are confirmed. Mother is sneaking around with Mr. Molina from across the street! What the actual fuck. Isn't that like shitting where you eat? Sneaking around with your neighbor. Betraying his wife, the woman who took you in and sheltered you in a moment of crisis.

The revelation of my mother's lack of moral character is just one more hit. I'm mortified for her. I have to carry her guilt and shame now as obviously she isn't carrying it herself. It's a load I don't need, but someone has to do it and I step up. Charlotte shares the load in her own way. She adds judgment and straight-up anger. She's a completely grown-up person now and quite comfortable with her opinions. I'm still so attached to my mother that I can't quite separate how I feel from how she feels and acts. I understand. She is so alone and desperate she'd rather drive herself off a cliff than face conflicting feelings of loss and loneliness, freedom and relief, of losing my father. It's all too much. So over the cliff she goes, straight into the arms of Mr. Molina.

Charlotte uses her newfound knowledge as ammunition and a veiled threat to my mother of what she knows. "You better stay in line with me, or I'll blow up the neighborhood." It's not said directly, just alluded to. "Where were you last night?" she inquires. "I went looking for you, but you weren't in your room." All with knowing smirks and implied threats of exposure. It's fun to watch. Mother bobs and weaves. "I went for a walk." I bet you did!

All of this adds to the tension in the house and has the unfortunate result of my being even more of a target. Since Charlotte is obviously a stronger and more powerful opponent, the focus stays firmly on me. The low-hanging fruit. Easy pickings. The dependent child.

But hold on. I'm not so dependent, and Charlotte's revelations have given me more of an expanded view of my mother. I need to pay more attention and look harder. Seek my own ammunition. Plus, I have a job, a car, and some minor resources. Maybe I can stand a bit more firmly on my own. But there's still Melanie to consider. Maybe coming back from school was also motivated by wanting to be home with Mel, but I don't think it was a driving force. How do I manage Melanie and break away at the same time? I can't. That's clear. I will have to wait and see.

MK has a suggestion, and I think it's a good one. "Why don't you come live with Jane Rhea and me?" I can have the couch rent-free. I'm sure she can't imagine having to go through another scene like graduation night with me. She has her own problems and I need to contain mine. She's the oldest of five girls in her family and also has a traumatized mother, so she's used to caretaking too. I feel loved.

My move to Jane and MK's is unremarkable in that I have few possessions to transport and Mother is aloof and distant, seeming to have no opinion either way if I stay or go. Melanie and I have a little talk, and I tell her I will come over all the time and we will still go places and hang out, but I can tell she is unconvinced and frightened. She is already learning to shut down. I know she's angry with me for leaving her. I know she depends on me for safety and relief from our mother, but I can't figure out how to keep her with me. It's beyond my ability.

I stow my stuff at MK's and am set up on the couch. There is one bedroom and MK's room seems like it was probably a dining room, but girls like us have no use for dining rooms.

Not a week goes by and Mother shows up at the apartment. She wants to talk to me, so we sit outside on the steps. She offers a deal if I will come home, which I really want to do because life in the living room is uncomfortable and the couch is a horror to sleep on.

Her offer is shocking. She wants to move to London, where I can go to ballet school and she will provide housing and pay for everything. She knows I want to be a dancer, but I know her, and I feel like there must be a catch. Why would she do this for me? I say I'll think about it. There's really nothing to think about, is there? Stay in Tucson, sleep on the couch, work at Coco's, or go to London? She knows she has dangled an irresistible carrot.

How we are going to live is a large question. Since my father died, I am not aware of how my mother supports herself. My father's mother, Grandma Smith, died just three months before my father and rumor has it stashed all her money in US Treasury bonds. There is a vague explanation of Mother inheriting Grandma's money. This will provide an adequate income if we are careful.

I wait two days before moving home. I would have just packed up and gone immediately, but I feel like I should make her wait. Make her think I was really considering the alternative. She needs me. Melanie is only four years old and of some solace to her, sometimes, but I provide a real partnership. An almost adult she can depend on, yet over whom she has complete control.

The plan is to fly to London with a stop in Montreal. I pack every stitch of clothing I own, having no real idea of what I need in London other than what I've seen in the movies. Cold and fog.

The flight to Montreal is long and I eat my way through it. Every meal and snack is met with enthusiasm. There is not much else to do other than read, sleep, eat, and go to the bathroom. Melanie seems nervous and scared, so we spend a lot of time talking about how much fun we're going to have and all the adventures we will go on. She is not convinced.

We have a long layover in Montreal, so Mother decides we will go into town and explore. Mostly I think she just wants to get out of the airport and eat something other than airplane food and peanuts. She is more discriminating in her tastes.

We go to lunch in a large restaurant overlooking the city. It's a beautiful room with an enormous number of tables with white tablecloths. The waiter comes over to greet us. "Bonjour." Oh, I know this. "Bonjour," I say, with my best kindergarten-speech French accent. He is not impressed, though I think he should be. The twist to his mouth and general demeanor display to us his complete disdain. Montreal is French Canadian. We are Americans and don't speak French. The rest of the meal is a test of wills. He pretends he doesn't understand a word we say. Mother struggles along with a smattering of French and a translation book. The tension has destroyed my appetite. Melanie is ready to get back on a plane and fly home. I'm happy to go with her at this point.

We make it to Heathrow Airport, go through immigration, and find a taxi into London proper. It's all very dark and gray but I am feeling grown-up, having stood in the immigration line by myself with my own passport.

We get dropped in front of our hotel in Kensington. It doesn't look like a hotel to me and once inside are greeted very stiffly by a woman who shows us to a small room with three beds and not much else. The bathroom is in the hall, the light switches are strange, and there is wallpaper everywhere, but I haven't slept in over twenty-four hours and I'm happy for what we get. Though it's nine o'clock in the morning, we all go to bed.

This is my first experience of jet lag. You are transported across time and space and deposited in a foreign land where they appear to speak the same language but not quite. What is a "loo"? Why say "biscuit" when I am obviously being offered a cookie? And why do you drive on the wrong side of the road?

When I wake up, it's pitch black outside. I've slept twelve hours and am now wide awake with nowhere to go and nothing to do. I am completely regretting my decision to move to London. I lie awake in my bed for hours in this cold, strange land and wonder what lies ahead: *Where will we live, where will I go to school, how will I get there, what will I wear, what will I eat, will I make friends, what will they think of me?*

In the morning, we discover a tray on the floor outside our door containing a pot of tea, milk and sugar, three bowls of cornflakes, a little rack of cold toast cut on the diagonal, and three eggs in egg cups. I guess we get breakfast with the room. We eat, navigate the hall bathroom successfully in our nighties, forget to bring clothes, then have to run back to the room in very small, scratchy towels without getting caught half naked in the hall.

There is a relief to being finally out on the streets, having recovered a bit with some sleep, food, and now fresh air. We walk to the "tube," as we are going to the "estate management" office to look for some more permanent lodging. Why don't they just call it a real estate office? What is the insistence on trying to make everything confusing?

At the entrance to the tube, I attempt to buy a newspaper. *The London Standard.* I see the headline "Nixon Resigns." Well, that's some good news! The man selling papers is a jovial fellow until I show up and ask for a paper. He says something in what I will come to understand is a very broad Cockney accent, and I don't understand a word. I'm just asking how much and apparently he is telling me, but for the life of me I don't understand. Finally, he yells at me and I just take all the change out of my pocket and offer it to him in my open hand. He helps himself and offers some departing shot, which gratefully I also don't understand.

It is apparent that we are strangers in a strange land. It's August 1974 and, with Nixon the crook and Vietnam, Americans are not popular. I am not used to feeling strange and not knowing the right thing to do. The lady at the pastry shop yelled at me when we bought pastries and it became apparent that I was going to eat mine right then. "You're not going to eat that on the street, are you?" That's simply not done here. All kinds of things are not done here, but there are other rituals that I find weird that must be done. For instance, in the shops you are to hand your purchase to the clerk and say "thank you" even though the transaction is not complete and they haven't done anything for you yet. Then the clerk thanks you and tells you the price of your purchase. You hand over your money and say "thank you" again. The clerk says "thank you" and puts your purchase in a bag and hands it back with yet another "thank you." You take your bag and say "thank you." If any of these steps is skipped or any thank-yous missed, you are considered a rude foreigner and get the very British cold shoulder. I have not been here twenty-four hours, but I already understand that I am uncivilized, rude, don't dress correctly, and am generally unwanted.

I have never been on a subway, much less a "tube" before. There are tunnels and signs to follow. You ride down wooden escalators and then another escalator. It occurs to me just how far underground we are and if anything untoward should happen, how little hope of survival or rescue there would be.

On the platform the walls of the tunnel are all tile with the name of the station in tile as well. It's charming and quaint but also gives me a feeling of disorientation because everything requires maximum thought. Nothing is routine. Everything is so new.

The train finally pulls into the station sounding like an old wooden rollercoaster. It's red and has wooden slat floors and upholstered seats. There are smoking and nonsmoking cars. Everyone has a newspaper. When the doors open the car disgorges its load of passengers while the waiting load attempts to get on. I get separated from Mother and Melanie in the process but find my way to them in the crush. Everyone says "sorry" at every push and shove. I don't think they really are; they're just British. Another custom learned. Say "sorry" and don't mean it.

At our destination we follow the exit signs to a clump of people waiting at what seems like a dead end. Suddenly a large door opens to reveal an enormous freight elevator that everyone piles into. The man running the elevator asks for our tickets and we're slowly lifted to street level. Well that was an experience. The mysteries of the tube.

# thirty-one

LIFE HAS BEEN TOO MUCH. MY FATHER DIES, IT'S MY FAULT, I GO TO TCU, I come back from TCU, I move out, I move back, we move to London. I am not all there and don't feel solid ground underneath me. Too much change. Not enough time to gather my wits. Everything here is strange and I don't like it. We have moved hotels as finding somewhere permanent to live has proved expensive and difficult. Mother propels me along through life, sometimes providing opportunities I wouldn't have otherwise, but in the process important steps for me are missed. Like me thinking things out and making decisions. Or me planning what or where I want to go. Or me actually being ready to move this way or that. I have a vague idea that I should at least try to audition for the Royal Ballet School. I have no idea how you do this or if they take Americans. I know this is the best place to study but it's far beyond my ability. I'm being catapulted through my life and sometimes I flounder midair.

I'm not at all focused on why I came here but on day-to-day survival. Where do we live? How much does it cost? How do you get anywhere? What to eat, where to eat? I could use some normalcy and routine, but instead Mother throws a new wrinkle into the pot. She has found a ballet school for me. No one asked me what I wanted. Okay, I'm only seventeen, but it seems like I should be consulted. I am too worn down to argue.

I am to go to the Stella Mann School on Finchley Road. I imagine a small manor house, or possibly a little castle where this mystical school in Finchley will be. We will take class in the old ballroom and get dressed in the dining room that has now been converted into the dressing room. We will eat lunch on the lawn. We have to be transported from the tube station in horse-drawn carriages as the property is too remote to walk. The reality is we walk up the rather unremarkable Finchley Road to a large white building with no obvious address or door. In London during the war, many buildings were bombed out and burned to the ground. Once rebuilt, instead of giving them the same number as the previous building, they gave them a new number. You go along a street looking for number 26. 20, 21, 22, 195, 196. What happened to 23 and everything in between? Why is everything here so hard?

Having finally figured out the address and found the door, we enter the three-story building and follow a staircase to the first floor (which would be the second floor in the United States but here the "first floor above the ground"). No castle or manor house. No ballrooms but a rabbit warren of little rooms.

Stella Mann's office sits directly at the top of the staircase, her desk facing the door so she can monitor every coming and going. Nothing and no one gets past her. Stella herself is a short, chubby older woman in a too-tight dress and black pumps. She speaks with a foreign accent but welcomes my mother into her office. I am signed up, money paid, and told to arrive tomorrow morning sharply at 8:30 a.m. for my first class at 9. I will take ballet, pointe, and character dance classes. I will study for the Royal Academy exams, and my teachers are both also teaching at the Academy and the Royal Ballet School. Sounds good but the building itself gives me pause. The studios are small and I have trouble imagining flying through the air in them. There isn't enough room.

On arrival the next morning, having fought my way against

the wind up Finchley Road, I am directed up the next flight of stairs to the dressing room. The room is full of my new classmates giggling and chattering as they go through the gymnastics of dressing in a crowded room. The required uniform is a black leotard and pink tights. There is Jane, obviously a senior girl, who has long dark hair and equally long legs; Janet, another American girl who was here last year and has a decidedly British accent (or so I think); Stephanie, previously of the Royal Ballet School, who is a pretty blond with long legs and a bit of an attitude; and Gillian, who is too short to be a dancer, a bit overweight, but with a remarkable spark and friendly demeanor.

We all shuffle down to class and pile our ballet bags in the corner, taking up valuable real estate in the very small studio. Miss Nuckey, our teacher, comes prancing through the door like a woman in charge. She wears a gray skirt, white blouse, and pink leather shoes with a small heel obviously designed for teaching ballet class. She's pretty with her hair twisted up on the back of her head and the longest neck I have ever seen, which gives the overall impression of a periscope on the top of her body. She strides along the barre surveying her new recruits, greeting the familiar faces and giving us new soldiers the once over. "Ah, you're an American?" she says with that now-too-familiar tone of disappointment.

We are too crowded at the barre, so everything is designed so as not to kick each other once we get past pliés, tendus, and ronds de jambe. She goes fast and I am sometimes unsure of what she says, but thankfully ballet is the language of familiar French words and demonstration. We move to the center, breaking into two groups for combinations and grande allegro. Nothing very grande about the allegro. In one tombé pas de bourrée, you are already across the floor, which is very disappointing to me because this is where I excel and the part I love most. I can fly, I really can fly, but there will be no flying here. We will sing like caged birds. All British precision and control. No American freedom and abandon.

After class we all retreat to the common room on the very top floor. Everyone smokes and I am happy to hear that the favorite subject is food. We are obsessed with food. What we ate yesterday, what we are eating for dinner (tea), and what snacks we are currently eating. Then boys—who has a boyfriend, who wants a boyfriend, who has broken up with a boyfriend. Then our teachers—what is known about them (which is really nothing) and what gossip we are currently spreading.

We have another teacher in the afternoon, Miss Taylor. She doesn't appear quite as prim as Miss Nuckey and is a bit nicer but also more distant. She teaches us national dance class, where we study and perform the traditional dance of different countries. She explains that the dances are informed by the climate and terrain of the relative country. The Italian tarantella is very exuberant and free, like the Italians. It takes up a lot of space and is performed with as much wild abandon as the British can muster. The Highland fling, designed with little steps on your toes, is for Scotland, a cold country with little flat open ground. Very interesting. Combined with my religion class from TCU, I am learning more about the world than I ever learned in history or geography class in high school.

Eventually, I come to realize that the British are not "cold" or so much reserved—they are just cold. It's only fall but already my short Arizona winter jacket is far from sufficient. People rush from warm place to warm place. No one stops to talk on the street. Here you have to move along with your head down and your collar turned up. It's not that people are unfriendly; they just want to get where they're going and to get warm. Once you get the Brits inside, they open up as they warm up.

Gillian becomes my best friend. Where the other girls are a

bit standoffish because I am foreign, she is drawn to me because I am different. I do funny stuff and say funny things. We are invited to a party and she calls me at home to find out what I'm going to wear. I say, "Pants, I'm going to wear pants." There is a very long pause on the other end of the line, and then she breaks out laughing for what seems a long time. "Oh, you mean *trousers*, you're going to wear trousers." Pants in Britain are what we call underpants. She was very worried that I was going to go to the party in my underpants. I am a source of endless amusement.

Gillian has gotten a job at the English National Opera House on Saint Martin's Lane. She is an usher, showing people to their seats and selling programs. She knows my situation at home by now—that I live with my mother and little sister and have almost no money of my own except what my mother will give me. I hadn't even considered the idea of getting a job, but now that Gillian has one and says it's good, I want to work there too.

I tag along to the opera house with her and she takes me downstairs into the bowels of the theater to meet Heinz, her boss. Heinz Kiefer is a tall, handsome man with longish hair and a German accent. He looks me up and down, tells me I have to be on time, and hires me on the spot. I will need a long black skirt, black top, and black shoes. We have to be at work at six o'clock, the house opens at seven, and we have to be at our respective posts at seven thirty. I will make twenty pence (about 45 cents) an hour, but the money is the least of it. Gillian and I finish class around five, take the underground to Trafalgar Square, and walk up Saint Martan's Lane to the opera house. At first I feel guilty, being a tagalong to Gillian, but it's clear right away that she likes having a pal and we become closer friends. The usher bond is strong.

Heinz gives me to Gillian to train. We work in the stalls, the ground floor seating area. Margaret, an older white-haired woman of about fifty, works in the dress circle, and Marge, a bitter, angry old woman of undetermined age who dyes her hair and wears red lipstick, an institution at the opera house, works the upper circle. Once the house opens, the people rush in to get their drinks and smoked salmon sandwiches at the bar and place their drink orders with the bartenders for the interval. The seating areas are not yet open, and Gillian and I are still downstairs in the commissary, finishing our tea and crackers with cheese and Branston pickle. We make our way upstairs through the gathering throng with an air of usherette importance. You paid, but we work here and are in charge of opening the doors!

We go downstairs to get our pile of programs, all counted out in stacks that must either be returned or money accounted for. "Twenty pence, please," I have learned to say with my best British accent, or I will have to tell my life story to every patron. "Oh, you're a belly dancer." Now, we all know it's ballet, but said with a British accent it often sounds like belly. They look at me as if I just said I worked as a prostitute.

Programs sold, people shown to their seats, programs or their cash equivalent returned downstairs, we either go back down to the commissary for more tea and crackers or hang out in the dressing room. It all depends on the show and the length of the act.

At the interval we sell ice cream. We stand at either side of the stall doors with big wire baskets full of ice cream, straps around our necks. Tiny little cups of chocolate or vanilla with little wooden spoons. "Twenty pence, please."

Then back downstairs to return our unsold wares to Peter, who is in charge of the program and ice cream distribution. Gillian has a crush on Peter and I'm sure they are soon to be an item.

The English National Opera has the main run of the house, but the English National Ballet is also a regular. This is even more exciting when Nureyev is dancing with them as a guest artist. He is the heartthrob of the ballet world but getting to be past his prime. Doesn't matter to me. He is a world-famous superstar of dance and I get to stand at the back of the stalls and watch him for free. He is magnificent. His dancing is not like in his prime when he was a wonder of the world, but it's still good. You can see the injury and pain in his left foot, but his mere presence and command of the stage and audience are riveting. You can't take your eyes off him.

They are doing *Sleeping Beauty* tonight and he is dancing with Eva Evdokimova, a Bulgarian beauty who is dancing Aurora to his cavalier. There is a place in the pas de deux where Nureyev holds her hand while she gets her balance, then she lets go to show her balance in arabesque on pointe. Sometimes, Nureyev gets tired of all the attention being on Evdokimova and gets a devilish look on his face before throwing her hand away before she's ready. What a jerk, but he's Nureyev and gets away with it. I hope Eva throws a pointe shoe at him backstage.

At tonight's performance, a man in a wheelchair is rolled into a box right behind where I stand selling programs. He is followed in by his wife, Dame Margot Fonteyn, formerly of the Royal Ballet, frequent past partner with Nureyev, and a world-famous superstar in her own right. I recognize her immediately. I had her posters plastered on my bedroom walls as a girl and also know that she married a man who became the Panamanian Ambassador and was then shot and paralyzed in an assassination attempt. I can feel a rustle in the crowd. Her presence has been noted, she is an icon of dance, and I determine to protect my idol. I don't speak to her. I never make eye contact. I just step sideways to stand right in front of the box and obscure the vision of anyone wanting to gawk. I assume my best ramrod-straight ballerina stance, daring anyone to approach or bother her. She is there to see her friend Nureyev, having a night out with her husband, and I decide she doesn't want to be bothered. It works. No one approaches; no autographs or photographs are requested. As the last bell chimes and the lights dim, I feel a light touch on my shoulder and a very quietly whispered, "Thank you."

Maybe that's not true. Maybe she never actually spoke to me, but that's what happened in my imagination.

# thirty-two

LIFE HAS BEGUN TO HAVE SOME ROUTINE AND FEEL NORMAL. I LEARN to take the blaring Americanism off how I talk and dress so there isn't constant attention on me, positive or negative. I've bought an army surplus topcoat. It's blue, wool, and warm and more fitting the current fashion than the fuzzy beige polyester jacket I showed up with. I have boots and bell-bottom pants. Everything is either navy, black, or gray. No one wears color. It screams American. The London fashion of the day is Biba, which I could never afford, but at least I can blend.

I get up early, ride the underground to Finchley Road and dance class, take class all day, then the train with Gillian to the opera house, work until about ten, then the train home.

We have graduated from hotel rooms to sublets. The first one on the Old Brompton Road is some lady's flat that still has all her stuff in it and isn't a place you can really call home. We regularly burn the toast in her confusing toaster, which prompts calls from the upstairs neighbors. They're probably afraid the crazy Americans are going to burn the place down.

A month later we move to a top-floor flat on Collingham Gardens, which requires climbing five flights of stairs. After a long day of dance classes and standing on my feet all night at work, these stairs are daunting. I stand at the bottom and stare them down, take them two at a time, and arrive breathless at the top. The apartment is straight out of another era with pitched roof, dormers, and leaded glass windows. Charming on a certain level but it's always cold.

After several months at Collingham Gardens, Mother announces she's bought a flat. I know she has money from my Grandma Smith, but I don't know how much. I guess enough to buy an unrenovated flat in London. It's lovely in a turn-of-the-century way with large rooms, picture molding on the walls, and French doors out of the living room onto a little balcony that overlooks Gledhow Gardens. It's on the Old Brompton Road but the address is Gledhow Gardens. Again, confusing. The houses in London are addressed by the gardens they surround, not the road they face.

Heat and hot water are the main issues as far as I'm concerned. This flat has little coal-burning fireplaces in almost every room, and Mom orders coal for them. We are heating our home with coal! Mother thinks this is charming, reminiscing about happy times as a child in Detroit where they used to mine coal. God help us, but now I can add a new life skill to my repertoire: starting and keeping a coal fire going.

The kitchen has a sink, some cabinets, and not much else. There is a box on the wall to the outside that acts as a refrigerator where we keep milk and butter. The hot water heater is a rectangular box on the wall above the sink. There is another one in the bathroom for the tub. The main problem with this system is you only get about three inches of hot water in the tub. It's an exercise in trying to submerge yourself as much as possible, employing strategic splashing, then getting out before you freeze. There is no coal fire in the bathroom.

I am beginning to understand how we can afford a first-floor flat with a balcony on Gledhow Gardens in London. On the surface the location and address are fancy, but the reality of life inside is a bit grim for anyone used to endless heat and hot water. My new bedroom used to be either the maid's room or a broom closet, as there's room for only a single bed and a dresser. The room has no coal fireplace, but the good news is the room heats up quickly from my body heat, and it does have a window onto the Old Brompton Road. From the street I hear taxis and a little traffic, but very early in the morning I hear the ironmonger driving his horse cart calling out, "Any old iron? Any old iron?" as he drives along, or the horse guards transferring horses from stables to, I assume, the palace. When it snows, it's beautiful, like being transported in time.

Mother has discovered the auction houses. Not Christie's or Sotheby's but the ones in the industrial part of town where you buy old furniture and you get whatever's in the lot. We have a mishmash of chairs, tables, wardrobes for clothes, and lumpy old beds.

Melanie is enrolled at the local school and is developing an even better English accent than me. I can't tell if she likes school or London for that matter because I am gone at school and work so much, and when I am home on the weekend, Mother has usually dragged her off to some museum or exhibition. Although I don't see her much, I'm not as concerned about her safety as I was in Tucson. Mother doesn't drive here and they take the tube and buses everywhere, so she's in far less danger. But the truth is I just give up. I blot her out of my mind. I'm up and out the door in the morning before she's awake and I come home late at night after she's in bed. Our lives no longer intersect. I'm ashamed to say it, but I'm relieved. She is my sister, not my child or my responsibility. Like a good, self-centered teenager, it's all about me.

We are becoming more distant, but tonight everyone is home and the three of us are having dinner together. Some sort of very British pie, brussels sprouts, and potatoes. The pie is fine and I can eat almost any vegetable or potato you put butter on. The butter in London is real and tastes like nothing I've ever eaten before. During dinner Mother says, "I met Roger Banister today." I can't place the name but know it's familiar. "He is the first man to run the four-minute mile," she continues. Okay, now I place him. Broke the record at the Olympics.

"Where did you meet Roger Banister?" I inquire.

"He's a doctor now and I went to see him today. He says I have MS. Please pass the brussels sprouts."

That's all she says: I have MS, pass the brussels sprouts. Multiple Sclerosis. All I know about MS is from what I've seen on a TV commercial that says it's "the crippler of young adults." What do I do? What do I say? She prattles on about her day until I finally interject, "How do you know?"

"Well, it's a difficult diagnosis because there is no test, just a multitude of symptoms. Remember when I went blind in one eye, and how I would complain of numbness, and how I would get so tired?"

I'm thinking, *And how you walk so funny, act so strange, get so depressed, fall down sometimes, lay down in the bank, seem desperate to control everything around you.* My brain is swirling but not with compassion. I'm angry and scared. How can she drop this bomb but not say more? Explain it to me. Talk about it! What does it mean, what should she do, what should I do, will she need a wheelchair, how long before it gets worse, will it get worse, has she had it since she went blind that time?

Dinner is over and I clear the table. She moves to the couch and turns on the TV. I can only imagine what she's going through. She has been diagnosed with some weird disease at the advanced age of almost fifty. I think MS is supposed to strike when you're younger, but maybe this happened because she never goes to the doctor. For anything. Doctors cost money. I only ever went to the doctor and got a physical so I could go to camp. My dad used up all the doctor money.

After her announcement, we settle into group denial. She is fine. She will be fine. There is nothing to worry about. She's been fine for all these years. She'll be fine for many more to come.

# thirty-three

OUR CLASS AT SCHOOL IS PREPARING FOR OUR ROYAL ACADEMY OF Dance (RAD) exams. There is a set barre, floor adagio, center combinations, and some allegro. I took my elementary exams with Maria in Tucson, so now I will take the intermediate. It's an unremarkable event, except you have to go to the RAD building to take the exam in a very large studio. I am nervous, don't think I did very well, and wonder at the whole idea of taking exams for ballet.

A week or so later I see Miss Nuckey at school rushing toward me in the hall. "You got 'highly commended' on your exam!" I almost can't comprehend what she's saying. *Me? Highly commended?* The order of scores goes: pass, commended, highly commended, and honors. She's waving around my exam paper like it's on fire. They give you notes and your score, but she doesn't let me see that and continues rushing down the hall. Well, I'll be damned. The American girl got a high score, the highest in her class, and put a feather in Miss Nuckey's hat.

At the opera house there are also big doin's afoot. The girl who works in the royal retiring room doesn't show up for her shift, and Heinz sends me. The royal retiring room is just what it sounds like: a room behind the royal box where the fancy people go to have their drinks and snacks during the interval so they don't have to mingle with the hoi polloi. I have never even been in the Royal Retiring Room, so I have no idea what to do or to expect. Heinz says it's an emergency and I'll be fine. There is already a bar set up so I should just bring an assortment of sandwiches and take my cues from them. Be polite and give them whatever they need or ask for. Tonight, it's the Chancellor of the Exchequer (the equivalent of the US Treasury Secretary). Not too fancy but fancy enough to get the royal box and privacy.

I rush to the box and await my fate. The bar is simple—bottles of gin, vodka, whisky, and brandy. The Brits don't do mixed drinks. No Pink Squirrels or Brandy Alexanders. They order gin and tonic, whisky and soda, vodka and orange. Even I, who have never tended bar, can handle that. The regular sandwich fare of the opera house is egg salad, cucumber, or smoked salmon made on small slices of white bread with the crusts cut off. I tidy the bar, labels facing forward to display the liquor bottles and types of mixers. I arrange the sandwiches on the center table, grouping by type. Cucumber in a circle, smoked salmon in the middle, and egg salad toward the back. I like egg salad but it seems the least fancy, so it gets short shrift.

Around seven thirty, they start to drift in. A young man comes in first, surveys the room, gives me the once-over, and leaves. A few minutes later a party of six come in, ditch their coats, and start to mill about. They order drinks and help themselves to sandwiches. The men are in suits and ties, the women in fancy gowns. I can tell who the chief honcho is as everyone wants to talk to him and his jokes and repartee all get big laughs. I hear others in the party addressed as sir and minister. I think I recognize the big man from the TV, but I'm still pretty new to British politics.

The first bell goes and I move about the room, retrieving paper plates and napkins and discarded drink glasses. The second bell goes and they start to file into the box. Whew! Round one survived. Tonight it's the opera *Aida*. I've been too nervous to pay attention.

At the interval it's pretty much a repeat of the same but they are a bit more subdued from the cocktails and food. I've tidied and replenished the sandwiches from the stalls. Bells, they go, I clean up, report back downstairs to Heinz.

"How did it go?" Heinz asks.

"Fine, I think. Everyone seemed happy. No one really paid me any attention or spoke to me other than to order a drink, and one guy took to serving himself."

"Good," Heinz says. "Go back for the finish and help them with their coats if they seem so inclined. Otherwise just stand by if they need anything."

Before the end of each act, a bell rings to tell staff to move into action. We get ice creams, sandwiches, drinks, and coffee ready for when the patrons come out. Ushers with ice cream trays loaded and ready, bartenders with drinks spread about the bar on little napkins with people's names on them. No one would ever pinch someone else's drink. This is Britain! Sandwich ladies stand behind their bars ready with snacks and coffee. The kiosk lady is at the ready with candy.

I make my way back to the retiring room and wait. I guess it was a good show as I can hear a lot of "bravos" and extended applause. But before the clapping is even finished my fancy folks are out of the box, headed for their coats, and out the door. As they leave, the young man who came in first to check things out appears. He walks over to me and hands me something without a word and is gone. It's a ten pound note! That's like twenty-five dollars. I make twenty pence an hour, so this is double my salary for a week. I'm liking the royal retiring room very much right now. Not hard at all, much more interesting than standing in the stalls selling programs and ice cream, and tips to boot!

There isn't always someone in the royal box, but when there is, I'm the regular girl. I guess there is something to be said for looking like a prissy ballerina. Couple this with the fact that I can make it up the stairs to the upper circle in about fifteen seconds to find more smoked salmon sandwiches when everyone else has sold out. My ballet legs and training on the stairs of the Collingham Gardens flat come quite in handy.

Tonight it's Beryl Gray, Director of the English National Ballet, and guests in the retiring room. As usual, I am in search of more smoked salmon sandwiches, preparing to mount my assault to the upper circle bar. As I round the corner on the stairs of the dress circle, grabbing the stair knob to propel me round, I see a small figure in a full-length black cape and hood, crouched on the divan. I pause midflight, pivot, close the distance between me and the dark figure in seconds and fall to my knees at her feet. I recognized the form before I ever saw the face. I ask softly, "Can I help you?" She lifts her head ever so slightly and replies, "I was late and they won't let me in."

It's Martha Graham. She has come to see "Nureyev and Friends," and they won't let her in! Some ignorant usher is enforcing house rules of not seating anyone after the lights have gone down on the Grande Dame of the modern dance world. I implore her to follow me, offer my hand, and help her to her feet. She is frail and tiny in what seems like full stage makeup. In her black hood and cape, she gives the impression of a fairytale character but not the good ones. Doing my best cavalier, I offer my arm, which she grasps tightly, and I escort her toward the boxes on the right side. "I will put you in a box. There are generally empty ones," I tell her.

I crack open the door of the nearest box, check that it's empty, and get her comfortably seated. Not an usher in sight. Once she's inside with the door closed, I continue my race up the stairs in search of smoked salmon sandwiches. I have done my bit to keep the world on its axis. I may never have my photograph published in *Dance Magazine*, but I like my private moment better. Tonight I was a hero to Martha Graham.

Gillian has started a thing with Peter as predicted. I don't know if I would call what they're doing "dating," as none of us has enough real money to go anywhere, but I know they are sleeping together, which I find shocking. What if she gets pregnant or gets crabs!? It all seems too risky to me; plus, I just don't get the appeal, but I bow to group pressure.

There's an usher, Malcolm, who likes me, so I agree to go out with him. Gillian has a boyfriend so I should get one too. Malcolm is an actor with an usher job just like I'm a dancer with an usher job. He's handsome, fit, and funny. Always trying too hard to be funny for my taste though. He's always doing some bit to attract attention and to try to entertain, but generally it has the opposite effect. We go on a date, but since nobody has any money, it's just the one required date where the boy takes the girl out to dinner. Now we are officially an item on the opera house gossip mill. I immediately regret my decision as now I have to flirt with him, sit with him in the commissary, and generally feign more interest than I have. He seems happy, but I don't have the emotional experience to foresee how in the long run this will lead to hurt feelings all around. His and mine. His for my lying, leading him on, mine for betraying myself, but I don't know any better. I am trying. Trying to do what seems like the right thing.

Nureyev is back with the English National Ballet and it's another night in the royal box. Bar set up, sandwiches procured, but tonight there is a long table with a white tablecloth and chairs in the center of the room. There are flowers on the sideboard and the table. Someone extra fancy must be coming, but no one tells me anything.

I'm at my post at the bar in the retiring room when an elegant woman comes in, surveys the room, and gives me a nod. Shortly thereafter a party of half a dozen or more mostly elegant ladies and a few rather effeminate men arrive. There is something rather familiar about a few of the faces, but I can't place them. In part, I'm too busy making sure drinks are poured and they have what they need. Then it hits me. Princess Margaret. It's Princess Margaret. The truth is I only figure this out when Nureyev comes in and yells, "Margaret!" and gives her a big smooch. He's not dancing tonight and has joined the fancy folks to watch the performance. It's exciting and nerve-wracking to see Margaret this close. I am in awe. She's royal family and almost queen, but Nureyev, my God, that man. He is dressed in snakeskin from head to toe. A Nehru jacket, short breeches like little boys used to wear, and boots, also snakeskin, that go just above the knees. His presence and physicality fill the room. He's flamboyant and gregarious. Margaret can't take her eyes off him, and neither can I. There is no worry tonight about doing anything wrong. I am invisible.

One of the ladies (turns out they are Margaret's ladies-in-waiting) comes over and tells me they all want smoked salmon sandwiches at the interval. They also want coffee, which was not previously requested. They go in to watch the performance, the bell rings, and I am off.

Coffee is logistically hard and will take time to brew, so I start with that. I brave the sandwich lady on the left side. I'm not generally friendly with her, but she's closest to the retiring room so this makes sense to me. I throw Margaret's name around and beg for help. "How can I get coffee for the retiring room, please?" I implore, looking like a helpless American. "Margaret's here?" She looks at me out of the corner of her eye and assures me she will deliver coffee in an urn fit for a princess. It's a bit territorial at the opera house. Ushers don't make sandwiches or do coffee. That's the purview of the sandwich ladies, but the smoked salmon sandwiches will prove more difficult. I start my search in the stalls, only two, then the commissary, nothing, then dress circle one, then upper circle four. Disaster! There's not nearly enough! I fly down the stairs, back to the stalls, where I am friendly with the sandwich lady on the right side. I ask her what to do, throw Princess Margaret's name around some more, and she volunteers to make more but it will take her a bit of time. Time? I don't have time! I rush back to the retiring room to see if the coffee is at least there. Finally sandwiches are ready and I rush back, skirt in hands just as the interval is starting, and rush up the steps to the retiring room.

I glide in as if nothing has happened and my heart rate is not over two hundred beats per minute. Everyone sits down at the table and one of the ladies in waiting asks, "Will you please serve now?" Serve? I've never served a sit-down in the retiring room before, but it's the "almost queen" and Nureyev.

Wine. They should have wine. I fetch a bottle of white from under the bar and show it to the lady-in-waiting for approval and she nods. Good, because it's all I've got. It's room temperature but I've been blindsided. I shove it into the ice bin under the bar as I place glasses for each diner. I fetch the bottle, which is at least wet, so it looks like it's been chilled, if not cold, wrap it in a napkin, and take it to my girl for tasting and approval. I'm not going to ask Margaret to taste the wine. No one seems aware of my heart rate or quandary and I'm relieved when she nods.

I look at my pathetic sandwiches on little blue and white paper plates wrapped in Saranwrap and think, *This just won't do.* There are small china plates on a shelf under the bar and I hatch a plan. Acting like "this is how we always do it," I retrieve the plates and find, thank God, that there are also linen napkins. I grab plates and napkins and return to the sideboard. With my back to the table, shielding my actions from sight, I remove the Saranwrap and slide each sandwich onto a proper plate. I walk around the table placing a napkin to everyone's left. No one pays me any attention; they just keep chattering, and Nureyev is pontificating about the first half of the ballet. I can carry four plates in one hand and resolve to use this technique to serve as I am not sure of the hierarchy of the group. Margaret is first, but then who? Do I serve the rest of the women next or Nureyev? I opt for fame and serve Nureyev, the rest of the ladies, then the gentlemen. No sirens wail or royal guards appear to haul me away, so I assume I guessed the right pecking order. With food and wine served, I step away behind my bar and become aware of the pulse pounding in my head like a Saturday morning cartoon character and realize I have been holding my breath. I let out a long, slow exhale, then inhale as inaudibly as I can. I am grateful for my invisibility. No one sees me.

I clear the plates and pour coffee. A few of the gentlemen have brandy. Saved by the bell! Off they go, back to the box, and I avoid my first stroke at eighteen years old.

After the second act, as they're all getting ready to leave, my girl catches my eye and gives me a wink. I take this as a knowing gesture of what it took to pull off dinner and I'm pleased. They've all gone and I exhale and shrink a few inches in height. Just then, my girl, the lady in waiting, comes back through the doors, up two steps, and extends me a hand. She gives me twenty-five pounds. What a night!

# thirty-four

HEINZ TELLS ME WE HAVE A PROBLEM. I'M AN "ALIEN," AND THOUGH I've registered and have diligently renewed my visa, I'm not legally allowed to work. I have a dusty green alien registration book, kind of like a passport that was issued by the Home Office to allow me to stay in the country and go to ballet school. But it doesn't allow me to work. Heinz advises I can go to Croydon, fill out some forms, get a work permit, and clear the whole thing up.

The Home Office in Croydon is akin to a bank. Lots of windows with no one there. A cheery little signs say, "I'll be right back," but it's a lie. London in the '70s is sparse and economically depressed. Yes, it's been thirty years since the war, but they had a big hole to crawl out of. There isn't much of anything and what there is, is pretty basic. With ten service windows, only two are manned. I get a number and sit on a bench to wait.

Everyone here is dealing with some sort of immigration or visa issue, so there's a palpable tension in my fellow patrons. Everyone's issue is life-altering. Every now and again the air is punctuated by a little cry of pain at some denial of permission, a gasp of horror at possibly facing deportation, a sigh of frustration at an unknown regulation, a piece of paper not known to be needed and not brought. That means returning home, then back to Croydon, the endless wait, and the unknown outcome. It's a place of pain.

My situation seems almost silly in comparison. I just need them to say it's okay for me to work at the opera house for twenty pence an hour, and I cannot imagine this will be a problem. No one wants my job selling programs and ice creams. They might want my job in the royal retiring room, but they don't know about that little perk.

I wait for six hours. Six hours on a wooden bench, parallel to the service windows, away from the wall, in the middle of the floor. I get up, stretch, walk around, pace, sit through lunch when no window is open. I am too terrified to leave and get food, lest my number is called in my absence. When I finally do get to the window, the young man behind the glass takes one look at my alien registration book and my work permit application and hands them back.

"I'm sorry, love," he says. "We have a million unemployed in Britain right now, over-immigration from other commonwealth countries, and massive inflation and economic problems. You're an American. I cannot approve your work permit."

I've waited six hours. Heinz had said this would be a formality, but now I see my life at the opera house fade before my eyes. It's only in this moment that I realize I'm here in the United Kingdom for ballet school, but it's the opera house that sustains me. The people, Margot Fonteyn, Margaret, Nureyev, Gillian, my pals in the usher corps, Malcolm, Peter, Heinz. We work toward a common purpose and overcome obstacles together every day. I love the camaraderie of it. Ballet school holds no such thrill. It seems vain and self-centered by comparison.

I break. Burst into tears, sobbing uncontrollably. There is no acting. No show I put on to try to get over. I can't take the hit. I can't imagine life here without my job. It's not the money because God knows there's little of that—it's the experience and adventure it brings me.

"Oh, love, I'm sorry," the man says again, reaching a hand through the little slot to console me. Then he notices my ring. I wear an aquamarine ring with diamond chips on the side that was passed down to me from my great-grandmother on my mother's side. It only fits my left-hand ring finger and I've worn it ever since I was allowed to have it as mine. In the early years I was only allowed to wear it to church or some fancy event. I like it because I loved my great-grandmother and because it's also useful in warding off unwanted attention.

"Are you engaged?" the clerk inquires as he pats my hand. My brain's well-worn path into fantasy comes alive.

"Yes!" I blubber with a little more volume than required. "And he's English. And if I can't work, we can't get married!" I snivel through my tears. Method acting. Find some anchor in reality and expand.

"Well! Why didn't you say so?" His little stamp comes out in a flash. My alien card and work permit application, still lingering on the counter, are promptly stamped and pushed back in my direction. Approved!

"Good luck!" he calls out.

I drift away from the window semi-hysterical. Still crying from the real emotions that had erupted only thirty seconds before but at the same time laughing at how fate, a ring, an assumption, all came together in a magical moment. It wasn't necessarily a lie, as Malcolm could ask me to marry him, but I know that would be a mistake.

I quickly walk out of the office and beat a fast track to Croydon Station. It's gonna be a great train ride home.

Life at home is deteriorating quickly. Try as I may to maintain peace with my mother, especially since her MS diagnosis, we cannot seem to keep from bickering. There is something she wants or needs from me, and I don't know what it is and I don't think she does either. I try this, I try that. Nothing works and everyone is unhappy and frustrated.

Gillian wants to move out of her place and suggests we get a flat together. She's found a place in Islington that we can afford. It's what's called a "bedsit" for six pounds a week. A bedsit is a room with beds for sleeping and chairs for sitting. In the United States we would call it a studio apartment, except it doesn't have a kitchen or a bathroom. There is a two-burner gas hot plate and a tiny refrigerator in the closet. The bathroom is common to all four apartments on the floor.

Islington is farther from the city center, ballet school, and opera house—all the things my life revolves around—but I am on my own and away from the tension of my mother.

Shortly after I move out Mother advises that since I have emancipated myself, I will need to pay my own school tuition. After a moment of panic, she adds that I can also have my social security benefit check, a death benefit from my father's passing that she's collecting every month from the government on my behalf. Well who knew? Turns out to be a wash between the benefit amount and what school costs, but I feel more grown-up.

At school I start studying for my advanced RAD exam. I've risen in estimation with Miss Nuckey but still carry the stain of being a foreigner. The syllabus is harder and more challenging, but my enthusiasm is waning. It all feels robotic and rote. Too much of the same thing every day. The movement is too rigid, the dancing too controlled, the studios too small. I long to bust out, but I have adopted the constrained British way of life. We don't "bust" and we don't fling ourselves around. We are proper and controlled.

Today on my tube ride home, they evacuate the Oxford Circus underground station just when my train is pulling in. The IRA is very active and they are blowing things up all over town, but it has never touched me so personally. They make bombs and pack them with coach bolts, long screws that they use as shrapnel and which are designed to maim and kill beyond the actual blast radius. I read about them every day in the paper and see reports on the news.

If you are going to be in an emergency evacuation situation, you want to be in Britain. I rush off the train and follow the mass of humanity up the escalators to safety. There is no panic, no shoving or pushing, everyone queues up and waits their turn. The unlucky timing of this disaster is that the Oxford station is further underground than most and there are two very, very long escalators you have to take to get to the surface. With the volume of people, I can't walk up the left side like I normally would but have to stand, patiently waiting for my turn. I understand panic as I want to run, escape, be master of my own salvation, but this is just not done.

Once outside I get my bearings and consider the long walk home. Islington is too far. If I were still living on the Old Brompton Road, I would have enjoyed the walk through Kensington, reveling in my escape and pondering my brief brush with death. I don't understand the IRA, but I'm new to this story—the long history of British imperialism, the struggle for independence and self-rule. Still, blowing up innocent strangers is wrong. Maybe I'm not "innocent" in their eyes.

All the buses are overwhelmed with the underground passengers forced off the trains and to the surface. I try to hail a cab, deciding to part with my hard-earned money for this extravagance, but there isn't an unengaged cab in sight. I begin to walk and end up at Piccadilly station. Everything seems to be normal here. People are going in and out of the station as if nothing has happened. I resolve to take my chances again underground. I won't be blown up, it's not my karma, and I will be useful to others if disaster does strike.

At the opera house, we have a code for an emergency evacuation and regularly do drills. When we hear the code, we're to rush (calmly) to our stations, walk to the exit doors, open them, and in our most commanding voice instruct patrons, "This way out." I've been here six months and I've never experienced the real thing, and the drills are quite dull.

The opera season is back on and tonight it's *Madame Butterfly*. I love this opera. The American sailor Butterfly falls in love with leaves Japan, promising to return to marry her. She has his son while he's away. After two years the sailor finally comes back but with a new wife. They want to adopt the child and take him away with them. I relate to this heroine, knowing I will surely be betrayed by love. She kills herself in the end. Take that, you bastard. I've never loved anyone enough to want to kill myself but look forward to the day. Plus, it's Puccini, and you really can't beat Puccini. His music is beautiful and haunting.

I often stand in the back of the stalls for the last half hour as Butterfly sings her final aria and then commits suicide, but tonight, just as she is on her knees, facing the audience, singing her guts out, knife in hand to commit seppuku, the safety curtain comes down, the orchestra music thins and stops, and the house lights come up. I haven't heard the code word as I've been inside watching the performance, but the lowering of the safety curtain is a clear indication that it's an emergency and we have to evacuate.

We are all in a stunned state, having been with Butterfly in her world as she faces heartbreak and her final decision. I am not allowed to indulge in this sentiment and must force my way out of Butterfly's world, calling, "This way out, please," as I push open the exit doors on the side of the stalls to the street. Everyone stands and begins to exit. Calmly, quietly, no rush, no panic, but orderly and swift. The patrons gain traction as they wake up from Japan and reenter London. We all know it's the IRA. Bombs with coach bolts.

There are plenty of false alarms but enough actual bombings that no one takes it lightly. Except the guy who left his program on his seat and has come back in to retrieve it. I give him a few sharp words, snatch another program off the floor, and shove it at him. I can see his reluctance because it's not "his" program. My problem is that I am required to evacuate all patrons before finally closing the doors and exiting myself. I really can't see getting blown up over a program. Then *she* appears, tiny little thing, tottering back into the house saying something about her coat. A quick survey of the seats and I see it. A mink jacket and turquoise scarf draped over the back of her chair. She comes at me like a halfback. She's seventy if she's a day, but she's not leaving without that mink. I pull up my long skirt, high hurdle a few rows, retrieve her coat and scarf, and return them, almost lifting her off the floor as I squire her to the exit. Butterfly died for love, but this lady is willing to go for her coat.

# thirty-five

THE QUEEN IS COMING! SHE'S NEVER COME BEFORE, ONLY MARGARET and other government ministers, and there is a marked difference in preparations. I am *not* to be employed in the royal retiring room. Humph! She has her own staff, her own people to do for her. Gillian and I are relegated to glorified porters stationed outside the double doors into the retiring room to open and close them for Her Majesty and entourage.

"Her Majesty." We Americans have a complicated relationship with Britain, the royal family, and the Queen. We are young and brash and want to take all the credit for winning World War II, but we also know where we came from and to whom we owe our laws and heritage. We don't sit around daily and study the Magna Carta, but back in our subliminal Neanderthal brains, we feel the pull of home and Momma. We love the steadfastness of the Queen; the glamour of Margaret; Charles, Anne, and Edward are an afterthought of privilege and class. Maybe it's the ears, but Charles is going to have a tough act to follow. We don't care that he was in the Royal Navy or flew airplanes. After all, the Queen drove ambulances during the war and knows how to repair an engine. That's our girl.

The day of the big occasion, the house is vacuumed and polished and vacuumed and polished again. Heinz admonishes everyone to wear a clean shirt. No spots, be on time, and for heaven's sake, just act normally. Right. It's the Queen!

She arrives promptly at seven o'clock in a convoy of the long black limousines the royals favor. Her retinue is large, seeming to consist of other royals, ladies-in-waiting, and staff. They come in off of Saint Martin's Lane and walk through the front of the house, through the stall bar, and down the right-side hall toward the retiring room. I am stationed on the left-side door, so my back is to the procession as they approach. Lacking foresight, I have been outmaneuvered by Gillian, who has a full view as they progress down the hall toward us. It's only fair. She's British. I am a dumping-good-tea-into-the-harbor American rebel. All may be forgiven, but all is not forgotten.

Just inside the double-door entry to the retiring room, there are five steps up where things slow down and bottle up a bit. With my back to the procession, I don't get a very long look at the Queen, but I'm struck by the lack of pomp. She's just a nice British housewife in her coat, good shoes, and famous handbag going to the opera. I do wonder at her being the last in the procession and at her having to wait as those ahead fiddle-faddle on the stairs.

"Get up and get in, for God's sake. You've left the Queen standing out here in the hall!"

Finally, the crush on the stairs abates and the Queen steps inside the doors. Gillian is in charge of signaling when we open and close the doors based on her sightlines. She finally nods at me, pleased that we have successfully completed our royal task, and we close our respective doors. But my door bumps. Like there's something on the other side that it ran into. I have a vision of the Queen face down on the stairs. Ambulances called. Me transported to the Tower by Scotland Yard. A beheading at dawn.

I tell Gillian in a whisper. She can see how the doors are not closed flush with each other and how my eyes are wide and scared.

I can still feel resistance against my door, but I hold it tightly closed. Gillian whispers, "Run!" We take off, long skirts gathered to our knees for maximum speed.

Timing is everything, they say, and I have managed to miss the American Bicentennial celebrations and now I'm about to miss the Queen's Silver Jubilee. Not that I care much for either as I've developed a real fear of crowds and crowded places. The IRA has left their mark.

I pass my advanced RAD exam, but just pass, no highly commended this time, no fuss. I go to Croydon again to see if I can get a work permit as a dancer, but they pretty much laugh at me. "There are twenty-five thousand unemployed dancers and performers in London alone. Without the status of soloist or above, no one is going to give you a permit to perform in the UK." No ring saves me this time. No serendipitous magic where forces align to move me along some predetermined path. I can work at the opera house selling ice cream, but there will be no prospects in the London dance world. The truth is I don't mind. I'm tired of being "the other." Tired of working so hard to be acceptable. I don't think about it much. It's time to go home.

Gillian has already moved out of our bedsit and it's a pretty hard life alone in Islington without her. We give each other love and warmest wishes when she leaves. We promise we'll write, but I know we won't. Somehow this friendship belongs at ballet school, the opera house, and in London. Without those ties, it won't survive.

# thirty-six

I PACK MY FEW POSSESSIONS AND TRANSFER BACK TO THE FLAT ON THE Old Brompton Road to gather the rest of my belongings. When I tell Mother I've decided to go home, she offers that she has decided to leave London too. She wants to enroll Melanie in school in the fall in the States. I don't know if my leaving influences her decision to go but it doesn't really matter. I pack while she stores her and Melanie's personal items and clothes they will leave behind. I haven't thought about what she will do with the flat, but it seems she'll keep it for now.

In our bustling about, I find a rather serious-looking letter tossed casually on the coffee table in the living room from the Home Office threatening her with deportation for overstaying her visa. How like her to have broken a rule, but she never tells me anything about it. Her plan is to escape in the night rather than try her hand at a trip to Croydon.

My plan is to fly to New York City and take an Amtrak train to North Carolina where Granny and Pompy have retired to what they consider proper, white, well-off, country-club life. Mother says she will meet me there and we can drive back to Tucson together. I don't have a better plan, so I agree.

Leaving London I allow myself a bit of sentimentality and longing. I've been here for two years and think I've changed significantly. Gone is the naive American girl with no knowledge of the world beyond her borders. I understand Europe and Britain a bit more—how this is a place shaped by age and tradition. How the proximity of so many people and cultures intermixing necessitates constant compromise. Not becoming false or not yourself but just enough not to offend. Everyone has prejudice, but when you get to know people who were once strange to you, the fear abates and there is great joy in learning the new.

The romance of London has been strong. Walking in Hyde Park when the daffodils bloom, coming out of the tube station at Trafalgar Square with Lord Nelson and the Lions, walking up Saint Martin's Lane to the opera house, Covent Garden, getting lost and finding yourself in a mews that hasn't changed since Queen Victoria, taking a taxi past the palace all lit up at night, the ironmonger in his horse-drawn cart. Little moments in time, some repeated daily, have become commonplace and served to rearrange me. Gone is the lost girl traumatized by her father's death and fearing change. In her place is a young woman of some accomplishment and bravery ready to take on what comes.

I fly out of Heathrow into JFK and catch a bus to Penn Station, where I'll catch a train to North Carolina. My timing couldn't be worse as I get to the station around 10:00 p.m. and my train doesn't leave until 9:00 a.m. the next morning. After midnight, there are very few people in the station other than the homeless and unfortunate stranded travelers such as myself. Being overly tired, I decide to rest my eyes and my body. I lie down on one of the wide wooden benches with the unfortunate little wooden dividers delineating each seat. Trying very hard to drift off, I am awakened by a poke in the ribs. It's an older, slightly portly New York City police officer jutting at me with his billy club.

"Wake up," he says. "I don't want to do the paperwork when you get robbed."

"Yes, Officer," I mumble and sit back up. I thought I had been very strategic and conscientious laying my bag under my head as a pillow to sleep, but he apparently had a different opinion.

I spend the night reading and wandering Penn Station. Finally, I board the morning train to North Carolina. Relieved to have somewhere comfortable to sit, I go to the club car to smoke and order a rum and Coke. I don't know why I order this drink. I've never had a rum and Coke in my life. Then I have another. I learned to drink gin and tonic in London with my ballet school girlfriends but never really got into it because I have no money for drinking. Plus, I have eating disorders, like any good aspiring dancer, and with two drinks in me I'll probably throw up. But I am a world traveler now and feeling very grown-up, so I'm drinking.

In my now-tipsy state, ignoring the rule that I must not eat and if I do must eat only diet food, I order a hamburger. A big fat American hamburger. London has a chain restaurant called Wimpey's where you can get a burger, but it's a tiny little bun with an even tinier hamburger patty. No lettuce or tomatoes. No pickles or onions. No secret sauce, ketchup, or mustard.

There is a nostalgia to the dining car on the train. It may not have the grandeur of the past, but still, with the white tablecloths and the waiters in their short jackets, it's a step back in time. At any moment you can imagine Cary Grant in his gray flannel suit coming in to sit down and seduce Eva Marie Saint.

My hamburger arrives with fanfare far beyond its worth. It's not coq au vin, cooked by some chef behind the scenes; it's a hamburger grilled in the kitchen in back, but oh, what a hamburger it is! A large, thick beef patty served on a bun of exactly equal size with mustard, enough mayonnaise that it squishes out the sides of your mouth when you bite it, lettuce, tomato, pickles, and a slice of onion if you are feeling daring. On first bite I feel the American continent reenter and course through my bloodstream. An energy of mystical proportions. I have come home to the vastness that is the country where I was born. We have so much. There is so much space and so many resources for anyone with the nerve to reach out and grab. To dare, to risk it all for a shot at something new, something better.

It was probably just the beef. In London, I'd become a vegetarian. Not through any social consciousness or moral decision but rather because meat is so expensive, combined with my limited cooking facilities and lack of funds and time. I existed on Jacob & Cos Cream Crackers, Irish cheddar, Branston pickle, Hovis bread, butter, bags of peanuts and raisins, and Cadbury chocolate bars. I haven't eaten meat in months and few vegetables. My eating disorder requires that I resist any food at all during the day for as long as I can, and then once my blood sugar drops sufficiently and finally overwhelmed by hunger, I'll eat whatever is immediately at hand. It doesn't really matter what it is, but I have to eat now or kill someone.

I am a little drunk. Two rum and Cokes on an empty stomach, now bolstered by my hamburger, I make my way back to my seat. Fueled by the protein coursing through my veins and the comfort of feeling like I'm "home," I settle into my seat and pass out.

Airline travel is disorienting, picking you up from one place in the world and then teleporting you to another space and time, but train travel picks you up where you are and shows you the entire journey. There are towns, the backyards of those unlucky enough to live along the tracks, fields of tobacco or corn or beans, lots of cows and horses. It shows you the path along the way and all the spaces in between. You know where you were, how you got there, and where you are now. I find this comforting.

I arrive in Southern Pines, North Carolina, smelling like an old mop but looking better than I feel. Youth is a great cover. Granny and Pompy pick me up at the train station. Granny hugs me and wants me to sit with her in the front seat of the car. I'd rather be in the back, alone with my odor and filth. I left London the day before, flew for eight hours, hung out in Pennsylvania Station for twelve hours waiting for my train, and have spent another dozen hours on the train down to North Carolina. Yes, I took a "spit bath" in the ladies' room and changed my shirt, but there is no getting away from my feeling of grime.

Their home is understated and meticulously beautiful. Gray-weathered wood with glass all along the front and back to showcase the Carolina pine trees, birds, and squirrels that share the property. Once inside you are greeted with the low hum and chill of good air-conditioning, white walls so as not to distract from the views, a mix of wood floors with Persian carpets and neutral wall-to-wall carpeting, antiques from my great-grandmother, paintings of old dead relatives, and paintings by Granny. She designed and drew this house and supervised the construction with the contractor. It's all space and light, and everywhere your eye lands there is order and beauty. I aspire to her sense of grace and comfort. The house welcomes you. The truth is, this is how Granny wants to live and you are just fortunate to be invited in. Not everyone is. And there are expectations that come with the invitation. You must be nice, mind your manners, never raise your voice, and never be messy or disturb the tranquility she has created for herself and my grandfather.

I spend the next few days eating breakfast, lunch, and going out to dinner every night. I sleep like the well-fed in the quiet of the woods and the safety of this place where "good" white people live and the police regularly patrol. I am again smacked by the structural racism of the American South. There are Black and

Hispanic people here, but they are relegated to service jobs—waiters, gardeners, valets at the country club. London was such a mishmash of races and cultures. There were a lot of Indians and Pakistanis, and Indian restaurants everywhere you went, with the aroma of exotic spices wafting down the street. There were people from all over the UK with all kinds of accents, people from all the Commonwealth countries, so many people from the continent—you got used to the variety of skin colors, dress, and way of speaking. I was never afraid in London. Never had the sense of being "other" (once I shed my blatant Americanism).

But here in North Carolina I feel the underlying tension, and there is fear. The divide is intentional and hostile. I go out of my way to say hello to the valet or the gardener but can feel their sense of my having tread on a boundary. I am required to slot into my place and join the social order here. It's very sterile, air-conditioned, cold, and pleasant if you want to spend your life playing golf and tennis and doing the exact same thing with the exact same people every day. I don't. I want to fling myself around and explore.

A week later, Mother and Melanie arrive, also by train from NYC, and we go and pick them up from the station. Just Granny and I go, as Pompy has some longstanding feud with my mother. This is his way of showing his general displeasure without having to actually say or do anything. Heaven forbid anything ever be discussed or resolved.

Mother is overly animated and loud, trying too hard to be cheerful with Granny, which has the opposite effect. Their underlying tension is immediately installed and my loyalties divided. I love my grandmother but do not understand her lack of compassion. I am only nineteen years old but can clearly see my mother has escalating issues, damage, and now a horrible disease. Why not a little kindness? You have so much, and she is constantly drowning.

Today Mother shows up with a new car. I wish she had involved me in this purchase as it's a four-door sedan of some nondescript '70s boxy styling, maroon, and not at all what I would have chosen. With reentry into the United States, I have resumed my role as partner and paramour. It's again my job to watch her, especially where driving is concerned.

We stay a few more days, and I am grateful to be off. Living in the schism of love for Mother and Granny, with my grandfather and his disapproval patrolling the perimeter, is exhausting. I am relieved to be gone.

The drive home is uneventful except for Mother's driving. She drives in whatever lane she wants, as fast or slowly as she is in the mood for, with no consideration for the fact that she is driving a lethal weapon, or that there are other drivers on the road, or that possibly a turn signal here and there might be useful, or at least courteous. I am once again in low-key fear for our lives, so I make little suggestions here and there, but it just seems to make the situation worse.

I sit in the front passenger seat holding my breath the entire trip home. I check my mirror with every lane change and the speedometer as we pass speed limit signs, always on the hunt for the highway patrol. My right foot is embedded into an imaginary brake pedal on the floor, my right hand clenched around the padded armrest on the door, my left hand ready to grab the steering wheel at any moment. I long for my own rearview mirror as Mother will take the shortest path around a curve by cutting across the lane. When discussed, she advises this is for fuel economy. It's exhausting. I give up our fate to the gods of the highway and hope for the same protection provided to "mad dogs and Englishmen."

I hadn't realized the liberation afforded me access to mass transit and Mother not driving in London. I can imagine her driving on the "wrong" side of the road with her entitled driving in polite British traffic, my little sister bouncing around in the back seat. I did worry about her crossing streets, but I've also noticed Melanie taking a more active role in all things lately. I imagine her pulling Mother back from stepping off the curb with traffic coming.

# thirty-seven

BACK IN TUCSON THAT AUGUST IT'S HARD TO RECONCILE THAT I'M BACK or why I went to London in the first place. I didn't achieve anything other than being two years older and no closer to my goal of being a professional dancer. And yet, I have seen something of the world, and it has changed me. I have hung out with royalty, sold ice creams, ridden the underground, braved the IRA, and had my first real long-term relationship. I've learned to eat strange food, the value of heat and hot water, and not to fear the differences between us. We are the way we are because of where we grew up, who our people are, and where we've been. I understand now the fear from people who have never been out of their town or their region or state. They have not experienced the difference in cultures or food or the pleasure of a kindness from a stranger you were taught to fear. Yes, taught to fear. I see this everywhere now. People being taught to fear what they do not know or what is strange to them.

I call MK and she comes over and picks me up in a little green Toyota pickup truck with a black and white decal on the side that says, "The Fancy Farmer Restaurant." She is studying at the University of Arizona and says she has a long story to tell me about what's been going on the two years I was away.

Her mother, Maudine, fell in love with a man, a very flashy man, who swept her off her feet. The kind of man who has the world on a string and a big wad of cash in his pocket. They got married, he built and opened a restaurant, built a very big house with a pool for Maudine and her five girls, a horse corral for MK's horse, bought cars for everyone—and a boat. Then it turned out he had used Maudine's credit to make deals all over town, conned all kinds of vendors—from the bank, the phone company, car dealers, restaurant suppliers—into extending him credit he didn't have, then crashed and burned and split town, leaving Maudine to carry the load of his debt, which is massive. The big house is being foreclosed, all the cars and the boat have been repossessed, and Maudine and all five girls are working at the Fancy Farmer Restaurant, trying to keep it afloat and dig out from under this mess. What a story!

Turns out he's a bigamist with eight wives (that they know of) in five states, and this is what he does. He preys on divorced or widowed women with assets, then cons the whole town into somehow supporting his shenanigans. When it all crashes and burns, he leaves town with a trail of ruined lives and chaos in his wake. Gee, sorry I never met the guy. Of course I will come and work at the restaurant.

There's a new professional ballet company that has started in town: the Tucson Ballet. It opens that fall. They are building studios in an old warehouse building. The new director is a Frenchman who has brought his wife as the star ballerina. There are professional dancers brought in from New York City. It's not much, but I am assured by everyone I talk to that there is great hope for the new company and bringing the little dance world in Tucson together.

I go to class and am not at all impressive to the Frenchman. He never speaks to me or seems to have an opinion either way about my dancing, good or bad, but my existence is tolerated in class. The feeling is mutual. He's short and has the kind of Napoleonic aura of a man who needs to compensate. He's arrogant and his French accent seems exaggerated, which is just enough to make his English unintelligible. I'm not having any fun but don't have any better options.

I go back to Maria's studio to see her, say hello, and take a class, but all the people from my old crew are gone and it's a whole other lot of girls. I don't belong here either.

It is announced at the ballet company that they're forming a junior company which will be run by the company ballet mistress. All of us younger dancers not good enough to be in the main company are selected and we will have our own junior company classes. Then *she* walks in: Michele.

She is tall and very pretty with short blond hair that flops over one eye. I am instantly suspicious. She is the ballet mistress for the main company but now will also teach our junior company class. While teaching class, she demonstrates combinations at the barre. There is a flow, a vastness, a connectedness about her movement that is mind-expanding. She not only demonstrates but explains what and why. How things should be done. It is a revolution to me. No more British rigidity or regimentation. She is all open and flowing. I try to copy everything she does.

In the ballet world, you are often taught by an older man or woman. Maybe they were dancers in an earlier life but are now well past their prime and can only indicate what they are asking for. There is limited ability to demonstrate the turn of the hip or the arch of the back they are looking for, so you are left to interpret and execute as best you can. There is often no accompanying explanation for what you are being asked to do or the correction you are given—it's just a kind of "do it" world. I once took a class at the San Francisco Ballet School from an ancient man who spoke only Russian and carried a stick. I didn't understand a word he said. He'd demonstrate, and if you got it wrong, he'd hit you with the stick.

Michele is young and still in her prime. Maybe a little heavier than she would want to be, but she carries it flawlessly. Her movement and technique are better than any of ours. All of her body seems to be connected in a way I have never seen before. It's not a head and arms and legs attached to a torso and pelvis, but one coordinated machine of a whole body. My dancing is immediately changed. It's not like I can do what she's doing yet, but I see well where I want to go.

The other half of my life is now fully entrenched at the Fancy Farmer Restaurant with MK and family. Waiting tables at a diner-style restaurant is hard, heavy work, but with MK setting the standard, I fit right in. I am the adopted daughter. Not quite family, but almost. Just like at Coco's, I go to work every morning at 5:30 a.m., open the doors at 6:00, and the regulars pile in. Same guys. Working guys. They just want breakfast, coffee, and a smile. Some days I provide the food and coffee but cannot manage the smile. I'm too mad. I don't know at what. I'm not mad at them, but they are there at my dead-end waitress job and I resent having to add the smile. You paid for breakfast and coffee, you get breakfast and coffee. The smile is up to me and I just haven't got it today.

I work until 2:00 p.m., run home, and change out of my polyester uniform that smells like every bite of food I served today and into my dance clothes. Dancers are particular about their dance clothes. Leotards and tights of some form are the base, but on top of that you decorate. Some for warmth, some for looks. A sweater on top. I am currently in favor of the huge, long, old sweatshirt, polyester leg warmers, one for each leg (that I got out of the lost and found) pulled up to the top of the thigh to just under the knee, cut-off tights rolled to the bottom of the calf, and white ballet shoes with white socks over the ballet shoes. Socks slouched at the ankle with just a bit of skin showing between the top of the sock and bottom of the tights. It's all about getting your muscles warm at the barre, but believe me, it's a meticulously put-together outfit. It's designed to say, "I just don't care how I look," when that's all you care about.

Even at just nineteen, I wake every morning with stiff muscles and joints. A hot bath, or at least a long hot shower, is required to work out the kinks and get the thing moving just to walk around upright.

Before class I sprawl on the floor and slowly stretch and wiggle. Hamstrings, spine, ankles just to get them moving. Then the slow, meticulous progression of exercises at the barre. I analyze every muscle, tendon, and joint and give extra attention where needed. Ankles are stiff today. Right hip is clicking and I can feel that tendon getting stuck at the top of the thigh bone with every front extension. Low back is compacted and needs a few slow twists to encourage vertebra separation. Slowly the circulation increases, body heat rises, and I start to sweat. The rigidity begins to pass. I start to feel all the individual parts separate so they can come together again just like they do every day. I hope I don't discover some injury just painful enough to require a compromise in movement. It doesn't take much. Most things will work out as I warm up, but now and again, some nagging stiffness or pain won't go away. It scares me. What if? It could all be over, but I push through.

It's odd how drawn I am to Michele but terrified of her at the same time. I am in awe of her dancing and gobble up every word of instruction, but there is something else. When she looks at me. There is intensity to the connection with this human being that I have never felt before. I barely know her, and yet I feel like she sees through me into my soul and I am naked. Naked on the toilet. Naked with all my deepest, darkest secrets scattered around me on the floor on display. Some shiny little qualities, but mostly turds. This makes me angry. I've lost control. I want to close off. I don't want to be seen so clearly. I don't know how to hide myself from her, so I shove all these feelings down somewhere. I live with a knot in my stomach around her. What is going on?! Who the hell is this woman and why does she have such power over me? How I think, feel, and act. It's exhausting.

What feelings? I have taught myself not to feel, but with her Svengali influence over me, my feelings break out of their enclosure and overwhelm me. I can walk numb through the world, but around her I am a live wire, the kind you see on the TV news flopping around and sparking all over some road. Try as I may, I cannot contain myself. I want to be near her. I'd be happy to follow her around like some mongrel puppy. Listen to her talk, the sound of her voice, watch her move, sit, stand, walk around. But that's impossible, so I settle for ballet class.

# thirty-eight

IN THE NEW YEAR MICHELE ANNOUNCES THAT THE JUNIOR COMPANY is going to give a performance this spring and that she will be doing the choreography. Rehearsals will begin right after company class every evening. I've hit the trifecta! Time with Michele, choreography from her, and a performance! I stand deadpan at this news, slouched at the barre, barely looking at her. I can't let on how thrilled I am. I don't know why, but I just can't. I think it's too obvious how much I love this woman and I know I need to hide it. So I hide it even from myself.

In rehearsals I act distant and bored, like none of it matters to me, but the enthusiasm in my dancing belies all this. The ballet is called *Joyous Moments*, the music is Pachelbel, and her choreography is joyous too. I've never had so much fun dancing. Her choreography is teaching me to actually "dance" just by the steps she creates and the way it's put together. It's free but it's logical. Everything makes sense, nothing is contrived. She lets simple movement and the corps work stand for itself. I feel beautiful doing it.

Today in class she absent-mindedly shows us a back hinge to the floor. Stand straight up, on your toes, stretch one arm high over your head, and hinge back from your knees to the floor to land on your shoulders. You use the extended arm to find the floor so you don't whack your head. She teaches this to Joey, one of the boys, and typical of me, I have to try it too. I always want to see if I can do everything the boys do. I do it twenty times. It's such a dramatic move.

After class I am a little wobbly on my legs. Even driving home my legs feel like they can't quite push the gas or the brakes. There is an unfamiliar weakness, but I brush it off as just being tired from having worked hard in class and rehearsal. At home I run a hot bath. Hot water is the cure for all ballet ailments. I sit down in the tub and both my thighs explode to twice their size. I sit in stunned silence in the tub, staring at my legs that have deformed themselves into huge gelatinous flesh bags, not the trim, muscled thighs of which I am so proud. I scream, which brings my mother running. Atypical of her. In high school I cut the end of my finger off in the cake mixer, and standing with my middle finger hanging by a flap of skin, the bone sticking out, screamed, in my best this-is-an-emergency voice, "*Mother!*"

She screamed back "*What!*" from the other room.

I'm sitting in the tub dumbfounded. I don't understand what is happening to my legs. I can't move. Well, I *can* move, but there is something terribly wrong. It's like someone has cut 90 percent of the connection to my legs. They are slow to respond and have no power. Mother has to help me crawl out of the tub. I'm like a newborn fawn trying to stand for the first time and failing miserably. I collapse naked on the bathmat, and even she can see how swollen and puffed up my legs are—two bloated bags from hip to knee.

I go to the doctor the next morning. I arrive with both thighs tightly wrapped in ace bandages, trying to hold things together. I walk stiff-legged because if I bend my knees, my legs fail, and I fall down. *What is happening here?* Do I have fast-onset MS? I know waking up paralyzed in your legs is one of the symptoms of the disease.

The doctor is our family pediatrician. I haven't seen him since I last went to camp. He is charming with the usual "how much you've grown" and "you're almost as pretty as your mother." He asks about what I did the day before. I recount my day—waiting tables, company class, and rehearsal. He doesn't seem satisfied.

"Did you do anything new or unusual?"

I remember the hinges and tell him offhandedly about that, but he snickers a bit under his breath, which seems rather unprofessional as far as I'm concerned. "You've torn both your quadricep muscles rather badly. You will need complete rest. No class or exercise for six weeks."

So matter of fact. So blasé, like I can take six weeks off. I have a performance in ten days!

It seems that the back hinge I was having so much fun showing off puts all your weight in your thighs while at the same time requiring these same muscles to stretch, almost completely to their full range. Putting a muscle in contraction, asking it to fully flex, and then fully stretch at the same time is how you end up with two torn quads. Maybe I could have done it a few times with no major injury, but no, I had to do it twenty times.

I hobble out of the doctor's office in a haze. *What shall I do? Where shall I go?* Oh, Scarlett, get a grip.

Two days later I go back to class. Michele knows, everyone knows, and I'm dramatic about it. There are no understudies in a company this small and we all know the rules: "The show must go on." I am determined to get better. It will ruin her choreographic structure to have me missing and I can't do that to her. Plus, I *want* to do the piece and perform!

Slowly, tentatively, I take just the barre but very modified. Just standing is challenging. I think about all the years I imagined myself wounded, bandaged, taken to the hospital with my parents, them sorry for all the bad things they had done and weeping by my side. This is horrible. I do *not* want to be hurt. Okay, the extra attention is good for five minutes, but ultimately I have things to do, places to go, and I am absolutely not into this tragedy thing. I am too strong.

Day by day I get better. Day by day I get stronger and do more in class and in rehearsal until I forget I was ever hurt. I wear the ace bandages for effect at first, but even those are discarded. Oh, the joy of being young and strong. At nineteen my body recovers so quickly. Ten days, not six weeks. The doctor doesn't understand the fitness level of the ballet dancer or my iron-willed determination.

We are in the final days and starting technical rehearsals at the theater when the Frenchman walks onstage to tell us that Michele is no longer with the company and he will be taking over rehearsals and the performance. Then he walks off. No reason given. *What the fuck is going on? Where is she? Why is she gone? How could she leave us?* I can only imagine the Frenchman saw the ballet and how great we looked and how wonderful the choreography was and he had to find a way to get rid of her. She's taller than he is by several inches, still young and beautiful, extraordinarily talented, and he can't take it.

Our joy is gone. We are all crushed, but there's the rule again: "The show must go on." So we persevere. This saying was obviously made up by some egomaniacal impresario who did something dastardly and is looking to cover his tracks. All the dancers gather to have a secret company meeting and talk about how much we love Michele and the ballet, so we are doing it for her and to celebrate the gift she has given us.

On the night of performance I imagine Michele has snuck into the back of the house up to the mezzanine to watch. I dance for her. I need her there to show her how she has revolutionized my life. There is no way she can miss it. I unleash my unbridled joy of doing this ballet for my imaginary friend watching from the shadows of the balcony.

A few days after the show, it's over. The company has folded and disbanded. The doors are locked. Michele is gone. Welcome to the dance world. Outside New York City, there is never enough money to support the amount of facility and work required to keep a ballet company. Some sports only require a grassy field and maybe some chalk lines. Ballet requires an indoor space with wood floors and a pianist. We need at least a dozen or so dancers and time to create and hone the work. Time where there are no performances, nothing to sell or see. Then performance and sometimes you get a stinker. The main company show is a turd. That's what the Frenchman gave us. Lots of complicated choreography starring his wife and fancy costumes. All "sound and fury, signifying nothing." No one wanted to see it. I'm sure he went home and relayed stories of trying to bring culture to some cowboy town, but that wasn't the case. He brought his wife and his ego but nothing of value. We can see the male ego on display every day of the week. We don't need it imported from France.

# thirty-nine

OKAY, NOW WHAT? I REORGANIZE. I REGROUP. WHAT SHALL I DO, WHERE *shall I go? Tara. I'll go home to Tara.* Well, I don't have a vast Southern plantation to go to—to regroup and plan my next move—so the Fancy Farmer will have to do.

I work, I wait tables, I'm cheerful. But the heart and soul of me are not in residence, or if they are, they are very sad and upset. I can work and move about the world with a bare minimum of effort or presence. I can be mostly absent while you order your eggs or BLT.

Why do I feel these losses so acutely? I am not the first dancer to have a company fold out from under them. Matter of fact, it's almost a dancer's rite of passage. If you haven't had a company or show fold right out from under you, leave you stranded in Omaha with no money and no prospects, you must be doing something wrong. The high high is always balanced by the low low. There is a price to pay for feeling like a physical god, and it's feeling like an emotional pig. You spend the day rooting around in the mud and filth of your pain and misery, looking for ways to feel the most damaging parts of it, feeling sorry for yourself. You're covered in it. You reek. Think of the *Peanuts* character Pig-Pen. I understand this character now. A wounded child no one can comfort or heal so he's allowed to wander with his pain.

Staring out the front windows of the restaurant as I take another order for a big fat hamburger for a guy, and for a girl, salad, dressing on the side, I see a new sign across the street. The restaurant is set well back in the strip mall, so it's across the parking lot and across the street, but the sign is enough that I can read: "Dance Studio." That's all it says and all I need. I almost don't go, such is my snobbery. Who are these people? And if I go in and never come back, will it hurt their feelings? I never consider the alternative that it could be great, could be just what I am looking for. You don't find salvation in a strip mall in Tucson, Arizona, across the street from your waitress job.

I wait a day but I can't resist. I have to investigate. I can see the sign clearly, but in my mind I'm in one of those sci-fi or horror movie scenes where the protagonist is trying to get to a door when suddenly the hallway stretches out, and as fast as she runs, the distance never changes, it just keeps getting farther away. It could have been the Arizona sun.

Standing in front of the studio, having jay-walked through traffic to force my brain out of the movie scene, I muster my courage and try the door. Unlocked. "Nothing ventured, nothing gained," as Mother would say.

It takes my eyes a good minute or so to adjust to the cool darkness inside the studio. Ballet studios often have few windows as we need all that wall space for barres and mirrors. Sunlight is for mortals. We are vampires of the night.

Speaking of vampires, the woman who bored down into my core and sucked the soul from my body stands there, her back to me, hands on her hips, in her green wraparound teaching skirt and sandals, talking to a rather short woman in leotards and tights. They seem engaged in a serious conversation and take no notice of my entrance.

Well that's rude. If you're going to be the light of my life and obsession for the next several years, you could at least play out this scene with a bit more drama. "As she opened the door to the studio, backlit by the blazing Arizona sun, Michele turned . . ." You get the picture.

I had no idea what had happened to Michele since the company folded. I assumed she went back to New York City. She was just gone to me and I had no expectation of ever seeing her again, but here she stands. As blasé as I can muster, I walk forward and introduce myself to the shorter woman, giving a slight head nod to Michele. She introduces herself as Deborah, owner of the studio, and indicates that Michele will be teaching ballet class there every day starting next week.

I didn't see it coming. I never see it coming. The little synchronicities of life, coincidences, if you will, that move and shape you. I have been taught that I have bootstraps I need to pull up and that I must work for everything I get, but no one tells you there is equally magic in the world that you just need to see and appreciate. Just ride the wind when it blows. That sometimes, all your pushing and pulling and reaching and striving is just busywork while you wait for the magic or while the magic waits for you to see.

Okay, so this new studio is a little studio in a strip mall in Tucson, but they can't all be the opera house and the royal family. Life has some highs and lows, but this isn't a low. London sounds exotic and glamorous and more important, but I can assure you, it wasn't, though it did show me the world. In London I lived a disconnected life. I went through the motions but didn't belong there. Here, I belong. Here, I have a purpose, though I don't always recognize it. It's hard to make anything important out of waiting tables on Sunday brunch with a line out the door and no end in sight, but here, I'm working to help my adopted family, Maudine and the girls, dig out from under their mountain of debt. I know I'm not really family but MK is as close to me as any human yet in life. We are the same in our damage, the missing father and our heroic attempts to replace him. Hard to recognize anything important in filling jellies and creamers for the millionth time. And yet, jellies and creamers do help make the world go round, just like smoked salmon sandwiches with the crust cut off at the opera house. It's all connected.

I've been back in Tucson for almost eight months now. My twentieth birthday passes with little fanfare in April, but *she's* back and my inspiration and enthusiasm for life returns with her. Class is fabulous, though there are only five of us. Three girls and two boys. This ratio of boys to girls is pretty unheard of in the dance world. Usually it's twenty girls in a class and some boy the teacher kidnapped from a gymnastics class on the promise that ballet will improve his gymnastics. Our boys are pretty good. Bill, previously of the Houston Ballet, has returned to Tucson and his family and is pondering his next move in life. Evan is an aspiring actor who is taking class the way actors do—in that your résumé needs to say actor/singer/dancer. He has a nice body but no feet. It takes years in dance class to get those ankles stretched out and the arches shaped so that when you point your toes, the line of the ankle and into the foot is a straight-line extension, giving the extended leg the illusion of being longer than it is. Okay, so he has no feet, but he is tall and nicely built with slim hips and a strong upper body. And he can partner, so we are going to overlook the feet.

Probably inspired by the fact that she has two strong couples, Deborah and Bill and me and Evan, Michele tells us she wants to choreograph a ballet if we are willing to work for free. None of us has anything better to do, so we all agree. I am happy to be in the same room breathing the same air with Michele, so I am in without question.

We rehearse every day after class. It's interesting to see her craft as she creates the ballet. The first piece is for both couples, and the theme of the movement is that we each will do the same moves, but Deb and Bill will do the movement modified to be closer to the ground. I have never had a ballet created for me or participated so much in the process.

"Can you do this with your leg extended but your back arched to reflect the same shape as Deb?"

"No" is not in a dancer's vocabulary. You do what is asked even if it looks god-awful at first. If the choreographer is satisfied, you have to believe it will get better with practice—and it does. You have to buy into her vision—and you do. I do. It's a trust fall. She won't make us look ugly. Some moves are thrown out. Some moves are changed by the way someone does them, and then we all have to learn how they did it. This is sometimes challenging. Deb is an old gymnast coming to ballet later in her life and has an amazingly strong center. I am a ballet dancer with a natural sway back, all arms and legs, no center. Sometimes Deb can do things Michele asks for that I cannot and it bruises my ego. I am the better dancer, but am I? I often cannot emulate a move Deb does that Michele likes and keeps. In my mind I try to blame Evan; he's not as good a partner as Bill is. If he were a better partner, I could do it, too, but it's not true. It's me.

The studio begins to prosper. Deb teaches an adult ballet class every evening and has gained a good following. Michele has attracted a few more dancers for the advanced ballet class, so we are humming along. There is some trouble with the landlord, parking is an issue, and so is the music and the noise from the studio, so Deb finds us a new space.

The new studio to be is much further west, so the drive will be longer, but it makes me happy not to be right across the street from the Fancy Farmer Restaurant. It's not like I'm ashamed of waiting tables to earn my living and keep body and soul together; it's good, honest work, but these two versions of me need their own orbit. I need my two worlds to be more separate.

That summer I also find a new space. It's a little studio apartment built on top of an existing house with a wooden staircase up to a long covered porch that runs the length of the building. The interior is one open room that parallels the porch, with a kitchenette on one end and a bathroom on the other. Perfect. It comes furnished with a single bed of some dubious origin and an old brown leather La-Z-Boy recliner. Everything a girl could need. I add a coffeemaker and a toaster oven to the kitchen, a small table and lamp next to the lounger, and a bookcase/credenza given to me by my mother as a moving-out present. It's my first apartment on my own in the United States and feels like a big step up from the bedsit in Islington.

I feel very grown-up. Not the fake grown-up I felt in London, where I was in a foreign country with the feeling that at any moment I could be asked (politely) to leave and would have to run back to my mother for resources. No. I am in my own country. I earn my own money, pay my own rent, buy my own food. I am a modern, independent woman with a job and a career.

I don't have much of a kitchen, so any real cooking isn't an option. Though more importantly, I don't know how. I can boil water and scramble an egg and know some basics, but I never had the inclination to learn. Charlotte, on the other hand, was always in the kitchen making angel food cake or beef stroganoff. Not me. I wanted to eat it, not make it.

I'm provided one meal with every shift at the restaurant, so I eat there. This generally entails a salad from the salad bar. Lots of lettuce, half a hardboiled egg, some black olives, and a lot of dressing. Blue cheese with a little vinaigrette is my current favorite. A good greasy hamburger or a sandwich would be a more logical choice, but I am a dancer with a demented image of my body (I'm too fat, or I will be soon), so I must eat only low-calorie diet food.

I work an eight-hour shift, eat my salad, then go to class and rehearsal. Fourteen hours on my feet and hard physical work. All on a salad, if that. I get home at the end of the day and am ravenous. In an actual panic. There is no one to leave an old, dried-up dinner in the oven for me. No one to buy groceries. There is no bread in my house, but there are corn tortillas, cheddar cheese, Doritos, peanut M&Ms, and red licorice. I do the shopping at Circle K and buy all my favorites.

In my low blood sugar panic, I open the Doritos and begin shoving them into my mouth as I prepare a tortilla with slices of cheddar cheese for the toaster oven. I rationalize that this qualifies as real cooked food. I shower, fueled by the Doritos I am still chewing, then settle in the La-Z-Boy to inhale my cheese tostadas. I make two more tostadas as my appetite is now awake and a beast that must be fed. Once the tostadas are finished, I get my book and settle in to read until I am ready for bed, but the siren song of a large bag of peanut M&Ms is calling to my still-lingering hunger.

There is a correct way to eat peanut M&Ms: You put them in your mouth two at a time, roll them around sucking off the candy shell, let them linger while the chocolate melts, then crunch down on the peanuts with the last bit of chocolate. Anyone who pops them into their mouth and begins crunching is an ignorant rookie.

This food melodrama is repeated every night like a religion. I set out only to have two tostadas from the toaster oven, but I always have four. I vow not to eat the M&Ms (alternating with red licorice), but I always do (sometimes both).

We were not allowed snacks or "junk food" growing up, or, God forbid, candy. Though Charlotte discovered Hershey's candy bars hidden in my mother's underwear drawer, we were never allowed candy except at Halloween.

So this is my food backlash and rebellion from my mother.

Even I can see this one. It is probably due to the sound nutrition of my youth that I survive this period. I am working physically harder than I ever have in my life and living on mostly sugar. I should have rickets and beriberi, but physically I am a beast, so I survive. My mental state is another thing altogether.

On days I don't work, I have nothing to eat all day. While in class or rehearsing, I am fueled by stored fat and adrenaline, but I am also aware of the "high" of not eating. I space out, have no focus, and sometimes get dizzy, and when we stop, I light a cigarette to provide the nicotine rush. It's an altered state I enjoy. I'm high.

# forty

AT REHEARSAL ONE DAY THAT FALL DEB LIGHTS A JOINT AND WE ALL PASS it around. I have smoked pot a few times, but always in strange, uncomfortable situations and I didn't enjoy it at all. So today is a real first. Smoking pot after rehearsal with Michele and my fellow dancers. I am feeling very grown-up again.

As the drug hits my brain I physically relax into my body. I am no longer tense and anxious with my brain going ninety miles a minute wondering what people think of me or if I am doing the right thing. Someone orders a pizza and we all inhale it without a thought of calories or getting fat. I am relaxed, comfortable, full, and content to be right where I am with who I am with.

I drive home relaxed and full but must force myself to concentrate on driving at the same time. I am conscious of being mentally compromised but feel with extra effort I can even everything out. I want to let go and just drift away, but I need to get home. To navigate effectively and arrive with my car and body parts in place, I must force my brain through the fog. I'm not sure the trade-off is worth it, but "I'll think about that tomorrow." Thank you, Scarlett.

I sometimes say hello to the boys who live downstairs in the main house under my little studio. I see them in all our comings and goings, but I have gotten rather pretty and attract a lot of unwanted attention from men, so I shy away. This afternoon one of them stops me to talk. "Hey, we bought a quantity of very good pot if you're interested?" After my experience at the studio last night, I am very interested. Enough to risk the company of boys, strangers at that.

"Sure," I reply. We go into the main house downstairs.

"This is Roger," who's just driven up and follows us into the house, "and that's Dave," he says, indicating the boy lounging prone on the couch. "And I'm David." Slightly confusing but I get it. "Move your ass, Dave, and let her sit down," David chides. "Would you like a beer?" David offers. I've never had a beer before, but I want to look cool, so I say, "Sure."

David, the one who invited me over, asks, "We are selling a lid of pot for $10 if you'd like to buy some?" After last night at the studio, I am eager to have my own stash.

"Yes, I would, thank you very much." Ten dollars for my very own bag of transformation—all mine to smoke whenever I want in the privacy of my own place. Yes, please!

Dave, who has fully awakened from his nap on the couch, joins us and begins to roll a joint using a shoebox lid to contain the pot as he crushes the dried flowers, then tilts the lid as he scrapes, allowing the unwanted seeds to roll away. Now cleaned, he crumbles the flowers into a folded-in-half rolling paper, rolls it around in his fingers until satisfied, then licks and seals the edge.

"Here," Dave offers, handing me the joint and a lighter. Grateful for last night's experience smoking at the studio, I do my best impersonation of a girl who has smoked many joints in her life: light up and pass it on. My nerves settle, I drink my beer, I avoid too many personal questions, but we laugh. They're nice. I like them, but I make a hasty retreat, give them $10, and make my excuses. I am so grown up!

Up in my apartment with my new stash, I set out to roll my first joint. A shoebox lid worked perfectly for the boys, so I fetch one from my closet. I crush the flowers, tilt the box lid, and let the seed roll to the other end. I have no rolling papers. I try using a cigarette paper, but it's too small to reroll. I wander around my little home searching for alternatives. I don't want to have to go downstairs and ask the boys. The only thin paper I have is the paper wrapping on a Tampax. Cut the ends off, slit it down the middle, cut it in half for size, sprinkle the pot in the middle, then roll like a cowboy. All of this is pleasing to me. I enjoy the ritual of it, not to mention the release of tension, the relaxation of my brain, the unwinding of the knot in my stomach. It's such a relief.

The next morning, I can't resist. I roll another joint as the coffee brews. It's not giving in to temptation as much as realizing I have found a solution. Why would I go about my day without it if it brings so much relief? You might be tempted to think I want to escape rather than face reality, and that may well be, but when reality gives you pain and confusion, why not?

*If work is a disaster*, I tell myself, *I won't do this again.* Surely I can take a few orders and serve eggs a little stoned. It's a bit harder to concentrate, but how much concentration does diner waitressing really take? No one notices, or if they do, no one says a thing. Plus, I enjoy my day more. Truth is, pot takes away my anxieties, or any feelings, really. I've had my fair share of hurt and evil and the pot serves to soften the blow. The feelings of being so overwhelmed, confused, and hurt are prevalent, and I have frequent thoughts of suicide. This started when I was much younger and felt so confused by my parents—my mother's lack of love, the change from Magic Mommy to the dragon that replaced her, my father's complete absence, except when his rage came out. The unpredictability that made the ground beneath me unreliable. When you are always being told you are "bad" and being punished for some imaginary transgression, it's hard to keep up a sense of well-being or self-esteem. I wanted to lash out, to hurt them the way they hurt me, but I knew this was wrong so I turned the anger in. I think I must be bad. I must be crazy. I come from crazy, so I must be too.

I understand the line in *The World According to Garp* where he says, “Keep passing the open window.” Passing an open window in a high building can be a tricky situation. Every time, I play out the scenario of launching myself out of it. So far I’ve been strong enough to pass the window. Haven’t thrown myself under a London underground train either. That one seemed gruesome, and on consideration, completely rejected. Haven’t driven myself into a brick wall or a tree. The scene I came up with was being trapped in the car, badly wounded and in serious pain, no one around to rescue me, so I suffer for hours, days maybe, until I’m rescued and survive with some major deformity or disability. You have to play these things out, and obviously it isn’t easy to off yourself.

Being stoned seems to kill the pain, but it takes some of the good parts too. It used to be that the dark thoughts and feelings were ascribed to my parents. Now I think they’re all mine and I have to take responsibility. I’m not a child anymore, and if I’m so grown-up then I can’t go around blaming other people for my problems. I have to find my bootstraps and pull!

Here is where it seems relevant to reveal that I am now stoned every minute of my life and will be for the next twenty or so years. I still function, and I still go through every motion, but that’s all it is. Nothing means anything to me because the things that do mean something to me are not allowed. Tit for tat. I don’t get anything from the world, so the world only gets limited access to me. It’s the best I’ve got. It’s the best deal I can offer and survive. Despite being constantly stoned, I am surviving, even thriving. Evidence of my continuing success is mounting. I have a real dance job that pays me a salary, my own apartment, a fallback job at the restaurant, and my own stash of dope. I am not only grown-up—I’m killing it.

Two weeks after buying my first stash and being constantly high, I show up to class to find Evan being very familiar with Michele. Too familiar for my taste and I look on with scorn. I can tell by her demeanor that she is wishing he wouldn't show this change in their relationship, but he is like a dog wanting to show his new dominance in the pack. I do *not* approve. How could she do this? Sleep with the boy with no feet. I thought she had higher standards. He wears Dr. Scholl's wooden clog sandals, for God's sake. I have only ever seen these worn by girls. It's an attempt to be cool and cutting edge, but really?

Michele has a boyfriend, but he is in New York City trying to make his fame and fortune in the art world. Good luck with that. I think he wanted her to go with him to NYC, but she was in a "been there, done that" frame of mind. She had already spent time in the City, with a few years with the Harkness Ballet, then touring with a guy doing guest appearances in various places. I never got the full story, but he was a big Christian and this eventually became an issue, so they broke up and she ended up the ballet mistress in a small start-up ballet company in Tucson. That's the extent of what I know.

I don't blame Evan—she's beautiful—but I do blame her. I withdraw my energy, attention, and approval. I barely pay any attention in class and my efforts are severely lacking. This is tricky, though, because I still want to look spectacular for her. More importantly, however, I want to look like I just don't care. *You want that boy? Fine, have that boy. I will be over here ignoring you. Dripping with apathy. That's what I am. Dripping with apathy.*

Rehearsal today doesn't go well. All the positive effort and energy I bring has now done a 180. I am absent-minded, surly, lack effort, and feel generally destructive. I suppose it's noticed, but hey, isn't a girl allowed to have a bad day? Michele makes a minor effort to reach out and see what's up with me, but she knows, so she shouldn't be surprised when she's rebuffed in my new withdrawal-of-love tactic.

It doesn't help that I of course have to dance *with* Evan all day in rehearsal. I have no choice but for Evan to suffer the same withdrawal-of-love energy as Michele, but to a lesser extent as he is the lesser offender. This goes on for three days until it is obvious that Evan and Michele have had their fling and she's called it quits. It's over and I have won. I don't know what I've won, but I can go back to my fantasy relationship without their reality getting in my way.

I spend every waking minute of every day high. The ritual of preparation in the morning has morphed into me rolling two or three more joints as I smoke the first one. These will be securely tucked into my cigarette pack to be smoked later in the day whenever my buzz wears off. I know it's bad, but I don't want to think about it. I'm doing everything and anything I want to do in life, and everyone else can go to hell. I am tired of trying so hard. Tired of always doing the right thing. I'll do whatever I want, and I'll get stoned and stay stoned all day long if I want to. My new "fuck it" and "fuck you" attitude is quite enjoyable. I've been a good girl for so long that it's exhilarating.

Michele is also choreographing a ballet for the three women in the company. Oh yes, Dianne. Dianne was the fifth girl of the original five in class. She's a bit older and married with a kid but very dedicated, is a good dancer, and comes to class every day. She's also a bit odd, but I like people who are a bit odd. People to whom you have to pay attention to see who they are. If all the balls just fall into all the normal slots right away, then everybody is the same and we might as well all be robots. Give me something different. Give me a quirk, or at least a tick.

The structure of this ballet, Michele explains, is that the three women will start off doing the opening together, then separate for solos and rejoin and complete the ballet with the newfound energy and relationships found in each solo. Or, I think that's what she said. The music is Chopin. Each section is to a different Chopin Nocturne, so it's all very romantic and dreamy.

I think my solo might have been better represented by me stomping around the stage. All arms and legs flailing and furious, but no one asked me, did they? So instead it's all romantic and lyrical. All dreamy and flowy. Can't we be more real? Can't we show the real drama playing out in this studio every day? Two women circling each other like boxers, a little jab here, a roundhouse landed there. Show the tension, the frustration, maybe even the real pain of life and love. Enough of the tragic romantic bullshit. Everything isn't *Romeo and Juliet* where they both die for love. The truth is Juliet would have had to marry Paris because she had no choice; she was controlled by her father and the societal clash between Montague and Capulet. Romeo would have left town and wandered the world, turning into an alcoholic underachiever whom his family would finally give up on and disown. Instead, we get Chopin and fantasy. The fairy stories Michele was also brought up on instead of the far more interesting story of two women slowly falling in love in a world where this is taboo. Nowhere more so than in the world of ballet and the overly feminized ballerina.

When you rehearse a ballet about being in a romantic relationship with someone all day, it's hard not to think you actually are. Both Deb and Bill, and now Evan and I, have started sleeping together. I know this sounds quite hypocritical on my part, but it's the order that was established from the beginning. Evan's foray outside the choreographic bounds with Michele was incorrect. Now we are back in order: two couples with Michele adjudicating at the head.

I like Evan, but there is no romance there for me other than the choreographed relationship of the ballet. I think we both want Michele, but since that's not happening, we settle for each other. He's a decent lover. I have nothing against a penis—they can be handy during sex and he's pretty good with his—but with no underlying emotional connection, the sex is only physical and not enough. There is the turn-on of being pursued, of being wanted, but with no wanting in return, it rings hollow, even for him. And so it's short-lived.

We're getting close to performance and Deb has been busy drumming up publicity. Today there's a newspaper guy and a photographer at the studio watching rehearsals. The reporter talks to Michele, and the photographer takes photos as we rehearse. Everyone acts differently while trying to act as if they couldn't be bothered. I stand around trying to look dramatic when we stop dancing and Michele gives notes. I pose in what I think are very attractive and photographically interesting positions. Michele is more serious and professional. It's a little nerve-wracking that some offhanded "ugly" could get memorialized for all eternity in the local paper. This performance should be "make or break" for the company. Do a good job and get funded again; do a shitty performance and it all goes away. Back to full time at the Fancy Farmer for me, Deb to another struggling dance studio, Michele back to NYC as another lost dancer, Bill with no distraction, and Evan stuck in the almost nonexistent world of the theater in Tucson? I don't know, and I don't ask.

It's our last run-through at the theater, and Michele gives me a new note about a lift in the double duet piece. A lift where she wants me to "really kick that lift and fly." I file it away for performance.

# forty-one

FINALLY IT'S PERFORMANCE WEEKEND: JANUARY 1978. WE'RE AT the downtown Temple of Music and Art auditorium. It's an old but large auditorium and stage. Plenty of room on stage and off. I'm licking my chops at the size of the stage. There will be no compromises in our dancing today. Backstage there is a large central space and big dressing rooms on either side for the men and women. We will do a matinée and evening performance. My only concern is having the energy to do both. In rehearsal you can slack off a bit here and there, and we don't always run both ballets all the way through back-to-back. In performance, there is no stopping—and we have to do it twice. I'm concerned. I don't know how to pace myself. I don't know how to do anything other than "full out," so it's going to be exhausting and just thinking about it makes me tired. Plus, I'm stoned so I have to fight through that as well.

Stage fright is strange. You know you're going to go on, you know you're going to do the performance, you know you know all the steps, but your brain suddenly tells you not to go on, that you won't make it through, and you'll probably forget the steps at some point. It's like the devil suddenly shows up on your shoulder and drags out any and every insecurity you ever had and feeds them to you one by one. Now I understand the origins of "the show must go on." It's a law of the theater created to help us all get through that terrible insecurity and get our asses out of the wings.

The performance starts well. My brain settles down within the first few bars of the music and concentrates on the task at hand. Relax your face, point your toes, mind your spacing, look at Evan with love, do your job. Then we get to that lift, the one Michele gave the last note about in rehearsal. It's a lift where I run a few steps toward Evan, take his hands, his and mine both crossed, do a big tour jeté, he swings me around, and I land on his upper back with my pelvis across his shoulders; he's in a small lunge on his front leg. As instructed, I run at him, take crossed hands, kick that tour jeté with all my might, arms extended, back arched to show the flight—and I sail right over the top of him and land face down on the stage.

When you don't know you're falling, you don't tense up, so I land and bounce a little. I was flying and enjoying the flight, very surprised to find myself on the floor. I hit my head, one hip, and one knee. Knowing this was not at all where I belong, I leap to my feet, grab Evan's hands, and continue the choreography. Evan is looking at me in stunned horror.

There is another rule in the ballet world that applies to partnering and pas de deux: "*Don't drop the fucking ballerina.*" That's it. Your main job as cavalier is to take care of your partner. In his defense, I kicked the shit out of that tour jeté and here we are. I recover much faster than he does and spend the next thirty-two bars saying, "I'm okay, I'm okay." What I really want is for him to dramatically sweep me up in his arms and carry me tragically off stage.

The boys now get to sit down while Deborah and I do a duet that is all flying and jumping. I am not really hurt, just so pissed off. I fell. On stage. How humiliating. I have made the whole thing Evan's fault in my mind, but it isn't. Adrenaline is a powerful drug and, fueled by this, the note from Michele, and the excitement of the performance, I flew right over his head in a way he had never before experienced.

So the duet is now getting all the emotion of that event and the retribution I need. We know I can jump, we've discussed this, but today, I truly outdo myself. After the fall, I am amped up on "go go" juice, embarrassment, and a bit of rage.

After the performance, we all gather backstage in the large common room. Michele has come down from the mezzanine where she watched the performance. We stand in a clump around her for notes. Her first question is, "Are you okay? Are you injured?" She should know I'm not since she just watched me dance the last two-thirds of the ballet.

"I'm fine," I mumble.

"It won't happen again," Evan offers, interjecting himself.

Deb and Bill both confess, "We didn't see a thing but heard a thump." They were upstage with their backs turned for the lift.

I have a bump on my hip, knee, and head, but nothing to speak of. Do I want there to be some compound fracture with a bone sticking through my skin, an ambulance called, and tragic hospital visits? Yes. I want Michele in tears weeping by my side. Not really. We've covered this before. It's persistent—that longing for the imagined, visible tragedy of my life juxtaposed with the sturdy reality. Everyone talks about my fall. "Oh my God, Emily, you're amazing," somebody says backstage, but there isn't sufficient concern in my mind. Yes, I'm fine, but I'd like a little more fuss.

Evan, Bill, Deborah, and I all go for lunch at some health food, hippie café they know and that I have never been to. Faced with vegetarian fare and lots of bean sprouts and hummus, I don't know what to order, so I order ice cream. It was the only identifiable item on the menu.

The evening performance is unremarkable by comparison, with the exception of my spiked and now-falling blood sugar. By the end of the second ballet, I am so tired I can barely stand, but the end of the ballet is pretty tame, so I get through.

Friends come backstage and there are congratulations and flowers all round. Michele seems pleased but quiet. Deborah is proud. I guess our funding will be maintained.

Another great tradition in the theater is waiting for the reviews; it's also one of the most unfair things about the theater. Many a good show is badly reviewed by an ignorant or outright nasty journalist and closes before its time. I'm not sure how the review came to wield such power. Go see the show and decide for yourself. Why do you need the newspaper and some stranger to tell you if some show is worth your time? I've seen plenty of bad dance and theater performances, but that doesn't mean they weren't worthy of my time. There is always something to take away. Sometimes it's just the question: why?

Our review isn't spectacular, but it's good. The reviewer talks about the good quality of the dancing and choreography and how our little company is worthy of support. Then he gets to me. "Smith took a heart-stopping fall in Saturday's performance but continued with barely a missed step. This is what is called professionalism." From there he goes on about how we are the best thing going for dance in town. Can't really beat that if you're going to fall face down on stage.

# forty-two

WE HAVE FIVE DAYS OFF AFTER THE PERFORMANCE. MICHELE HAS GONE to LA to visit her father and I'm spending my time working at the Fancy Farmer. I don't know what anyone else is doing. I drive over to Evan's and see a strange car in the driveway. I don't go in because I don't know who's there. As I back out of his dirt driveway, I see a note tucked into the clasp that holds the mailbox shut. I read it. I don't know why I do this but I do. It says: "I dropped by to see if you were home. Call me later please. Sharon." He has a new girl. Can't say I'm surprised or have any right to be angry or jealous. I've ignored him for the past few weeks as much as a person who rehearses with and sees him every day of their life possibly could. I know who Sharon is. She's a ballet groupie. I can't blame him, but I am disappointed. I'm lonely.

Michele is supposed to be back from LA, so I get up enough courage to drop by. We've hung out plenty of times, but always with the rest of the troupe at Deb's. We eat, drink beer, and get stoned. This would be me dropping by her house alone and uninvited. What the hell—I'm going. I can't resist the urge to see her.

I see her car parked next to her place, which is actually a tiny trailer, the kind you can pull behind your car, with a big outside awning and chairs. I can't imagine how she lives in there because it's so small and she is so tall and long. I'm nervous but more excited to see her. I knock, she answers. I can tell she's surprised but pleased to see me and invites me in warmly. We sit at the little dinette or on the floor and she shows me all the music she's brought back from LA: Bette Midler, Donna Summer, Earl Klugh, Al Jarreau. We talk and play music. I've never been alone with her this long. Never just sat and talked. She plays me each album and talks about her favorite tracks, talks about seeing her dad, tells me how awful LA is—"a toilet," she proclaims. We talk about everything and nothing. I make her laugh, but it's well past one in the morning and I'm fading fast.

I don't want to leave, but I worked today and have to be at work early in the morning. I'm tired and need to sleep, still catching up from the exhaustion of the last several months of rehearsal and performance. We hug goodbye and I get in my car and start the engine. I'm just backing out of the parking spot when Michele appears at her door and calls me back. I turn off the engine and walk back to her door.

She beckons me inside and says, "I don't want you to go," and kisses me. The Earth quietly tilts on its axis and slows rotation. We kiss for a few minutes, then she sits down at the dinette and I kneel on the floor and lay my head in her lap. I know it seems wrong with all the tension that has led up to this moment, as we should be ripping each other's clothes off, but I could have fallen asleep right there. Just enjoying the quiet peace of knowing I love her and that she loves me. Understanding what all these feelings have been about, that I'm not crazy and that it's nothing bad. I'm not mad or lost or out of my mind. I'm just in love. I feel such relief and peace.

After a while, she gets impatient with me and says she's going to go take a shower, that she hasn't showered since she got home. She tells me to get undressed and get into bed—that she will be right out. What ensues is the world's longest shower.

I wish the story of what happens next were different. I wish I wasn't so tired. I wish I wasn't stoned. When we kissed, every tensed-up nerve in my body relaxed and then fired off with a new electrical current. We make love, but it is the fraught lovemaking of a girl who needs to sit quietly and understand what's just happened to her. To inhabit her body in a new way with a new mind and awareness. My nervous system just got plugged in and properly connected for the first time in my life. Prior to now it had been jerry-rigged and crosswired; only now is it straight-line connected.

I sleep soundly tangled in her arms and legs but eventually dawn and light wake us. Oh, shit! I'm supposed to be at work. I was supposed to be at work an hour ago. I throw on my clothes and leave in a panic. How to ruin something that should have been beautiful.

Outside I find my car still sitting in the street, driver's door wide open and keys in the ignition. I guess I was a little distracted. I pray the battery isn't dead. It starts and I drive home in a daze to shower, dress, and dash off to work.

Maudine is sitting in the front booth drinking coffee and reading the paper. I guess she got the call when I didn't show up. I apologize profusely. I care but I don't really. On the scale of things, what happened to me last night against not being on time at the Fancy Farmer Restaurant is not equal. I'm hostessing now and strut around the restaurant in my own little world. What I really want to do is jump up and down and scream my lungs dry: "I'm in love with Michele and she loves me!" but I can't, so I settle for strutting. Now I get it. I get the sex thing and the love thing.

But we have a problem. I am *not* a lesbian! Lesbian was the worst thing you could be called on the playground when I was a kid. That's not me. I am a ballerina, for Christ's sake. An icon of femininity. The most extreme feminine representation of the female. Pink tights, tutu, tiara, the whole shebang. There is no way I can be a lesbian. It's just not possible and doesn't fit in my image of myself, so it's just Michele. It's just about *her*.

Two days later, Michele comes to the restaurant with her boyfriend Komo, who has just returned from NYC. They come in for breakfast. What a terrible thing to do to me. This is the first time I've seen her since that night and now here she is with Komo. Thank God I'm hostessing and don't have to wait on them, but still. I'm working and in a servile position and it makes me feel small, plus she comes in with Komo. How can she not think that this would hurt me? Kissing her, sleeping with her, making love to her was like a high dive off a bridge. I was terrified, but there was no way I could *not* do it no matter the outcome. I'd risk life and limb for her, and now she is bringing her boyfriend to where I work to eat breakfast? Come on! Show a little respect. A little consideration.

I run around the next few days in my new little body with my new little brain, but I'm about to explode. I need to tell someone, talk to someone, but there is no one I can tell. I decide to tell Mother. I go over there to pick up some things and I ask her to sit down. I say I have something to tell her. I have no idea what her reaction will be because I haven't thought it out. I just desperately need to tell someone.

We sit formally in the living room, face to face with her on the couch, me on a chair. I tell her that I have fallen in love with Michele and that we slept together and wait for the explosion. The shock, the yelling, the disapproval, possibly cursing, hitting, and throwing things. I get none of that. She cocks her head a bit to one side and says, "Well, I'll be damned." Then, after a pause, she tells me, "Ya know, given the same opportunity at your age, I probably would have done the same thing."

Then she stands up and walks out of the room. I can't believe it. She stole my thunder. She managed to make it about her! She'd have done the same thing? Well you didn't, did you? You are not allowed to co-opt every experience in my life. This is me, my thing. Ask me how I feel. Ask me if I'm okay. *Talk to me!* She's let all the air out of my balloon. My earth-shattering revelation gets nothing more than an offhanded comment. Deflated, I skulk out the back door and into my car. Next time I have momentous news I will find someone more excitable to tell.

Rehearsals finally start again, and it's good to be back in the studio and to see everyone. The performance was so successful with the local dance scene that the company has grown by a few members. That feels good. Strength in numbers. Growing is good, more people around is good. There is too much Michele on my mind anyhow.

I don't know how to act. I don't act like Evan did after they slept together, obviously showing a new familiarity. No. If anything I act more distant. I am thoroughly besotted in love and feel like everyone knows it and can see my hopeless situation. I don't know how she feels. We don't talk. She teaches class and starts choreographing a new ballet and I'm just supposed to act like everything is normal.

This goes on for ten days. Not a personal word passes between us. Even corrections in class are few and far between. That day, Deb announces, using her Executive Director voice, "We're having a company meeting before class this morning, so everyone gather round please. Michele should be here in a minute."

Michele shows up a few minutes later with Komo, which is unusual. She doesn't look at me seated on the floor with the rest of the company. I have a feeling that Komo is there to prop her up, to protect her. She's dressed in street clothes, not clothes for teaching class. Oh, this can't be good. She perches on the windowsill and says something about needing to branch out and pursue other things and that she and Komo are moving to Los Angeles. She is leaving the company—and me. I guess it *was* a high dive off a high bridge. I just didn't realize I hadn't landed yet. I didn't realize how far down the bottom was. I was free falling and today I land, but I land in the shallow water where the rocks are and break every bone in my body.

I sit on the floor hugging my knees, disintegrating inside as she gives her little speech. When it's over the other dancers get up and wish her well and hug and kiss her, but I don't move. Komo ushers her out the door and into her car and they're off.

I don't give a flying fuck about her branching out or that she needs to pursue other things. I need a fucking explanation, but I get nothing. Nothing but watching her walk out the door, out of my life. My teacher, my inspiration, my choreographer, my love, my hope, my life—*gone!* Was it too much? Was it a mistake? Just say so. I can take it. But to just up sticks and walk out, walk away from the company, all the dancers, and everything we've built and worked for makes no sense. I'm sorry. Sorry for making you love me. Sorry for loving you back. Is that what you need? Just don't leave without a word.

This is what drugs were invented for. When you can't deal with or don't understand what you feel, you need to get very, very high. You need to leave this world and your brain and your heart and disappear. You need to leave the planet, exit the world. Thank God there were no high buildings nearby. I would *not* have been passing any open windows.

Rehearsals continue, with Deb and the boys stepping in to finish the ballet Michele started. What do I care? Everyone laughs and jokes around, but I can't join in. Even though there are echoes of Michele in the choreography—she set the movement vocabulary and structure of the piece—I find no soul. It's all technical steps and movement. She hasn't given it life; she had only passed on arms and legs.

Everyone moves around me like I'm not there. I'm not. I'm at the trailer, replaying that night. I'm at the meeting when she said she was leaving. I'm at any little moment I can salvage from my mind to remember her. What did she say? What did I say? Could I have said something different to change it all? If I had, would she still be here? Would I be happy?

Every day is a long series of me trying to come out of my shadow world and into the present moment. Someone speaks and I need to respond. There is laughter and I need to join in. I could care less about the present moment. I am desperately trying to understand the past.

This goes on for days, weeks, months until the next performance. Because we no longer have an artistic director, Deb has brought in local choreographers to fill out the bill for performance. Some of it is interesting, but mostly it's boring modern dance choreography with no point. It could have been Frederick Ashton and I wouldn't like it. I'm not there, so I have no basis to judge.

There are two modern dance ensemble pieces, one about birds, the other about nothing, as far as I can tell. A jazz piece choreographed by a local newscaster who used to dance. Deb choreographs a schmaltzy duet, and Bill and another girl do the pas de deux from *Don Quixote.* It's like a variety show. The reviews are tepid. They say the dancing is good and we are working hard (code for the reviewer was bored).

I get a letter from Michele. She says she has spent the last several months in LA getting herself back in shape and has gotten a job as principal dancer with the Arizona Ballet in Phoenix. She invites me to come to her next performance. Tucked inside the letter is the program, featuring her on the cover looking spectacular.

I may be still in love with her, or more accurately completely obsessed, but I cannot find the will to suffer such rejection, the torment I have lived the past several months, get in my car, and drive 120 miles to see a performance and her in some unknown state of affection. The letter contains not a word of feeling, just news. She worked hard to get in shape, found a great teacher, she and Komo are no longer together, she ate a salad for lunch. Good for you. I'm not going.

A week later, just as we finish rehearsals for the day, I see Michele's little orange Fiat Le Car through the front windows of the studio as she pulls into a parking space. In she walks, cool as a cucumber, to warm hugs and greetings. She's just coming off her Phoenix performance. I get the feeling she was expected by everyone but me. I guess we don't talk to the dead.

Everyone sits on the floor. Pleasantries are exchanged, stories told, and a large bag of Doritos passed around. I sit a little off to the side, trying to recover myself and my blood pressure. I finally start to breathe again, grateful for the Doritos that help by giving my face the activity of chewing to settle down. I don't look at her much. I pick at my tights, squirm to get comfortable. *What is going on and why is she here? Is she here to see them? Is she here to see me?*

Others drift off until it's just Deb and Bill, Evan, me, and Michele. Deb and Bill give their goodbyes. Michele says to me, "Can I sleep at your house tonight?" Hallelujah! I will have her alone and all to myself. I am house-sitting for Dianne, so I tell her the address. I say goodbye to Evan and we all leave, lock up the studio, and get in our cars.

Time and the anticipation of her arrival is endless. I will finally understand what happened. I will finally get some answers. What did she feel? What did she want? Why did she leave? How does she feel now? I am so relieved but terrified at the thought of talking to her and what she might say that I hyperventilate and have to go find a paper bag in this unknown kitchen to calm myself down. Smoke a joint. That's the solution. That's always the solution.

She finally arrives and we hug warmly but there is a scrim between us. There has always been a barrier, a cheesecloth on the lens of our relationship to keep the focus soft and the sharpness blurred. But today it feels a little thicker and a little colder. We are just going through pleasantries when Evan walks up.

The front door is open to the warm but still refreshing Arizona breeze. Still dependent on swamp coolers, open doors and windows are the norm during the spring and fall. There is a long sidewalk leading to the front door and I see him walking purposefully toward us, clopping away in his Dr. Scholl's. Why is he here and who invited him? How did he get the address? I get up to open the screen door and greet him, but what I want to do is to slam the door in his face. She's mine now, go away!

He greets me in an overly familiar way so as to suggest we are still together, which we are not. It's a performance for Michele and a way of claiming me as his, not hers. He is here to claim her as well. He is here to interfere. Mission accomplished. The mood in the room instantly changes, and Evan dominates the conversation. I am too young to understand what he's doing, but I hate him for it.

The hours drag on and he's still here. Michele finally says she's going to bed and Evan gets up to leave. He kisses me on the mouth, and I feel like a forest boundary that's been peed on by a wolf. This is mine, my territory. I'm not his. I'm not anybody's. I don't know if I'm hers, but I'm definitely not his. How arrogant he is.

Once he leaves, I go looking for Michele. She's gone to sleep in Dianne's little girls' bedroom. I knock but there's no answer. I crack open the door to find the room dark with Michele, all five-foot-ten of her, squeezed into a little child-size bed. She's asleep on her side, facing the wall with her back to the door. I kneel down next to the bed and whisper, "Are you asleep?" No answer. "Will you wake up and talk to me?" No answer. I want to scream but I don't. I back out of the room and softly close the door.

I cannot say I am an expert in human relationships, having grown up with two damaged parents who taught me no skills on how to get along with or relate to people, but I know this is over-the-top fucked up. I don't know what to do. I get into bed in the master bedroom and stare at the ceiling for a while. Finally, I can't take it anymore and go out to the living room, roll a joint, and explore the music selection.

An album by The Association seems appealing. I play the song "Along Comes Mary." I play it loud and over and over. It's about a girl who plays games in love. Seems appropriate for my current situation. Then I play "Cherish." Over and over. Also appropriate.

When I wake up the next morning, she's gone. Not a note or any word—just gone. Well, I hope she got the musical message. She's fucked me up beyond belief, and I love her dearly.

# forty-three

REHEARSALS START AGAIN. EVAN HAS GONE TO LA AND BROUGHT BACK a dancer named Hama who is going to choreograph a jazz piece for the company. Hama is Japanese, stands about five-four, has long, jet-black hair, and speaks with a heavy accent. I don't think his English is that good to start with, but add the accent and I struggle. I also struggle because I have only taken a few jazz classes in my life, so all his movements and choreography are strange to me. He is obviously a talented dancer and I like his choreography, but I am a stick-up-the-ass ballerina and not in the mood to apologize for it. I try. I try hard, but I've been thrown into the deep end and feel I look a fool. Add to this that I'm stoned. It's like trying to learn a new language that I must use conversationally every day. I forget the choreography and do the steps badly.

I get another letter. The Arizona Ballet has folded and Michele has moved home to Cincinnati where she grew up and her mother lives. She's enrolled at the University of Cincinnati going for a degree in art history. She's living with a man named Michael who has helped her renovate and open a ballet studio in a large old building on Vine Street. The renovation consisted of sanding the floors and putting up ballet barres in what is a huge studio with massive windows. She has been awarded a commission to choreograph a ballet for a festival in Indiana and wants to know if I will come for two weeks to learn the piece and perform it at the festival. What? I'm gonna say no? Of course I'll come.

All I do is think about her. Constantly. I'm obsessed to the point of delusion. I want to hold her, kiss her, sleep with her, go on a picnic, drive cross country, dance in the same ballet company, be the subject of gossip and jealousy, build a life together. My life exploded after one stupid little kiss. One kiss that unlocked the truth of who I am that I still can't face.

I know she's in love with me. I was there. There at the studio with her every day while it happened. There in the bed with her when it all came pouring out. She's run, but it keeps rearing its little head. Run away from Tucson, come back, run away, please come to Cincinnati. She can't stay away.

How do I reconcile this? I'm out here reinventing from scratch. Am I the only one? I've gone mad. If I thought I was shut down before, this is a whole new level. There is a parallel track and this little freight train is barreling down it. I understand. I've found the missing pieces, and now I'm furious.

But still, this cannot be. I know who I am, and I cannot be a lesbian. Mother's reaction notwithstanding, I know what the world thinks and it's not good. It's just *her.* I will not be labeled or categorized. You can put ten naked women in front of me right now and I don't care. *It's just undeniably her.*

I tell Deb I'm going. That I can't pass up the opportunity to dance in the festival. I say I'll only be gone two weeks. She knows why I'm going and it has very little to do with the festival.

It's the end of May 1979 and I fly out of Tucson late at night and arrive in Cincinnati early in the morning. Michael picks me up at the airport. I guess this is Michele's way of introducing us. How fucked up is this? I don't know what she's told him about me. I don't know what to say. Add to this the airline lost my luggage and I haven't slept. All I want is to shower, change clothes, and take a nap. And food would be good. Food is always good.

We arrive at a tiny top-floor apartment. It's all slanted ceilings and dormers. I wonder how Michele navigates without hitting her head. She is apparently in class until 2:00 p.m. Oh goodie. I get to sit around in my dirty clothes with no prospect of clean ones until they find and deliver my luggage. Neither sleep, a shower, or food is offered. I sit in the tiny living room and make small talk with Michael until Michele gets home from class.

When she does finally arrive, she is greeted by Michael with overplayed kissing on both sides. It's all good, folks. Calm down. I know he's your boyfriend. I don't think you're a lesbian. I'm playing with the idea of what I am, but I have no idea what's up with you.

Michele wants to introduce me to her mother, so we drive over to her house. I know very little about her mother other than that she is a psychiatrist and she and Michele have a problematic relationship. I am introduced in my rumpled clothes and dirty face. Her mother is sixtyish, well-dressed, stern, and feels disapproving. I have no idea what she has told her mother about me or our relationship. Likely nothing. She hasn't told *me* about our relationship. We stay briefly, just long enough to get the feeling of being not wanted and off we go. We are going to the studio now.

The building is on Vine Street, not far from the University of Cincinnati campus. It's painted red brick and four stories tall with massive arched windows. We climb the stairs to the third floor and Michele opens a set of large double doors to reveal a huge studio. There will be no running out of room or dodging seams in the plywood floors here. The floors are freshly sanded and finished. It's magnificent. Huge and full of light.

She leads me into an adjacent room with a large kitchen and a bathroom tucked in the corner. It's old, probably from the '40s, but it's clean. There is another small room just off the kitchen with windows onto the side street and a fire escape. There is a bookshelf in the corner and a single mattress on the floor with a pile of sheets on top.

Michele offers, "I was thinking you could stay here. You have everything you need—a kitchen, bathroom, and bedroom. It will be just your space and it's separated from the studio so no one will bother you." Can you be thrilled and horrified all at the same time? I am. The building is architecturally beautiful, the studio more than you could ask for, the location right on Vine Street in the heart of the hip and happening university part of town. But I will be in the empty building by myself at night, the kitchen is ancient, the bathroom has an old toilet, a sink on the wall, and a metal shower stall. It's the vastness of it that's terrifying. How can I know if someone has snuck up the fire escape and is lurking in a corner? Romance and fear simultaneously. Smoking pot makes you paranoid.

I don't know that I thought about where I would stay. I can't stay with Michael and Michele in their tiny apartment, I wouldn't want to, so the studio seems like an obvious and very acceptable alternative. Except for the ghosts and the monsters that creep up the stairs, crawl up the fire escape, and hide in the corners.

My life in Cincinnati begins to take on its own rhythm. I wouldn't have believed anyone who'd told me I'd be in Cincinnati for eight months, but that's exactly what happens. I blame it on Michele.

I wake with the dawn (I have no curtains), shower, tidy up, and get dressed for class. Michele shows up around 8:30, class is scheduled for 9. Dancers start to drift in and we populate the studio, with everyone finding their favorite spots at the barre.

Michele has advertised her new studio well and connected with some of the dancers from the Cincinnati Ballet, so there is a mix of professional and nonprofessional dancers. There is a snobbery from the Cincinnati Ballet dancers that is unnecessary. Everyone in class knows who they are, and some of them are very good, but not that good. Ballet breeds insecurity. It's never enough and you're always competing—to get in a company, to stay in a company, to get a part, to keep a part.

There is a boy named Jimmy who shows up at the studio and decides we're friends and adopts me. Jimmy is maybe five-eight, has a good body if he were carrying twenty fewer pounds, dark hair, big eyes, and the exaggerated personality of someone working very hard to be someone else. He's gay but I don't think he knows it yet, or if he does, he's trying unsuccessfully to hide it. How easily I can see it in other people. We all take class together every day. I feel I must do very well to show what a good dancer Michele can turn out.

I was supposed to come to Cincinnati for two weeks, learn the ballet for the festival, go home, then fly back for the performance. As I settle in, I start to feel little draw to return to Tucson and the company. Add to this the reality that Michele hasn't scheduled any time to choreograph or rehearse, and the two-week deadline is upon us.

The Tucson studio in the strip mall with plywood floors and no Michele has little allure compared with being in Michele's orbit, her studio, her classes, and the quality of dancers here. If I quit the Tucson company, I'll have to get a job. Even with no rent or utilities to pay, I need to feed and clothe myself. There happens to be a hip restaurant across the street, and I easily get a job. I have no car here, no way to wander or explore very far afield. I talk to Michele to be sure I can live in the studio for a while longer, call Deb with my decision, and tell my mother. No one is surprised, but the choreography isn't getting done and the performance deadline is looming.

School has begun to dominate Michele's life. Even with the studio, she seems to spend all her time when she's not teaching class at the university. We have a few rehearsals here and there; she tells me the piece for the festival is called "Sea Creatures." It's mostly on the floor trying to look like fish and crabs and things. I don't mind it, but it isn't fun and it hurts my knees. Fish don't do a lot of jumping.

It's mid-May, with the performance scheduled for the first week in June. Tonight she wants to rehearse late after class. Rehearsal doesn't go well. She doesn't seem pleased with how things are going. I don't know if it's the choreography she's struggling with or me, but I suspect it's probably me. Seemingly in frustration, she goes off to shower in my bathroom. Technically, it's her bathroom as it's her studio, but I live here, so it's my bathroom. She comes out in my towel, fetches me from the studio floor where I am laying, and leads me into the bedroom. She kisses me, her towel drops to the floor, and I'm done. I say I need to take a shower, too, but she pushes me down on the bed. I don't know if it's the lack of conversation, the lack of time spent together other than in class, the lack of intimate connection, or the lack of a shower, but I'm not really into it. I need to be seduced. I no longer feel connected to her the way I was before. I need to be intimately connected, be in love, whatever words you want to use to describe it, and it's not there. The sex feels mechanical and unemotional. I'd even take fucking over this. At least with boys I can feel the passion of a hard dick between my legs.

There is a car honk from downstairs. Michele gets up, right in the middle of making love to me, gets dressed, and says she has to go. It's Michael downstairs to pick her up, she says. None of this feels good. No matter how infatuated I am or was, something breaks.

Three weeks later, we travel to Indiana for the festival, and it seems like a lot of work for very little reward. A week after that she tells me the festival went broke, declared bankruptcy, and we won't get paid.

I'm leaving. I don't know when or how, but I'm finally going to get myself to New York City. Dance capital of the world. There is nothing here for me anymore.

I'm marking time. I'm still here but I don't want to be. My relationship with Michele has disintegrated. Not my obsession, just the relationship. I go to class because I can't resist, and I can't really make excuses because I'm living at the studio. But the magnetism that drew us together seems to be pushing us apart. Like we realize we can't have what we want from each other, so we're destroying it. She is. I'm braver. I've been inventing myself since I was very little. Okay, I'll give you the movies thing, but those were role models for what was possible. The irrepressible Scarlett, the overcome-all-odds Jim Thorpe, the transformation of Charlotte in *Now, Voyager*, the truth-seeing Scout. I don't want to paste a life on top. I want it to explode out of me the way she has, but now she can't go with me, and it breaks my heart, and I have to go.

There is a boy from class named Derek. He is a beautiful specimen of the male body—tall, dark hair, blue, blue eyes, broad shoulders, narrow waist and hips, and he's decided I am his girl. We go out to dinner once, but mostly he comes over and we fuck enthusiastically. I don't know if it's the sex or the fact that I can rub him in Michele's face. I don't have any deep emotional connection, but at least he talks to me and lets me know he wants me. I'm pretty sure he's gay, so we are a perfect pair.

I display my hickeys and rug burns strategically in class. I want Michele to see that I have moved on from her. That I don't care the same way she doesn't care. I can get sex anywhere. That's not what I'm looking for.

Derek and I discuss New York a lot. He's an actor, or at least an aspiring actor/singer/dancer, so NYC is his nirvana too. We talk about NYC so much that finally, sick of ourselves and in a moment of spontaneity, decide we're going. Now.

We're both broke, but Derek has an old, broken-down Volkswagen with a nonfunctional heater and holes in the floorboards, so driving seems the obvious choice. My friend Jimmy has moved to NYC and is now living in Brooklyn and says we are welcome to come stay with him. Never mind that it's February and freezing cold. Why did we have to wait until February?

Derek and I set off around seven at night. He had to work that day, but once we decide to go, we can't wait. A Volkswagen isn't the most comfortable car on a good day, but on a freezing February night driving across Ohio, Pennsylvania, and New Jersey, it's a conveyance of last resort and something only the young and foolish would choose. We spend the first few hours pretending we are okay and the next few hours wrapping ourselves in every article of clothing we have. I spread my packed clothes out all over the car floor, trying to create insulation. We talk about how to get the heat off the engine and into the car, but it's more a conversation to stave off hypothermia than any real plan for mechanical modification.

We cross a bridge over the Delaware River with huge sheets of ice floating on top. Derek cries out, "Hey, this is real Valley Forge stuff!" We stop at an all-night diner to try to warm up. My hands and feet are frozen, and I wonder how he's managing to drive with frozen feet, but I don't ask. I don't want to know. I just want to get to NYC. We'll deal with whatever comes after that.

We cross the George Washington Bridge at dawn with its huge American flag hanging down over the roadway. I know we came from the west and not by ship, but I feel like a true American immigrant. A refugee looking to make my way in the world.

There are a lot of ways a human being needs to be fed—physically, emotionally, mentally, and spiritually. I have managed the first and skirted around the rest. I know there is more and I have come to the center of the world to find it.

I am starving. Starving for love, starving for knowledge, starving for more. The Statue of Liberty in the harbor welcomes me and my fellow immigrants. I can't see her from the bridge, but I know she's there. I know she holds a torch aloft to light my way. I know the words on her tablet. I am a "huddled mass" unto myself, a "wretched refuse" indeed, "homeless, tempest-tost." I yearn, I beg, I will myself to breathe free.

I am twenty-three years old, five-foot-six, and weigh 110 pounds. I am a solid, strong, long-muscled female with a will of iron and a determination to succeed. I don't care how or even at what—I just know I will.

# Epilogue

I WILL SPEND THE NEXT SIXTEEN YEARS IN NEW YORK CITY PURSUING my career in dance—the great love of my life. I will fall in and out of love. I will have adventures . . . meet famous or soon-to-be famous people. I will succeed and fail. My mother will get sicker, and eventually Charlotte and I will need to go back to Tucson to intervene. Melanie will grow up.

There are a lot more stories, so I have started the follow-up book, which encompasses all my years in NYC until I finally leave for Los Angeles . . . and therein lies another tale or two.

# Acknowledgments

Without the support of my friends Kathleen and Jamie I would never have had the courage to keep going. They read early drafts of the book and didn't say it was shit, so I kept going. Kathleen let me talk and remember stories. Jamie told me about a writing group I might like and agreed to be my backup file storage lest my ancient computer crash and lose everything.

The writing group turned out to be "Show Up and Write" with Brooke Warner, a Zoom meeting where Brooke talks for five minutes about the craft of writing, and then we all write with our Zoom cameras on. No talking, just writing. The camaraderie and accountability of the group got me through the end of the book.

The next steps were coaching, editing, and finally publishing with Brooke and She Writes Press. Brooke took me from a scared, dyslexic, misspelling, poorly punctuating writer and gave me a little confidence. I always wondered what "editors" do and now I know. They make writers better writers—at least Brooke did for me.

It took a village and still does. Kathleen and Jamie still support. Brooke holds my hand when necessary. Anne had the unwieldy task of copyediting. Addison shepherds me through the final stages to a physical product with a book in my hands or on your Kindle or your audiobook.

I am eternally grateful. I couldn't have done this without every one of you.

# About the Author

Photo credit to Jamie Trachtenberg

Emily Sayre Smith grew up in Texas and Arizona, spent two years in London, worked as a dancer wandering around the United States for a few years, and settled in NYC for sixteen years and LA for twenty. She currently lives in Palm Springs, CA.

Hers has been a strange and wandering career path, starting life as a classically trained ballet dancer, then gym owner, construction manager, and now author. She took a gun out of her mouth in April of 1998 and went to an AA meeting. It stuck so she's here. "I can't tell you how liberating it is *not* to kill yourself."

Emily stumbled back into writing in one day's desperate attempt to put off cleaning house. She hates cleaning house but has rediscovered a love of writing. "I've been writing in my head my whole life. I just didn't realize what I was doing."

*Smartass: A Memoir of a Mouthy Girl* is her first book. She's halfway through the follow-up to *Smartass*, which as yet is untitled. Sober twenty-six years . . . it took a village and some good therapy. She really needs a housekeeper but is afraid to break the spell.

## **Looking for your next great read?**

We can help!

Visit www.shewritespress.com/next-read
or scan the QR code below for a list
of our recommended titles.

She Writes Press is an award-winning
independent publishing company founded to
serve women writers everywhere.